Introduction

Related study material is available on the Laurence King website at www.laurenceking.com

Marketing
Fashion

Harriet Posner

LAURENCE KING

LAURENCE KING

Published in 2011 by Laurence King Publishing Ltd
361–373 City Road
London EC1V 1LR
Tel: +44 20 7841 6900
Fax: +44 20 7841 6910
e-mail: enquiries@laurenceking.com   ·
www.laurenceking.com

Text copyright © 2011 Harriet Posner
Published in 2011 by Laurence King Publishing Ltd

A catalogue record for this book is available
from the British Library

ISBN: 978 1 85669 723 1

Design: Draught Associates
Series designer: Jon Allan
Picture research: the author and Annalaura Palma
Senior editor: Peter Jones
Printed in China

Front cover: © Stephane Cardinale/People Avenue/Corbis
Back cover: Courtesy adidas Originals

Dedicated to the memory of Rhona Posner, my dear
mother who first ignited my passion for the world of
retail and beautiful design and Boris Trambusti, a unique
force in fashion, an inspiration to students and the person
responsible for getting me into fashion education in the
first place.

Marketing and branding play a critical role in today's fashion industry; they are stimulating and exciting disciplines that inform many of the strategic and creative decisions involved in design and product development. Marketing bridges the gap between the intangibilities of fashion and the concrete realities of business. It can be viewed as a holistic system connecting the commercial goals and value system of a business organization with the personal ideals, desires and actual needs of consumers.

Fashion is by its very nature a marketing tool. Marketing is part of its DNA; it is inherent in its substance and spirit. Think about it; if it was not called fashion, it would be plain apparel or garments, and these words contrive to kill the very essence and flamboyance of fashion itself. Fashion allows us to dream; it can transport us from the mundane to the glossy world of models, catwalks and fantasies. In the magical realm of fashion, clothes transmute into season's must-haves, a garment's shape and proportion becomes a silhouette, a colour transforms from plain brown into glamorous mocha and a simple sheath of black fabric becomes a little black dress. It is hardly surprising that fashion is so seductive, when so much of the media focus centres on the more glamorous aspects of the industry. Acres of press coverage are dedicated to the reporting on the biannual designer catwalk shows; beautifully styled fashion spreads display tantalizing looks created from the new season's collections and magazines flaunt innumerable glossy adverts promoting an assortment of fashion, accessories and perfume. Fashion is a complex cultural phenomenon but it is also a global manufacturing and retail industry, the scope of which is immense. The industry extends to the agricultural, chemical and fibre industries that produce and supply the raw materials for textile manufacturing through to those working at the more glamorous end of the spectrum in the world of styling, art direction, photography, advertising and media. Marketing operates at every level of the fashion system and affects the entire industry **supply chain** from product development through to retail; it is as relevant to couture, luxury labels and designer brands as it is to independent niche labels or to the mass market and volume apparel businesses. Marketing is the common denominator that ties it all together.

Matthew Williamson Spring/Summer 2010.

"When clothes leave the factories where they are made, they are merely 'garments' or 'apparel'. Only when the marketers get hold of them do they magically become 'fashion.'"
Mark Tungate

What is in this book?

Marketing Fashion aims to offer you a contemporary visual guide to the fundamental principles of marketing theory and branding practice. The book explains key theoretical concepts, illustrating how these might be applied within the ever-evolving context of the global fashion and retail industry. Readers are led through the marketing process from initial research through to the creation of marketing and branding campaigns. Examples and case studies drawn from a broad range of fashion businesses help explain key concepts, and comprehensive lists of industry resources and suggestions for further reading are provided at the end of the book.

Marketing Fashion provides many useful tips and inspirational ideas aimed at assisting the reader to:

- Study and understand marketing theory and practice
- Understand how fashion marketing and branding principles are put into action
- Design fashion products that can be marketed with ease
- Recognize the importance of research and market analysis
- Analyse fashion consumers and understand their needs
- Create exciting and effective marketing and promotional campaigns.

How the book is structured

Chapter 1 – Structure of the Fashion Market sets the scene and gives an outline of the basic structure of the fashion industry. It explains the different levels of the fashion market and provides information on key fashion cities and important industry trade fairs.

Chapter 2 – The Marketing Toolkit introduces key theoretical marketing tools and concepts, illustrating how they are applied in practice within the context of the global fashion and retail industry.

Chapter 3 – Research and Planning explains how key marketing tools are utilized within the planning process. The chapter emphasizes the importance of thorough research and analysis and examines the purpose and value of both primary and secondary research, outlining key areas to consider when gathering market and trend intelligence.

Chapter 4 – Understanding the Customer focuses on research and analysis of customers. It explores ways in which a business can analyse its customer base so they are best able to understand customer requirements and target products and marketing strategies accordingly. It explains customer segmentation – how to group consumers into clusters that have broadly similar characteristics, needs or fashion traits. The reader will gain an understanding of the impact of psychology on consumer purchasing behaviour and learn techniques for creating customer profiles.

Chapter 5 – Introduction to Branding introduces readers to the fundamentals of branding and explains why brands are such valuable assets. The chapter shows how brands are created and explains the importance of brand identity as a strategic tool for building a relationship between a brand and its customers.

Chapter 6 – Fashion Promotion covers the main types of promotional activities employed within fashion and retail, together with trends in contemporary fashion promotion, such as the Internet, viral marketing and designer/high-street collaborations.

From catwalk to store, the fashion dream must be promoted and maintained.

Chapter 7 – Careers in Fashion Marketing outlines potential career paths and provides information on a selection of key roles relevant to those seeking a career in fashion design, marketing, PR or fashion management, and details the skills and competencies required.

Who is this book for?

Fashion marketing is now an essential area of study for all who plan a career in the industry. Students studying fashion, textile or accessory design, fashion management or buying and merchandising will all find that marketing will be included as part of the curriculum. Fashion, however, is never static and fashion marketing does not always conform to standard theoretical formulae. To be successful within the world of fashion marketing you need to build upon basic principles and adapt ideas so as to meet the challenges of each new market situation. The book aims to educate but also to inspire and readers are encouraged to use the material as a platform for further research and enquiry.

"Today, a designer's creativity expresses itself more than ever in the marketing rather than in the actual clothes."
Teri Agins

The adidas '60 Years of Soles and Stripes' launch event in Milan, Italy. Rather than using a runway show, the adidas Originals 60th anniversary collection was promoted at a unique house party event which provided a sneak preview into the global brand campaign.

1.

Fashion is a global market with a complex structure that operates on many different levels to reach everyone from fashionistas to those who just purchase clothing as a necessity of everyday life. The range and scope of fashion is immense; from an ornate haute couture gown made by hand in a Paris atelier to a simple mass-produced T-shirt manufactured in China, this opening chapter will provide you with an outline of the basic structure of the fashion industry and explain these different levels of the market. The chapter also features information on the industry's most influential fashion centres.

Fashion market sectors

The fashion market is broken down into specific sectors so that companies are better able to analyse market data and monitor their business results more effectively. Market statistics can be compiled and analysed by one or more of the following criteria:

- **Market or product category**
  Apparel, accessories, perfume or homeware. The apparel market can be further subdivided into womenswear, menswear and childrenswear
- **Product type, end-use of product or fashion style**
  Denim, lingerie, sportswear, formal wear or contemporary fashion

The diagram gives an indication of some of the key market and product sectors within womenswear, menswear, childrenswear and accessories. As new niche markets develop, so the chart can be adapted to include emerging sectors, for example, clubwear, urban wear, and surfwear.

Fashion market sectors

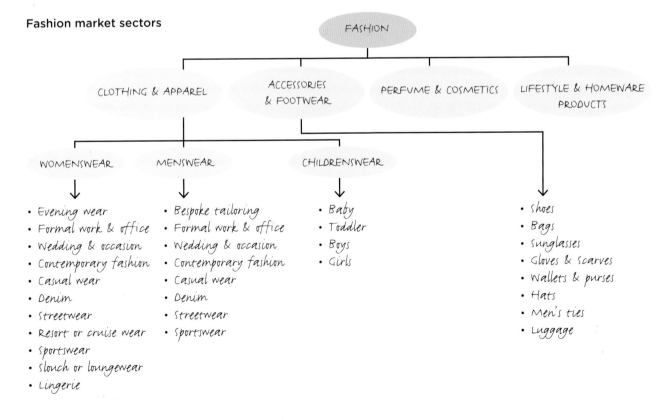

- **Market level**
  Couture, luxury, mid-market or value market
- **Location of market**
  Global, international, national or regional

Market information

Fashion analysts publish market reports and data analysis on most of the key international fashion market sectors. This information is helpful in assessing the relative size of specific markets or estimating future market potential.

Womens-, mens- and childrenswear Data from Verdict Retail, part of the Datamonitor Group, indicates that in 2009 consumers spent £19.1 billion on womenswear with spending on menswear and childrenswear at £9.0 billion and £4.6 billion respectively. The market in the US is considerably larger; for 2009 the womenswear market was US$104 billion, menswear US$51 billion and childrenswear US$33.5 billion. The childrenswear market is typically defined as clothing for children under the age of 14. The main sectors are infants' clothing (babies and toddlers under two years old), girls' clothing (ages 2–14) and boys' clothing (ages 2–14).

Accessories Accessories and footwear are important sectors, contributing a high percentage of the sales turnover for many brands. Global sales of fashion and leather accessory goods across the LVMH brands, including Louis Vuitton, Fendi, Christian Dior and Marc Jacobs, accounted for 34 per cent of the group's overall turnover in 2008, with sales of just under €3 billion in the first half of 2009 (www.lvmh.com 2009). In the UK, the women's accessory market was worth £700 million in 2007, with bags accounting for £468 million. Data from Mintel showed that between 2002 and 2007, sales of handbags in the UK increased 139 per cent with year on year growth of 30 per cent. However, the impact of the recession slowed this growth to 18 per cent in 2008. The fashion accessory market in the US was worth around US$16 billion in 2008 and predicted to reach US$20 billion by 2012

Below left
Bags and accessories displayed at Louis Vuitton.

Below
The Chanel eyewear collection for Spring/Summer 2009 is promoted in a window display.

(Packaged Facts 2009). Footwear sales in the UK during 2007 were worth just over £6 billion and data from the American Apparel and Footwear Association puts footwear sales in the US at just over US$59 billion.

Perfume The fragrance and perfume market is a vital business sector for luxury fashion brands. Fragrance and cosmetics sales at LVMH, for example, accounted for 16 per cent of the group's revenue in 2007 and 2008. Introducing a fragrance as a strategy for growth is not a new phenomenon. Paul Poiret can lay claim to be the first fashion designer to launch a line of perfumes and cosmetics in 1911; the House of Worth introduced a branded perfume in 1925; and Gabrielle 'Coco' Chanel launched the world famous Chanel N° 5 in 1921. The global fragrance and perfume market is predicted to reach sales of US$ 33 billion by 2012 (Global Industry Analysts, Inc 2008) with the European share of the world market estimated at 46 per cent in 2008.

Lifestyle and homeware This market can provide opportunity for a fashion brand or retailer wishing to develop and diversify its business. Ralph Lauren is a brand famous for its lifestyle and homeware products, and US fashion retailer Anthropologie offers an extensive range of bedding, curtains, cushions, tabletop and linens as well as lifestyle products such as bathroom products, candles and stationery. The Spanish retailer Zara has stand-alone home stores offering a similar range of products.

Other markets – denim and sportswear The global denim market is reputed to be worth about US$50 billion annually and data provided by the NPD Group, Inc indicates that denim accounts for 17 per cent of all apparel purchases, with jeans making up 73 per cent of this figure. Over 800 million denim jeans are bought in the world each year. Fashion industry analysts at Mintel predict that by 2012 the UK jeans market will exceed £2 billion, with the men's sector forecast to top £1 billion, women's jeans £846 million and children's jeans in the region of £136 million.

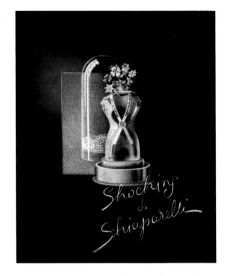

Top
An advert for Shocking, the fragrance launched by Elsa Schiaparelli in 1937. The curvaceous bottle, shaped like a woman's torso, was modelled on the physique of Mae West and designed by the surrealist artist Léonor Fini.

Above
The Jean Paul Gaultier signature fragrance takes its inspiration for the bottle design from the Schiaparelli original.

Left
A poster advertises the launch of John Galliano's first signature fragrance in 2008.

Fashion market levels

Fashion can be divided into two overarching levels:

- Haute couture and couture
- Ready-to-wear

Haute couture

Haute couture is literally defined as 'high sewing' or 'fine sewing' and is fashion at its highest level. Haute couture operates at a quality and standard way above that of luxury designer ready-to-wear. Prices are extremely high (an haute couture dress can sell for a six-figure sum) so there is an unwritten rule of limiting sales of any garment of over £100,000 to one per continent to ensure the exclusivity that clients expect. For lesser-priced garments, sales are usually confined to no more than three per continent. Haute couture clients view themselves as art patrons and consider these clothes to be a collectable form of art and an investment. The term 'haute couture' is protected by law and governed by very strict rules set by the Chambre Syndicale de la Haute Couture in Paris. To be classified as a bona fide haute couturier a fashion house must create made-to-order garments for private

Haute couture sits at the pinnacle of fashion. Although only a small sector of the overall market, its influence on designer and high-street fashion is of great importance. Designers distil ideas from their own couture collections and use them in a more commercial format for their ready-to-wear collections. In turn the designer and luxury brand ready-to-wear collections set the trends followed by mass market fashion retailers. When trends work their way down from the top of the market to the bottom, it is known as a trickle-down effect.

Basic hierarchy of fashion

TRICKLE DOWN
Ideas from couture and designer catwalk shows filter down through the fashion market and are used as inspiration for ranges created by high-street retailers.

BUBBLE UP
Ideas from street fashion and cultural subgroups gain momentum to become a trend that bubbles up through the hierarchy of fashion, eventually reaching the top when expensive designer versions are created.

HAUTE COUTURE & COUTURE

HIGH-END FASHION
LUXURY DESIGNER & PREMIUM BRANDS

MIDDLE MARKET
DESIGNER DIFFUSION BRIDGE LINES
AFFORDABLE LUXURY RETAIL BRANDS
MIDDLE MARKET RETAIL CHAINS

MASS MARKET
HIGH-STREET MULTIPLE RETAILERS

VALUE MARKET
VALUE FASHION RETAILERS
DISCOUNT RETAILERS

clients. They must also produce two collections a year, employ a minimum of 15 full-time staff, run an atelier in Paris and show a set minimum of runway looks, or 'exits', as they are known, of evening and daywear. In the 1980s and 1990s the Italian designer Valentino showed over 180 exits for his haute couture show, now he produces only 40. Very few design houses are approved as haute couture establishments and allowed to show in Paris; Chanel, Dior, Jean Paul Gaultier, Valentino, Giorgio Armani, Jean-Louis Scherrer, Elie Saab, Dominique Sirop, Stéphane Rolland and Franck Sorbier are all recognized as true haute couturiers by the Chambre Syndicale.

Haute couture relies on the expertise of many highly skilled artisans and craftspeople who labour behind the scenes to produce all the luxurious embroideries, trimmings and accessories required by the haute couturiers. Traditionally Paris has been home to a large number of studios or ateliers specializing in millinery, shoemaking, embroidery, beading, creating decorative flowers, buttons and costume jewellery. In 1900, Paris had over 300 *plumassiers* or feather specialists; today the Lemarié atelier is virtually the only one still in existence. Chanel bought the business along with five other specialist craft ateliers: Michel, specializing in millinery; shoemakers, Massaro; embroidery house, Lesage; button and costume jewellery makers, Desrues; and the gold and silversmith, Goosens. While many argue that something as arcane and extravagant as haute couture cannot or should not survive, it seems that demand has not diminished. Chanel employs around 200 couture specialists, while haute couture sales at Christian Dior couture were worth €765 million in 2008, an increase of 35 per cent on the previous year. However, haute couture is a relatively small business in fashion terms; couture at Dior accounts for only 4 per cent of overall LVMH sales. The real value of haute couture is its power as a marketing tool. Global names such as Chanel, Armani and Dior receive valuable press coverage of their haute couture collections, raising the status and desirability of their **brand** and keeping it in the public eye.

Fashion designers that are not recognized by the Chambre Syndicale can still produce exclusive custom-made clothing but this must be marketed as couture rather than haute couture. Prices for couture can still be high. The British designer Giles Deacon produces two or three couture pieces a year and a dress may cost more than £40,000. The price of a Vera Wang wedding dress can be in the region of US$25,000, although in an attempt to keep customers happy during the recession, Wang introduced what she calls **demi-couture** with a lower price tag.

Ready-to-wear

Fashion product that is not custom-made for an individual client is known as **ready-to-wear** or off-the-peg clothing. Ready-to-wear garments are premade, come in predetermined sizes and are usually mass-produced and industrially manufactured. Ready-to-wear fashion is

Above
Christian Dior haute couture for Autumn/Winter 2009/10. Gowns created for this exclusive market are sumptuously embellished with hand-worked beading and embroidery.

available at all levels of the market including:

- High-end fashion
- Middle market
- High street
- Value fashion

Middle market fashion product is designed and priced to cater for customers wishing to purchase at a level between luxury and mass market. A designer or fashion brand that has established itself within the high-end market, may decide to introduce a secondary **diffusion line** or **bridge line**, as it is known in the United States, so that they can extend their brand into the middle market. See by Chloe could be classed as a diffusion line, as could Betty Jackson Two, the secondary line to the main Betty Jackson range. High-street retailers such as Banana Republic, Cos, Hoss Intropia, Whistles and Reiss can also be considered as mid-market. The term middle market is not particularly inspiring and is not always perceived by retail brands as a position they wish to aspire to. Some combat this by re-stating their market level, claiming they offer affordable luxury or masstige (prestige for the masses, or mass luxury) rather than mid-market fashion. Affordable luxury and masstige fashion are seen as an important market opportunity now that so many fashion consumers view luxury as something that should be available to all, even those with limited budgets.

Mass market fashion is a term used when referring to high-street multiples or fashion retail chains such as Gap, Topshop, or Zara, available on high streets in most major cities or towns, or internationally, as in the case of Gap or Zara. At this level of the market, terminology can become slightly confusing as 'high street', 'fast fashion' and 'mass market' are descriptions also used in reference to retailers such as Primark, New Look or Kiabi at the lower end of the market.

According to Just-style, the **value sector** was worth €50bn across Europe in 2008, experiencing growth while the rest of the pan-European fashion market suffered a decline of 5.2 per cent. Value retailers such as Primark, French retailer Kiabi and Germany's Takko are expanding their chains throughout Europe. Primark already has stores in Spain, Germany and the Netherlands, and Takko in Austria, the Czech Republic, Hungary, the Netherlands, Lithuania and Estonia. Worried by the increasing number of value retailers encroaching on its market, the Spanish fashion chain Mango launched a new low-cost line in August 2009 called 'Think Up' in a bid to stay competitive. The new 90-piece range is marketed with the slogan, 'Low cost ideas for creative living'.

The demarcation between different levels within the fashion market is becoming ever more complicated and hard to pin down with clarity. An increasing number of fashion companies are implementing strategies to extend their businesses or brands in a bid to appeal to a wider range of customers. As the Mango Think Up example illustrates, a retailer or fashion

Top
This Banana Republic window illustrates how the mid-market retailer offers fashion with a luxurious feel at affordable prices.

Above
High-street fashion multiple retailer, Gap presents its Spring 2009 collection at Mercedes-Benz Fashion Week in New York.

Brand Pyramid

A fashion brand is constructed to make money from merchandise designed for different levels of the market. At the top of the range, the most expensive and luxurious product may be exclusive and available in limited quantity. These couture and ultra-premium ranges may operate as a loss leader but act as a promotional tool to secure the brand's status. To make money, brand companies must extend their offering to a wider range of customers. An example is the **brand architecture** of Armani described below.

Armani Privé: couture and ultra-premium, top-of-the-range product with very high **price points**. Targets customers in the 35–60 age bracket. Armani Collezioni: priced approximately 20 per cent lower than the main line, this collection is aimed at the discerning customer who cannot afford the signature price points. Emporio Armani: targeted at the young professional aged 25–35. Diffusion line providing contemporary Armani designs. Armani Jeans and A/X Armani Exchange: both aimed at a younger age bracket of 18–30. These collections have a more casual and relaxed style; they make the Armani brand accessible to more consumers.

Below left to right
Armani Privé
Armani Collezioni
Emporio Armani
Armani Exchange

Brand pyramid model

Exclusive couture and top-of-the-range collections. Expensive and limited availability. May not always contribute to overall brand sales income but will generate press coverage and increases cachet of brand.

Main signature collection, available in larger volume than exclusive top-of-the-range product.

TOP OF THE RANGE

MAIN READY-TO-WEAR COLLECTION

DIFFUSION COLLECTIONS & COLLECTIONS WITH WIDER MARKET APPEAL

FRAGRANCES, COSMETICS, SUNGLASSES, LOW-PRICED ACCESSORIES

Entry products more affordably priced. Brand businesses generate a large proportion of their income thorough licensing the brand name for use on a variety of products.

Money is made through selling mass-produced apparel and accessories aimed at the larger global market.

brand can extend its appeal by introducing more affordably priced product. Alternatively they can reposition upwards by offering luxury and premium products aimed to attract a more discerning customer willing to pay a higher price.

Other fashion markets

In addition to the basic fashion sectors described so far, there are other markets, such as vintage fashion and sustainable fashion, that have emerged during the twenty-first century. Vintage or thrift fashion refers to collectable

Left
Sheena Matheiken of the Uniform Project wore one of seven identical dresses every day for a year. Each day the dress was styled and accessorized using a variety of vintage and thrift accessories so as to create a fresh new look. In the photograph on the left, the dress is worn with the inverted pleat at front and the buttons at the back. In the right-hand picture the dress is reversed.

second-hand garments, shoes or accessories from the past sold in specialist vintage or charity shops, or on sites such as eBay. The market has grown in prominence as an increasing number of consumers choose vintage or thrift as a way to make a fashion statement, stand out from the crowd, save money or be more sustainable and consume less.

One highly innovative initiative utilizing vintage and charity shop fashion accessories was instigated by the Uniform Project Foundation, a non-profit organization advocating a socially responsible future through creative means. The foundation's mission is to embrace a sustainable culture through design, fashion, social media and business philanthropy. The project was started in May 2009 by Sheena Matheiken, a creative director at an interactive ad agency in New York, and Eliza Starbuck, a design consultant. The idea was to wear one dress for a year as an exercise in sustainable fashion.

Eliza designed a basic dress for the project that could be worn front or back, or as an open tunic. The dress was made from durable, breathable cotton, a fabric suitable for both winter and summer. Seven identical versions of the dress were produced so that Sheena had one for every day of the week. Each day, Sheena transformed the dress and fashioned a fresh new look by layering and styling it with a variety of vintage, thrift or hand-made garments and accoutrements. Extra items were sourced from eBay, vintage boutiques, charity shops and flea markets, or donated by friends and bloggers. The project was an ingenious exercise in sustainability and a great way to promote vintage, but there is also a serious side to the Uniform Project, as its main purpose is to raise funds for the Akanksha Foundation, a grassroots movement revolutionizing education of underprivileged children in India.

Sustainable fashion, also known as ethical fashion or eco-fashion, is another growing sector of the market. An increasing number of fashion companies endeavour to ensure their collections are ethically sourced, or at least some elements of their product offer are produced sustainably. According to the 2009 Mintel report on ethical fashion, sales of sustainable fashion in the UK quadrupled over the five years leading up to 2008, increasing by £40 million to £175 million.

Issues of sustainability and ethics affect every aspect of the fashion supply chain, from production of raw materials, clothing manufacture, distribution and marketing through to retail. Determining what is or is not sustainable is extremely complicated, not helped by the fact that sustainable fashion is used as an umbrella term to describe a range of practices that include:

- Use of certified organic fibres such as cotton or linen
- Use of renewable fibres such as bamboo and maize
- Recycling of fibres and garments
- Use of natural dyes or low-impact dyes
- Breaking the cycle of consumption by creating a long-lasting product
- Fair-trade raw materials and fibres
- Ethical labour and ethical farming practices
- Reduction in energy consumption
- Minimal or reduced packaging

It is claimed that the fashion industry is 10–15 years behind the food industry in terms of public understanding and with so many issues to get to grips with, many consumers find the topic confusing. The biggest problem is establishing what can or cannot be termed eco, sustainable or ethical fashion. A growing number of designers, fashion retailers and industry bodies are working together to clarify the issues, set clear standards, introduce regulation and clear labelling and raise the profile of sustainable fashion. Opportunities to sell and promote wholesale collections are improving, with London Fashion Week and Prêt à Porter Paris® both now incorporating sustainable fashion within their remit with estethica in London and So Ethic in Paris.

Below
The luxury fashion label, NOIR was founded in Denmark by Peter Ingwersen. The company's mission is to ensure that international minimum standards on human rights, labour and the environment are adhered to for the **sourcing**, manufacture and creation of the NOIR, BLLACK NOIR and Illuminati II collections. The guidelines of the UN Global Compact, the International Labour Organization and the International Chamber of Commerce are used in a bid to provide fashion that is created based upon corporate social responsibility principles. Ingwersen's aim is to prove that high-quality fashion is not incompatible with social responsibility and ethical practice.

Fashion cities and trade fairs

Paris, London, Milan and New York have traditionally been the most influential centres of fashion; each of the fashion capitals has its own specific characteristics derived from its history and the development of particular artisanal or manufacturing skills.

Paris

Paris is the spiritual home of fashion and the epicentre of haute couture. The haute couture shows take place each year; Spring/Summer collections are shown in January, and Autumn/Winter in July. Men's ready-to-wear works on a different timescale: shows in January feature collections for the following Autumn/Winter; June is the showcase for the next Spring/Summer. There are only about 30 menswear shows so this is a much smaller event than Paris Fashion Week, which hosts approximately 100 womenswear ready-to-wear shows; Autumn/Winter in March and Spring/Summer at the end of September/early October. Paris Fashion Week is extremely important and many designers

Below
Prêt à Porter Paris® is a leading international fashion trade fair and recognized brand name associated with several key fashion industry trade events in Paris, New York and Tokyo.

from all over the world choose Paris to show their seasonal ready-to-wear collections, knowing that the fashion press and buyers from the most prestigious boutiques and department stores will flock to the city to view the runway shows. Rick Owens, from the United States, Ann Demeulemeester and Dries Van Noten from Belgium, Viktor & Rolf from Amsterdam, Vivienne Westwood, John Galliano and Stella McCartney from the UK, Costume National from Italy and Zucca, Comme des Garçons and Junko Shimada from Japan are just some of the foreign designers showing in Paris.

As well as Paris Fashion Week, there is also Prêt à Porter Paris® at the Porte de Versailles, a trade show where over a thousand exhibitors from a variety of different fashion markets exhibit their product. Prêt à Porter Paris® is an international brand with several sub-branded shows: Atmosphère's in Paris; The Box, an accessory fair that takes place in both Paris and New York; The Train, a fashion and accessory trade fair held in the Terminal Warehouse building in New York's Chelsea district; and Living Room, held in Tokyo for womenswear, menswear, fashion accessories and lifestyle products. Première Vision, or PV, held twice a year – in February for the following Spring/Summer season and September for the next Autumn/Winter – is the largest European textile trade show and a major date in the calendar for international designers and buyers. The fair is an important trade opportunity for textile suppliers from all over the world but it is also used by fashion designers and buyers for its focus on colour and trend prediction.

London

Ever since the Swinging Sixties and Mary Quant, London has been famous for its street style and avant-garde fashion and this remains one of the city's biggest claims to fashion fame. Today, it is designers themselves who are London's greatest fashion export. John Galliano, Alexander McQueen and Stella McCartney have all gone on to work in fashion houses in Paris, and many other hard-working British or London-trained designers have found employment in New York, Milan, Hong Kong, China, India and Japan. London is a magnet for fashion students from around the globe. After graduation some stay on, start their own labels and make London their base.

London Fashion Week has become a major event on the fashion circuit with designers like Vivienne Westwood, Paul Smith, Betty Jackson, Nicole Farhi, Erdem, Luella Bartley, Alice Temperley and Matthew Williamson. London's reputation was given a major boost when Burberry returned to show its Spring/Summer 2010 collection on the catwalk at London Fashion Week in 2009. For wholesale brands there are trade shows such as Pure London, which gives a platform to over 800 brands; Betty Jackson, who presents her main collection at London Fashion Week, shows her diffusion label Betty Jackson Two at Pure. Although not traditional fashion trade fairs, the Spring and Autumn fairs at the NEC in Birmingham and Top Drawer and Pulse in London showcase companies selling gifts and fashion accessories, such as bags, scarves, hats or jewellery.

Above
Grey herringbone suit in Harris Tweed by British Company, Old Town. The company uses British fabrics for all of their men's and women's clothing. Historically the UK was a centre of textile production. Harris Tweed is a trademarked fabric made famous by Vivienne Westwood, who used the worn, renowned fabric for her collections in 1987/88, and Nike, which used the fabric to make a special-edition trainer in 2004. Scotland still has a strong reputation for other wool fabrics and knitwear made from lambswool and fine cashmere.

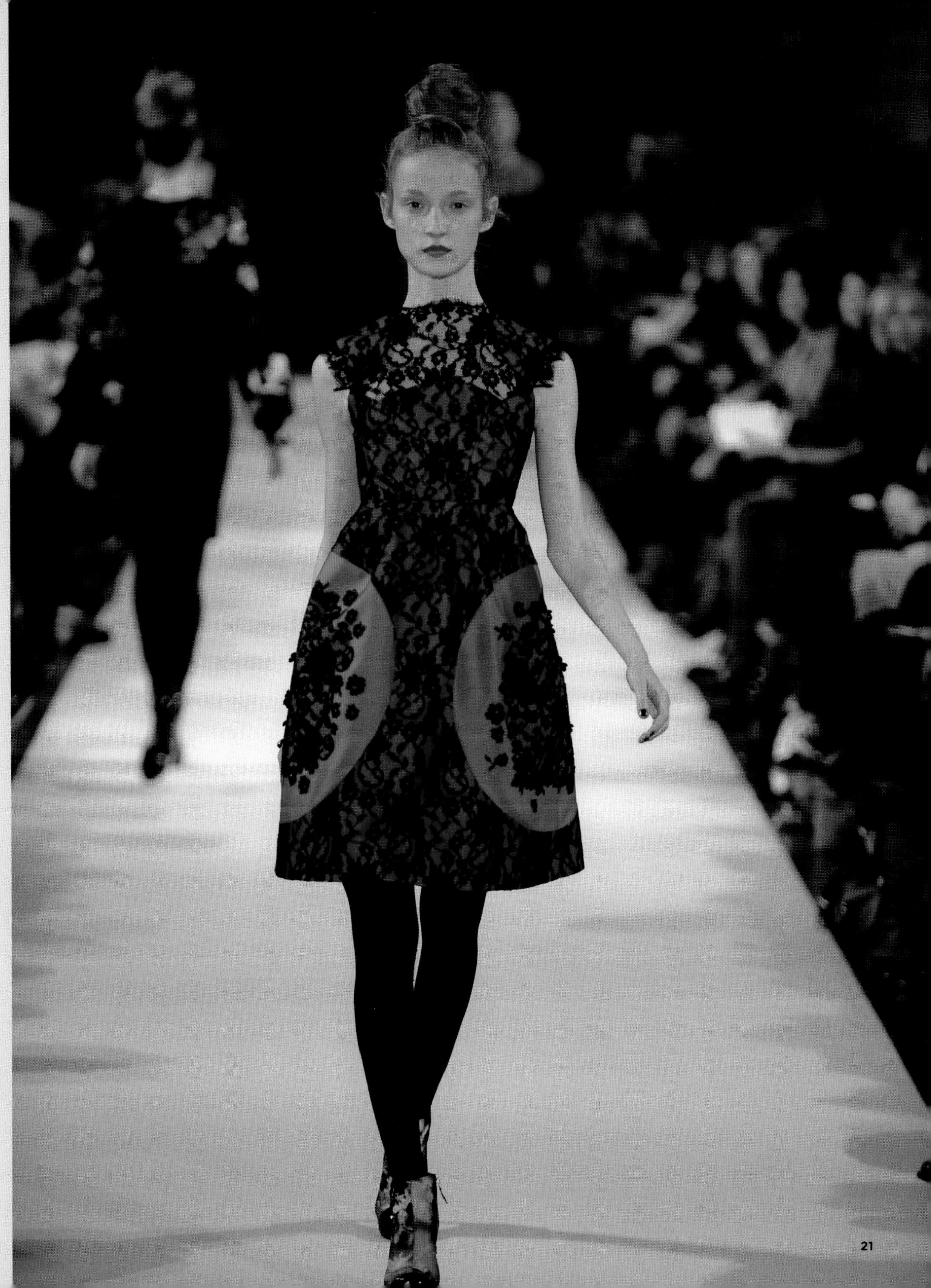

London Edge

The London Edge trade fair caters for the alternative clubwear market. Within this market there are several niche categories such as gothic, punk, cyber, techno, glam rock, heavy metal, rockabilly, industrial, underground, festival ethnic and biker. London Central trade fair focuses on urban streetwear, showcasing brands covering the skate, hip hop, surf and hippy end of the youth market.

Milan

Italian couture, or alta moda, can be traced back to 1951 when the Marquis Gian Battista Giorgini held the first haute couture fashion show in Florence for a select few designers and clients. Rome took over as the centre for high fashion in Italy during the 1960s but lost ground during the 1970s and 1980s to Milan, which became the commercial capital for Italian ready-to-wear. Today, Italy is an important country for the design and manufacture of luxury and mid-market fashion, with particular expertise in leather goods, footwear, knitwear and high-quality ready-to-wear for both men and women. Milan is a major trade centre where most of the design houses have their headquarters and where the majority of Italian fashion shows take place. It is also an important location for Italian fashion magazine publication, so satellite industries such as styling, photography and modelling also gravitate to the city. Italy is well known for its textile industry; Florence and Prato are important centres for the manufacture of yarn and knitwear, Como produces silk fabrics and the Piedmont area manufactures wool textiles. Key industry trade fairs

and catwalk shows are held in Milan, Florence and Rome. Milan hosts Milano Moda Donna for women's ready-to-wear and Milano Moda Uomo for menswear. AltaRomaAltaModa in Rome shows Italian couture and high-level ready-to-wear and Florence is the location for the Pitti Filati knitwear and yarn fair, Pitti Uomo menswear and Pitti Bimbo childrenswear trade fair.

New York

New York is the heart of the US fashion and apparel industry and some of the world's most recognizable brands, like Ralph Lauren, Tommy Hilfiger, Kenneth Cole and Liz Claiborne, have their offices and design studios in the city. American fashion is renowned for its relaxed, fluid, casual and chic style, epitomized by designers like Lauren as well as Michael Kors, Donna Karan and Calvin Klein. Retailers like Nike, Gap, Banana Republic and Esprit also have strong global appeal for their accessible and desirable fashion.

Historically, apparel and textile manufacturing was one of the United States' largest sectors. It has suffered a decline due to competition from manufacturing counties like China, but the industry still employed over half a million workers in 2007.

Mercedes-Benz Fashion Week (formerly Olympus Fashion Week) attracts 100,000 trade and press visitors and generates US$466 million in visitor spending each year, according to the New York City Economic Development Corporation. Calvin Klein, 3.1 Phillip Lim, Anna Sui, BCBGMaxazria, Carolina Herrera, Davidelfin, Diane von Furstenburg, Donna Karan, Isaac Mizrahi, Michael Kors, Zac Posen and Narciso Rodriguez are just some of the names that show at this prestigious event.

Above left
The tent at Mercedes-Benz Fashion Week, New York.

Above
Michael Kors runway show for Spring/Summer 2010 shown at Mercedes-Benz Fashion Week

Other fashion cities and trade fairs

India, Sri Lanka, Australia, Hong Kong and China and Japan all hold their own fashion week events to showcase designers and promote their region's fashion industry. In the US, Los Angeles plays a vital role in promoting fashion on the West Coast. The city is gaining a reputation for fashion design with acclaimed labels Rodarte and Band of Outsiders based there. In 2009, Rodarte, designed by sisters Kate and Laura Mulleavy, won the Council of Fashion Designers of America's (CFDA) Womenswear Designer of the Year award and Scott Sternberg's Band of Outsiders won the award for CFDA Menswear Designer of the Year. LA also holds two major international textiles and sourcing fairs, GlobalTex and L.A. Textile. Portland, Oregon is an important centre for fashion and active sportswear companies. Nike, Adidas, Columbia Sportswear, Jantzen swimwear and Keen footwear all have headquarters there as do eco-fashion brands such as Nau, Entermodal and A Fortes Design.

In Europe, Berlin hosts Bread & Butter, an international specialist trade fair for streetwear, denim and sportswear brands. Düsseldorf holds the CPD womenswear and accessories fair, and HMD (Herrenmode Düsseldorf) for menswear. Spain is well known for the manufacture of footwear and leather goods; the country holds two international footwear and leather trade fairs – Modacalzado + Iberpiel in Madrid and Futurmoda in Alicante.

Above
Sweden is gaining a reputation for cutting-edge and directional denim brands. One denim label making a name for itself is Dr Denim, started in 2003 by the Graah family in Göteborg. Their Autumn/Winter 2010 collection was exhibited at, Terminal 2 in Copenhagen, Bread & Butter in Berlin and Modefabriek in Amsterdam.

2.

This chapter outlines the fundamentals of marketing and introduces the basic concepts and tools underpinning marketing strategy. A useful framework for planning is known as the **marketing mix**. *This long-used marketing tool is explained and updated to integrate more recent marketing theory. Key principles of* **segmentation**, **targeting**, **positioning**, **differentiation** *and* **competitive advantage** *are explained, with information on how fashion designers create a distinctive* **signature style** *and determine a* **unique selling proposition** *for their brands.*

"Marketing is not the art of finding clever ways to dispose of what you make. Marketing is the art of creating genuine customer value."
Philip Kotler

What is marketing?

Marketing is intriguing in that it has been variously described as a business function, business philosophy and also as a management or social process. Marketing should really be viewed as a holistic system connecting a business with its customers. Professor Philip Kotler, who has been described as the godfather of modern marketing, believes that what makes a company is its marketing. Kotler considers marketing to be both a science and an art. It is strategic and creative, requiring systematic research and analysis as well as innovation, intuition and gut instinct.

The range and potential of marketing can be almost limitless; it may start way before any product has been designed and continue long after a customer has purchased. This scope and multi-dimensional nature could make a clear definition appear rather illusive. However, the next section will address this issue by presenting four definitions that capture the essentials and simplify the complexities of marketing. The key points raised by the individual definitions will then be examined in more depth.

Marketing definitions

Each of the definitions chosen below highlights a particular facet of the marketing dynamic. Viewed together they reveal the broad scope of marketing.

"Marketing is the management process responsible for identifying, anticipating and satisfying customer requirements profitably."
– Chartered Institute of Marketing (CIM) UK

"Marketing is the human activity directed at satisfying needs and wants through an exchange process." – Kotler (1980)

"Marketing is the social and managerial process by which individuals and groups obtain what they need and want through creating and exchanging products and value with others." – Kotler (1991)

"Marketing is creating, communicating and delivering value to a target market profitably." – Kotler (2008)

Collectively these definitions summarize the fundamental elements of marketing as:

- An understanding of customer requirements
- The ability to create, communicate and deliver value
- A social process
- An exchange process
- A managerial and business process

While the fundamentals of marketing may be similar for any industry, the exact nature of their application will differ from one sector to another. In the following pages we will see how each of these elements of marketing can be applied in the context of fashion, and, in particular, how they relate to the connection between the consumer and their clothing.

An understanding of customer requirements

The definition from the Chartered Institute of Marketing draws attention to the significance of identifying and anticipating the needs of customers. Naturally this is an important first step in being able to design, produce and deliver merchandise that satisfies or indeed exceeds consumer desires, requirements or expectations.

An underlying concept of marketing is to produce what people want to buy, not just what a fashion designer wants to design or fancies making. It is important to research consumers in some detail, identifying who they are and what they might want. While it is true that many professionals within the fashion industry do have an intuitive understanding of their customers, this in itself does not eliminate the need for research. Predicting future fashion and market trends and working to anticipate what consumers might want is a significant issue for the fashion and apparel industry. Information gathered from market research, retail analysis and trend forecasting is used with the aim of determining the trends, styles, colours or technologies most likely to appeal to customers in the coming seasons.

Some high-street fashion retailers can go from design to delivery in a matter of weeks, but the reality is that many apparel and manufacturing businesses start their initial research and design developments months in advance of a season or product launch; adidas, for example, can take 12–18 months to develop and produce a new product. This lengthy process time, also known as the **lead-time**, is one of the reasons why anticipating the future is so crucial. Marketing research, forecasting and consumer research will be explained in more depth in Chapters 3 and 4.

"Marketing should be an ethos (rather than a department) that pervades every facet of a business."
Martin Butler

Communicating value
Boden Owner's Club Manual

Boden is a British mail order and online clothing brand selling to over a million customers in the UK, Europe and the United States. Boden produce colourful, quirky and distinctive womenswear and menswear collections and Mini Boden, a line for children and babies. Inspired by the high standards of US mail order companies, Johnnie Boden started his pioneering upmarket catalogue in the UK in 1991. The Boden website was launched in 1999; now approximately 62 per cent of UK sales and 72 per cent of US sales are taken over the Internet. The Boden brand has been built up so successfully because it offers fair-priced, well-made clothing with a colourful sense of fun and style, delivered directly to the customer's home. When Johnnie Boden launched the catalogue this was a novel idea. The Boden catalogue and website are used not only to sell the product but also to communicate the Boden lifestyle and brand ethos. The Spring/Summer 2009 catalogue included an insert entitled, *The Boden Owner's Club Manual*. The small booklet is jam-packed with information on the details and quality of garment design and the value of the Boden product.

Right
The designers behind the Boden brand believe design details make a difference, so *The Boden Owner's Club Manual* is used to highlight the hidden extras that make a Boden trenchcoat so special.

Below
Johnnie Boden uses the cost-per-wear principle to calculate the true value of a pair of Boden chinos. By dividing the retail price by the number of times the trousers have been worn over the years, it is possible to determine their value per wear. The message is that although the chinos might not be the cheapest on the market, they are good quality and will stand the test of time.

We couldn't resist a slightly *decadent* trim on the underside of the belt.

To deliver a *commanding contrast*, we attach our ecru buttons with the same colour thread we use to make our coat.

Note the nice rich seam stitching – yet another thing that lifts this coat *out of the ordinary*.

9

Step 4:
Appreciate the hidden extras

We believe that when it comes to clothing, no detail is small enough to be overlooked.

We're never happier than when we're agonising over an unexpected feature others might find trifling – such as the contrast trim on the reverse of our Trench Coat belt. Some of the detail we've created in a whole host of our products is purely for an 'audience of one'. But *you'll know it's there* and that's reason enough for us.

8

The *Boden* *Owner's* *Club* *Manual*

10½ EASY STEPS to *ultimate* Boden enjoyment

$$\frac{price \; £}{times \; worn} = value$$

✳ **VALUE FROM THE BOTTOM UP**
My chinos from the end of the last millennium cost £42. I've washed them about 500 times – that's less than 9p an outing so far. They still look and feel fantastic and they've got plenty more mileage left in them.

7

Creating, communicating and delivering value

Successful business relies on a strong and effective interrelationship between the activities of creating, communicating and delivering. If one of these aspects fails, it will affect the efficacy of the total result. It is no good creating or advertising wonderful products if they are not delivered. Similarly if products do not match the quality levels expected by customers, or service is not up to standard, then value will not have been delivered.

So what exactly is value? Value does not just refer to low price or what might be termed 'good value'. In this instance it is used to express a much larger concept and refers to the range of potential issues that customers might value, care about or connect with emotionally. Value may be contained within the product offering – the actual fashion range or collection – but it can also relate to the inherent value or status of a brand. Value is also linked to the overall service a company might provide and to customer experience and satisfaction. The concept of value works both up and down the supply chain; whatever is delivered must not only be of value to consumers but must also create profit and value for the business as well.

Remarkable marketing

"Remarkable marketing is the art of building things worth noticing right into your product or service. Not slapping on marketing as a last-minute add-on, but understanding that if your offering itself isn't remarkable, it's invisible."
Seth Godin

The company LittleMissMatched was founded in the US by three entrepreneurs who recognized a great marketing opportunity – how to solve the age-old problem of the disappearing sock.

"Why do we have to wear socks that match?" the entrepreneurial friends pondered. *"Why not start a company that sells socks that don't match, why not sell them in odd numbers so even if the dryer eats one, it doesn't matter."*

LittleMissMatched only ever sells socks in odd numbers, three in a pair! Now that is remarkable. And if you get three odd socks that co-ordinate in fun and colourful ways then in essence you get three combinations per pair instead of just one. Revolutionary! Not just boring socks but a crazy way to express yourself and be creative. With a core philosophy of 'nothing matches but anything goes', the kooky founders of Miss Matched Inc. thought they had created tweenie sock heaven. They saw their market as girls from four years to teens, but to their surprise the idea caught the imagination of a much wider audience. Now LittleMissMatched is a full lifestyle brand with a range of products for children and adults, including colourful and mismatched gloves and hats, sleepwear, flip flops, bedding, stationery, gifts and hair accessories.

Above
LittleMissmatched has a unique take on marketing. They offer three socks in a pair; while each of the socks co-ordinates with the others in the set, none of them are a complete match. This novel approach solves the problem of 'the missing sock'.

Marketing as a social process

Marketing is a social process where individuals or groups can create and exchange products or information with each other. Fashion has a unique ability to be used as a vehicle for social connection and communication. Individuals often choose to dress in a specific and recognizable style so that they can express their ideas visually and signal membership to a like-minded group, joining what is known as a **style tribe**. This is a term for a collection of people who dress in a common distinctive style. They may not actually know each other directly but might share similar values and cultural attitudes; by adopting a specific mode of dress, tribe members can shape their identity and gain a sense of belonging.

Style tribes – Exactitudes

Exactitudes (a contraction of exact and attitude), is a project by Rotterdam-based photographer Ari Versluis and stylist Ellie Uyttenbroek. They started working together in 1994 to systematically document the conspicuous dress codes of numerous fashion style tribes around the globe. Selected individuals are photographed standing in an identical pose in a studio setting. The resulting photographs are placed in a grid framework that serves to amplify the striking similarities of each member of the style tribe.

The Exactitudes project illustrates clearly the subliminal influence and pull of a style tribe. The people photographed by Versluis and Uyttenbroek were spotted in the street and had no personal knowledge of the others photographed in their tribe. Although only 12 individuals appear in each tribal collective, responses to the work via blogs indicate that many people who viewed the photographs were able to identify themselves in one of the featured tribes.

We frequently purchase clothes either consciously or subconsciously based on what peers, friends, colleagues or celebrities are wearing. When consumers promote products or pass on style ideas to each other it is known as **peer marketing**. In many cases this can prove to be a far more powerful marketing tool than advertising or promotion controlled directly by a company. When a marketing message spreads rapidly from person to person it is known as **viral marketing**. The rise of web-based communication and proliferation of blogs, social networking and sites such as YouTube has been instrumental in the growth of this new marketing medium. Viral marketing utilizes the connectivity amongst individuals to capture attention and create a buzz. Forward-thinking fashion companies such as Levi's and Louis Vuitton are already integrating viral marketing into their promotional strategies.

Exchanging products and value with others

Marketing is an exchange process. The commodities for exchange are the goods and services and the currency is of course money. However there are other commodities of value to bear in mind, such as ideas, information,

"Buzzmarketing captures the attention of consumers and the media to the point where talking about your brand or company becomes entertaining, fascinating and newsworthy."
Mark Hughes

Opposite
Exactitudes, a project by Rotterdam-based photographer Ari Versluis and stylist Ellie Uyttenbroek documents the dress of fashion tribes from around the world.

Top left
Pin-ups – London 2008
Girls inspired by 1940s and 1950s pin-up style. Pencil skirts and blouses with cinched-in waists accentuate the figure. Retro-styled hair is adorned with accessories or hats.

Top right
Yupster boys – New York 2006
Yupster = yuppie + hippie. Grown-ups that don't grow up, this tribe of urban creative professional hipsters came of age during the first wave of indie rock and hip hop. Yupster uniform: T-shirt that communicates values or affiliations, zippered hoodie and all-important cross-body bag.

Bottom left
Geeks – London 2008
Skinny boys in V-necks and specs display their fashion geek credentials.

Bottom right
Charitas – Rotterdam 2007
Power ladies dressed to impress in suits or skirts and structured jackets; handbags at the ready, these women mean business.

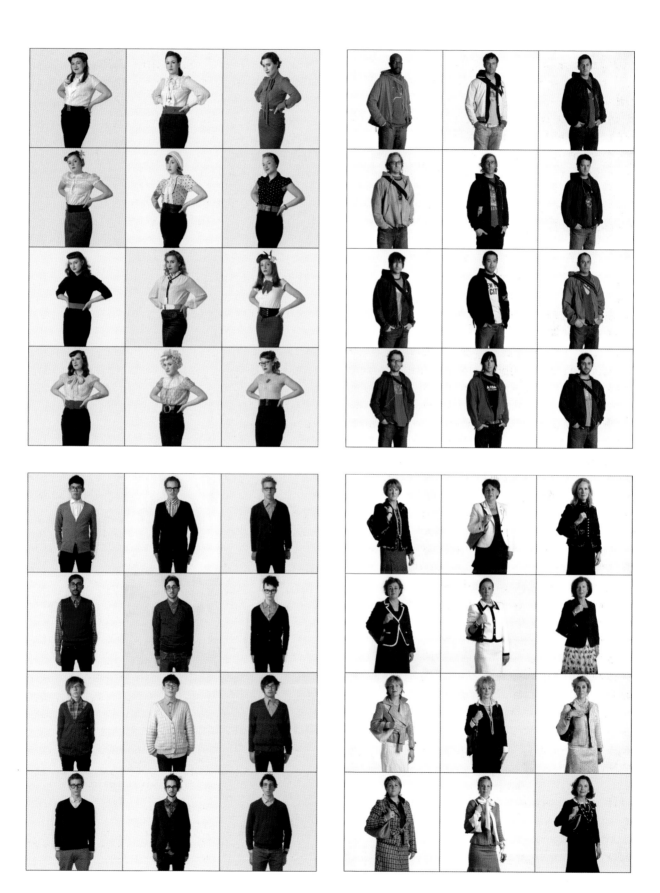

connectivity and emotion. Viewed creatively, the exchange process can be seen as a trade system with exciting potential to generate a diversity of assets for both consumers and businesses. A business model that incorporates this wider view is **co-creation**. This is when a company creates its products or services in co-operation with consumers. **Crowdsourcing** is a type of co-creation where tasks such as design, which would normally be carried out internally by company employees, are outsourced to the public, thus allowing the larger collective or 'crowd' to get involved. The Internet has been a pivotal instrument in the development of co-creational projects. Its potential and connective power offer opportunity to "tap into the collective experiences, skills and ingenuity of hundreds of millions of consumers around the world" (www.trendwatching.com). Within the apparel sector, there is an increasing number of casual clothing companies building businesses around the concept of co-creation. They understand and connect with a particular group

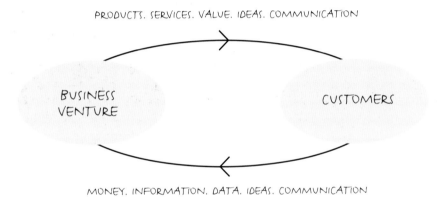

PRODUCTS. SERVICES. VALUE. IDEAS. COMMUNICATION

BUSINESS VENTURE

CUSTOMERS

MONEY. INFORMATION. DATA. IDEAS. COMMUNICATION

of creative, technologically competent consumers, happy to express themselves and share ideas online. This consumer cluster, termed Generation C by analysts at trendwatching.com (the C stands for content), is not related by age but by an attitude to sharing creative content via the Internet. The benefit of crowdsourcing is that it democratizes the process of design, shifting emphasis from manufacturers towards consumers, or users as they can also be termed. This 'user-centred innovation' has advantages over manufacturer-centred innovation in that users can create exactly what they want rather than relying on manufacturers to do it for them. Crowdsourcing allows value to be created jointly by a company and its users. It opens up the possibilities for exchange and brings diversity and new ideas into a company. Although users may offer ideas for free, they are usually rewarded with a prize, small fee or sometimes a percentage of sales if their design is chosen. The benefit of crowdsourcing is that it allows a company to communicate with its consumer base, gain knowledge of their needs and preferences and reduce risk by producing product or designs that consumers want.

Consumers get involved
Threadless

Threadless was one of the first clothing companies to place crowdsourcing at the heart of its business model. Launched in 2000, the Chicago-based T-shirt company opened up the design process to any creative individual willing to submit designs suitable for printing on the T-shirts. The concept is managed as an online competition. Each week design submissions are posted on the website; the six T-shirts receiving the highest number of votes from the online community are put into production and sold via the online store. Winning designers receive a prize worth $1,000. This system of crowdsourcing is effective because users are motivated by the possibility of winning and the opportunity to have their work available for sale, while Threadless minimizes risk by only manufacturing the designs chosen by their customers. Encouraged by the popularity of Threadless and the success of crowdsourcing, new casual apparel companies, such as Yerzies and nvohk, are adopting and developing this co-creation business model.

Run Rhino T-shirt from Threadless.

A managerial and business process

Marketing must be managed as an integrated function of business and the ultimate aim is not only to satisfy customers but also to ensure a profitable result. As the Chartered Institute of Marketing's definition states:

"…the management process responsible for identifying, anticipating and satisfying customer requirements profitably."

Now let's examine the key strategic tools available to the marketer. The first of these is the **marketing mix**.

The marketing mix

The marketing mix provides a framework that can be used to manage marketing and incorporate it within a business context. The concept of the marketing mix is that several strategic ingredients need to be considered and blended effectively to achieve the marketing and strategic goals of a company. The principles that underpin the marketing mix were first shaped in the US during the 1940s and 1950s. The term was originally coined in response to the idea that marketing managers were considered as "mixers of ingredients". Neil H. Borden, Professor of Advertising at Harvard Business School, originally listed 12 marketing variables, but in the 1960s, E. Jerome McCarthy rationalized these into four simpler variables – product, price, place and promotion – known as the 4 Ps of marketing.

The marketing mix can be thought of in a similar way to a recipe where the four ingredients of product, price, place and promotion can be blended in varying proportions giving emphasis to whichever aspect is most appropriate to the company, brand or product in question.

The mix employed will be unique to each company or situation, so there is no correct formula. Fundamentally it comes down to ensuring that the product is right for the specified market, that it is priced correctly, that the balance of merchandise is correct, that it is in the right place at the right time and that customers are aware of the offer or service through appropriately targeted promotions. Whatever the market level, an effective marketing mix will need to weigh up a company's overall objectives while also taking into account any changes and challenges operating in the market at any given time.

Product

For apparel, 'product' relates to product design, style, fit, sizing, quality, fashion level as well as performance and function. In the fashion and textile industry, product is rarely a singular item. Commonly it will be a complex range or integrated collection of product. Designers are generally required to construct well-balanced collections or wholesale or retail ranges that include a variety of different product categories offered at appropriate price points for specific target markets. When taking a strategic marketing approach to product, some useful questions to consider are:

- Are the products suitable for the specified market?
- Do the products meet the tangible needs of consumers?
- How will the products satisfy the intangible desires or aspirations of customers?
- Does the total product offer or range address the variety of needs relating to the target customers?
- Is the balance of the range or collection correct? Does it have enough choice and variety within it?

"Marketing is still an art, and the marketing manager, as head chef, must creatively marshal all his marketing activities to advance the short- and long-term interests of his firm."
Neil H. Borden

Product attributes and benefits

Product attributes refer to the features, functions and uses of a product. **Product benefits** relate to how a product's attributes or features might benefit the consumer. At the most basic level, clothing has core attributes, which offer protection, and safeguard against exposure and nudity. At the next level there are the tangible attributes, integrated into the design, manufacture and function of the garment. These are intrinsic to the product itself and offer concrete and physical benefits to the consumer. So a raincoat made from a water-repellent fabric will have the intrinsic attribute of being waterproof and have the benefit of keeping a wearer dry. Such a garment may be presented in-store with accompanying marketing material informing consumers about the specific attributes and benefits of the design or waterproof material. An item of clothing can also have what are known as intangible attributes. These are more abstract in nature and connect to the ideals, perceptions and desires of the consumer. These intangibles are extremely important for fashion as consumers do not really buy a product but a set of expectations and interpretations, each person perceiving a product's combination of attributes and benefits according to their own particular needs and viewpoint.

The total product concept

The example of the waterproof coat illustrates what Theodore Levitt called the augmented product or the **total product concept**. Levitt's model describes four different levels to a product.

- The generic or core product
- The actual or expected product
- The total or augmented product
- The potential product

Below
The Regatta women's jacket (left) and men's jacket (right) have several important functional product attributes: made from Isotex 1000 XPT, an extreme performance fabric, the jackets are waterproof, breathable and windproof. The jackets also incorporate technical and functional design details such as taped seams, a detachable hood, a centre front zip with storm flap and a map pocket.

Synthesizing the practical with the emotional
A waterproof coat

A waterproof coat or jacket is a good example of a garment that can be designed with many practical features and tangible attributes. A coat made of a fully waterproof material has the obvious benefit of keeping the wearer dry in the rain. For someone who wanted a coat to protect them during outdoor or country pursuits, a loose-cut practical waxed jacket might provide the benefits they require. If in addition it had a detachable inner lining, then the benefits of flexibility and keeping warm could be added to the list. At an emotional level, a consumer might choose a waxed Barbour country jacket, not only because of the durability, warmth and protection it offered, but because emotionally, the wearer connected to the heritage and values of the Barbour brand. The wearer might feel 'earthy' or 'connected to the land' when they wore it. They may appreciate quality and tradition and practicality. A different consumer, on the other hand, who wanted to feel 'active and alive' or 'daring and adventurous' might purchase a lightweight waterproof with high-performance features, even if they wore it in an urban setting or to go to the shops. The wonderful benefits of a high-performance or practical country jacket are likely to be of no interest to someone who wanted to feel alluring, fashionable and chic while they kept dry. For this consumer the silhouette or shape of the coat may be of major importance, along with the fashion status of a brand name. They may desire a designer label raincoat with a belt so that they can cinch in their waist and show off their figure to best advantage.

Each of the garments described provide the functional benefits necessary for specific uses or activities. But clothing provides more than the merely functional. The clue to understanding this is to view attributes from the consumer perspective and try and determine what consumers might feel, desire or aspire to when they purchase fashion product. Each attribute will generate a set of emotional meanings that augment the tangible or physical benefits. This is why fashion in general and branding in particular can be so powerful – they have a unique ability to confer the intangible and create a short-cut straight to the emotional.

American actress Maggie Gyllenhaal looks sophisticated and urban in a belted trenchcoat.

French actress Fanny Ardent makes a simple, classic raincoat look alluring and desirable.

If we consider a waterproof coat such as a classic trench, then at the most basic level the product is a coat. At the next level it is a waterproof coat with specific design features and styling details offered at a particular quality and price. The next tier up is the total or augmented product. This represents everything that the customer receives when they purchase the raincoat, including all elements that contribute to added value, intangible benefits, branding and emotional benefits. The total augmented product relates to everything that is currently being offered, but there is another highly significant layer to consider and that is the potential product. This is everything that could be offered or might be offered in the future. For fashion the future happens very fast and designers spend most of their time working on potential product. They must innovate and update, moving product design forward each season with new design ideas, fabrics and technologies. The concept of potential product is therefore of vital importance.

Levitt's model highlights another important point. "Consumers don't buy products or product attributes. They purchase benefits and emotional meaning." This means that potential product must also be about identifying innovative ways to deliver extra value and benefits to the customer.

The total product concept

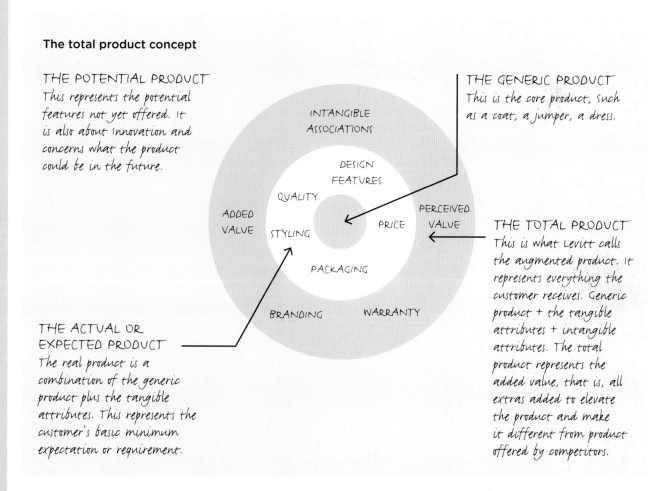

THE POTENTIAL PRODUCT
This represents the potential features not yet offered. It is also about innovation and concerns what the product could be in the future.

THE GENERIC PRODUCT
This is the core product, such as a coat, a jumper, a dress.

INTANGIBLE ASSOCIATIONS

DESIGN FEATURES

QUALITY

ADDED VALUE

STYLING

PRICE

PERCEIVED VALUE

PACKAGING

BRANDING

WARRANTY

THE TOTAL PRODUCT
This is what Levitt calls the augmented product. It represents everything the customer receives. Generic product + the tangible attributes + intangible attributes. The total product represents the added value, that is, all extras added to elevate the product and make it different from product offered by competitors.

THE ACTUAL OR EXPECTED PRODUCT
The real product is a combination of the generic product plus the tangible attributes. This represents the customer's basic minimum expectation or requirement.

Price

In this context price means manufacturing costs, wholesale and retail prices, discounted prices and of course margin and profit. For marketing purposes it is possible to view pricing from two perspectives; one is from the point of view of cost, what an item actually costs either to produce or for a buyer to purchase. It considers tangible expenditure so that a cost price can be calculated. The second standpoint, selling price, looks at the situation from the customer or end-consumer's perspective. It considers what might be a realistic selling price and factors in issues such affordability and perceived value. Perceived value reflects the apparent worth of a product; this may not directly relate to the actual cost of production or wholesale purchase price. An understanding of customers' perceptions of value is therefore very important, as is knowledge of competitor pricing within the marketplace.

Above
The display in the John Varvatos Malibu store features a range of products including jeans, shoes and accessories. The product mix offers customers an opportunity to buy into the Varvatos collection at a variety of price points.

Research is an essential element in understanding pricing both from a customer or end-consumer perspective and in terms of what the competition is up to. And of course, prices change frequently so research helps gain insight into:

- How customers perceive price
- What customers consider good value
- How much customers are willing to pay for specific products
- What customers will pay more for
- How much competitors are charging

It is rarely only one item that will need to be priced. A well-balanced selection of product will need to be constructed and a coherent pricing strategy devised not only for each individual item but for the entire offering.

Price architecture

A pricing structure will have to be planned or built up from the lowest cost items right up to the most expensive. This is known as the **price architecture**. Within the price architecture there should be products offered at:

- Introductory or low price points
- Medium prices
- High price points

It is customary to create a price band for each of these tiers. For example, a high-street retailer might set their lowest price band at £15–49, the mid-price band at £50–99 and the top band at £100–200.

Price architecture is dependent on the type of market, the market level and the product concerned. The proportion of styles and the stock volumes within each of the tiers is adjusted so that the business can satisfy the greatest number of customers and generate the highest potential sales margin and profit.

Price architecture

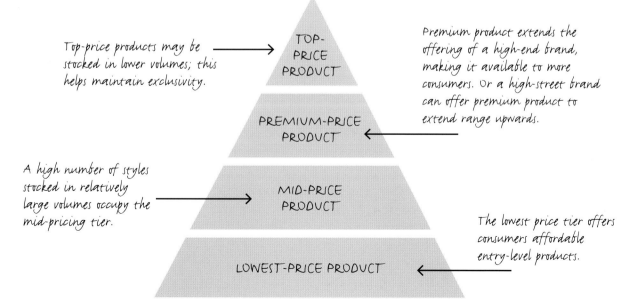

Top-price products may be stocked in lower volumes; this helps maintain exclusivity.

TOP-PRICE PRODUCT

Premium product extends the offering of a high-end brand, making it available to more consumers. Or a high-street brand can offer premium product to extend range upwards.

PREMIUM-PRICE PRODUCT

A high number of styles stocked in relatively large volumes occupy the mid-pricing tier.

MID-PRICE PRODUCT

The lowest price tier offers consumers affordable entry-level products.

LOWEST-PRICE PRODUCT

Each retail price band can then be further subdivided with specific price points. The top price band might, for example, have only four price points, £115, £125, £150 and £200. The lowest pricing tier might have something in the region of eight to 12 separate price points. Skilful setting of price points and consideration of the number of styles offered at each price within a pricing band are essential elements to the planning of a balanced range. It may not be possible to achieve the desired profit margin on every style but judicious flexing of prices should help to increase margin on enough product so that a workable margin is achieved overall.

Pricing calculations

The following examples outline some quick pricing calculations that can be used as a rough guide for understanding pricing parameters. The most useful overall tool is to monitor retail prices on a constant basis and take note of actual prices within the market.

Cost-plus calculation

The **cost-plus pricing** formula can be used as a guideline to determine the cost of producing an item and calculate the minimum price that must be charged to recoup the original financial investment. The total cost of producing the product is derived from the fixed and variable costs. Fixed costs, such as rent, salaries and insurance, remain the same whatever amount of product is produced or sold. Variable costs are expenses that vary in direct proportion to the quantity of garments manufactured and include the cost of raw materials, packaging, labour and shipping charges. The minimum price that should be charged for the product is calculated by dividing the total costs by the number of units produced.

MINIMUM PRICE = (Fixed costs + variable costs) / number of units

If a manufacturer produces 2,000 units of an item with fixed costs of £10,000 and variable costs of £5,000 then the cost per unit will be £7.50.

10,000 + 5,000 / 2,000 = 7.50

If the manufacturer were to receive £7.50 for each of the 2,000 units, then they would get their money back but would not make any profit. In order to achieve a profit, a **mark-up** percentage must be added. To achieve a mark-up of 40 per cent, the selling price per unit will be £10.50.

MINIMUM PRICE = (Fixed costs + variable costs) x
(1 + mark-up percentage) / number of units
(10,000 + 5,000) = 15,000
(1 + 40%) = 1.4
15,000 x 1.4 = 21,000
21,000 / 2,000 units = 10.50

The cost-plus pricing formula is dependent on the actual volume of product sold, so if the manufacturer does not sell all 2,000 units at £10.50, then a profit may not be achieved. If only 1,000 units were sold then the price per unit would need to be raised to £21.00 in order to get a return on the investment.

Mark-up and margin calculation

A retailer wishes to purchase 2,000 units from a manufacturer. The manufacturer opens negotiations at £12.00 per garment. The retail buyer can gauge the potential retail price by multiplying the wholesale price by a **mark-up factor**. If the buyer calculates a retail price by doubling the cost price, then they will have used a mark-up factor of two. This will achieve a mark-up percentage of 100 per cent and a margin of 50 per cent. Mark-up calculations work on a cost-up basis; that is, they view pricing from cost price and work upwards. **Margin** calculations look at the picture from the perspective of the selling price.

MARK-UP PERCENTAGE = (Cost price x mark-up factor) – cost price/cost price x 100
(12 x 2) = 24
24 – 12 = 12
12 / 12 = 1
1 x 100 = 100

MARGIN = (Selling price – cost price) / selling price x 100
(24 – 12) = 12
12 / 24 = 0.5
0.5 x 100 = 50

A fashion buyer will monitor retail prices within the market on a regular basis and will have a clear idea of the retail price they wish to sell a particular garment at when they enter into a price negotiation with a manufacturer. If a buyer works with a mark-up factor of 3.5, they will achieve a margin of approximately 70 per cent (excluding taxes).

Looking at the garment and knowing current pricing in the market, the buyer understands that the maximum selling price they can charge for such a garment is £39.99 and that if they buy it in at £12.00 they would have to sell it at £42.00 in order to achieve the correct margin. The buyer therefore negotiates with the manufacturer and an eventual cost price of £11.50 is agreed.

The final margin calculation is set out below.
(39.99 – 11.50) = 28.49
28.49 / 39.99 = 0.71
0.71 x 100 = 71 per cent margin

* Calculations do not contain adjustments for sales tax.

Place

In essence, place is about getting the right product to the right place at the right time and in the right amount. It concerns logistics and the various methods of transporting, storing and distributing merchandise and the means by which a company's products reach their target customer; termed as 'route to market' this relates to **distribution** and **sales channels**. The key sales channels by which apparel product reaches the end-consumer are:

- Direct routes such as the Internet or purchasing via telephone.
- Service-orientated channels; in other words a retail store, or what is termed as **bricks and mortar retail**.
- Catalogues – some companies start by producing a catalogue. They may then expand to open stores or operate a **concession** within another store. Most printed catalogues now also operate a second channel online.
- Public events such as sports or fashion events, or craft or country fairs.
- **Trunk shows** for invited customers (see caption).

Routes to market for the fashion trade can be via the following channels:

- Trade fairs
- Agent's showroom
- Company-owned showrooms either at head office or located in key global locations
- Internet
- Via a sales team
- Direct from manufacturer
- Via an agent
- Trunk shows

Above

Stella McCartney talking to customers at her Autumn 2009 trunk show at the Chicago store of Barneys New York. A trunk show is a special preview event where a designer will show off their latest collection to a select group of invited guests and customers. Usually guests will be able to purchase or order items during the event. Trunk shows are commonly held in a boutique or in the designer section of a department store and are excellent for marketing as they allow a designer to reach an audience that would not normally attend catwalk shows. They also provide an excellent opportunity for the designer and retailers to obtain vital pre-season information on which styles will be successful.

Variations might exist between retail stores in different national or international locations. Customer requirements or purchasing patterns are likely to differ, so a store in Germany might carry a different selection of styles and colours compared to one in southern Spain. Equally, the size range of garments may need to be adjusted to take into account variations in physique prevalent within different cultures. The merchandise offer will also be determined by the dimensions and layout of the retail space. Not every location will be able to display the same volume of stock, so the selection will need to be modified to suit the practicalities of the store.

Trade fairs and exhibitions
Timberland takes a stand

Industry trade fairs provide an important opportunity for companies to showcase their new product ranges and sell to retail buyers from around the globe. The advantage of a trade fair or exhibition is that buyers can view and compare a variety of brands all showing at the same event. Shows will be sector specific; Première Vision in Paris for fabric or Pitti Filati in Florence for yarn spinners, CPD in Düsseldorf for womenswear and accessories, or Bread & Butter in Berlin for street and urban wear, for example. Thousands of trade buyers typically visit these fairs; 33,500 visitors from over 59 countries attended the Igedo fashion fairs in February 2008. Exhibiting companies invest heavily in creating show stands that represent their brand and their products to best advantage.

The Timberland trade-show stand for its Outdoor Performance range is created using re-purposed industrial objects and natural recycled materials. Shipping containers have been re-deployed to create selling booths where clients can view the Timberland product range and place orders.

The innovative trade-show stand, designed by Michigan-based design firm JGA, reflects Timberland's commitment to environmental sustainability. The highly distinctive design is constructed from 98 per cent 'earth conscious' materials (53 per cent re-used, 18 per cent renewable, 27 per cent recycled), and 88 per cent of the stand can be recycled at the end of its use.

Timberland trade-show stand for their Outdoor Performance range. Graphics set the mood in the central 'meet and greet' space where trade buyers are welcomed onto the stand by Timberland sales representatives to view the product ranges and place orders.

JGA also designed the stand for the Timberland Pro series. The highly flexible build is designed to accommodate different trade-show footprints. Sales rooms display the Pro Series products and provide worktable seating for 8–10 people.

Promotion

Promotion is about communicating with customers and includes all the tools available for marketing, communicating and promoting a company and its products and services. The combination of promotional activities, such as advertising, sales promotion, public relations, personal selling or sponsorship, is known as the **promotional mix**. The idea behind this is similar to the marketing mix and relates to the mixture of promotional tools that can be employed to achieve a company's promotional objectives. Some of the most recognized promotional vehicles for fashion are the advertising in high-profile fashion magazines like *Vogue* or *Harper's Bazaar*, *Grazia* or *Marie Claire*; catwalk shows that gain extensive media and public interest; and the PR and razzamatazz that surrounds celebrities and their endorsement of designer fashion. There are, however, many more innovative and creative ways to promote fashion. One way for a retailer or fashion wholesaler to promote their business and provide something extra for customers is to produce an in-house magazine or seasonal brochure. Producing a high-quality, multi-page publication is a costly and intensive process, so companies that choose to do this usually publish on a biannual basis, timing editions to promote Spring and Autumn collections. The style and content of the publication must reflect both the underlying values of a brand and the attitudes and interests of targeted customers. Magazines and brochures are also a great vehicle for communicating essential information such as contact details for head office or customer services and locations and addresses of stores. Further promotional ideas will be discussed in more depth in Chapter 6.

The marketing mix today

The drawback of the marketing mix is that it tends to focus on the internal needs of the company rather than the ever-changing requirements of customers. The traditional 4P marketing mix was primarily developed during the rise of mass consumerism to market the tangible benefits of product – the limelight falls on issues surrounding producing, pricing and promoting product. Newer thinking believes the consumer should be at the heart of the matter. An expanded 7P version of the marketing mix has been developed to address this change in emphasis; it includes three further criteria, physical evidence, process and people. It can be a common mistake to consider fashion as a product-based industry, however – it should really be viewed as service- or people-based. Fashion retail concerns the experience of shopping, so service which incorporates the extra Ps could be viewed as a marketing tool of the highest importance.

Physical evidence

Consumers increasingly demand more in terms of value, experience or extra service, and as the ability of fashion retailers to match each other's product offer rises, so the criterion of physical evidence plays an ever more important

Below
Massey & Rogers produce beautiful printed items such as bags, brooches, tea towels and greetings cards. They take great care with presentation – their set of three bird-print tea towels are packaged with cotton tape and branded with a simple swing ticket.

role in differentiating one retailer from another. Physical evidence relates to issues surrounding packaging, brochures, business cards, website design and usage, carrier bags, staff uniforms, in-store décor, ambience, facilities, retail fixtures, store windows and signage.

The fashion experience is about so much more than just the clothes or accessories themselves, it's all the little extras that make a difference. The label in the garment embroidered with the designer name, the well-designed and beautifully crafted swing ticket, the carrier bag so special that it is kept as a treasured souvenir, or stunning windows and store displays that capture the imagination and make a shopping trip feel thrilling. All these extras are vitally important aspects of the marketing mix. They are persuasive factors that add value, enhance customer perception of a retailer or fashion brand and elevate one company above another in the hearts and minds of consumers.

Creating a world of beauty and artistry
Prey UK

Prey is a unique boutique retailer situated in the historic city of Bath in the UK. The shop has been described as an Aladdin's cave of beautiful objects; it is the ultimate micro department store, selling a diverse range of fashion, jewellery, accessories, fragrance, gifts and homeware. The whole ethos behind the Prey world is to delight customers and provide an ambience of beauty and artistry. This philosophy is apparent throughout the store, but one of the most delightful features is the beautiful packaging and exquisite illustrated carrier bag. The Prey bags are a treasure in themselves, far too gorgeous to ever throw away and a tempting inducement to buy into the Prey world and purchase from the boutique.

The Prey UK carrier bag is beautifully designed and crafted. The intriguing illustration artfully tells a story. The woman appears to be walking a dog but when the bag is reversed it becomes clear that it is a bird of prey.

Creating a Camper Universe
Camper Together with
Jaime Hayon

Fashion is becoming increasingly about experience so the design and feel of a retail store is highly important. Many fashion brands employ high-profile architects or innovative designers to help them create stylish, exciting and dramatic retail spaces. Camper is a modern footwear brand resonating with fun, imagination and creativity. On a practical level, Camper makes shoes for wearing and walking but at the same time they believe they make shoes for 'imagining'. The Majorcan company has a unique approach and philosophy that enables it to integrate several opposing and contradictory ideas and their stores provide a window through which they can exhibit their shoes and communicate their unique viewpoint to the world. To this end they created the 'together' concept, collaborating with Jaime Hayon. The distinctive retail environments conceived by this young Spanish artist bring the spirit of imagining and Camper Universe to life. The store-galleries located in Barcelona, London, Paris, Palma de Mallorca and Madrid showcase the designer's idiosyncratic modern take on traditional forms and shapes. Hayon's quirky, baroque touches, reflective surfaces and gold flourishes meld with the Camper philosophy to establish an intriguing contemporary setting in which to display the shoes and delight shoppers.

Jaime Hayon's designs for the Camper store in Cherche Midi, Paris.

Process

Process describes the customer's experience of the brand or service from first point of contact onwards. It considers the experiences and procedures they may have to go through in order to make a purchase and includes issues such as information flow, ordering, payment, delivery, service and return of products. In the modern marketing climate, with increased reliance on marketing and selling via the internet, process is a potent tool, especially for businesses wishing to build customer loyalty and ensure customer retention. Whatever the exact nature of a business, it is always worthwhile to take time to review the process customers go through when they make a purchase or use a website, to see the steps from the customer perspective rather than just what might be efficient for the company.

A customer purchasing a wedding dress will go through a series of steps from first consideration to final purchase and ultimately wearing the dress on her wedding day. The first step may be looking at wedding magazines and doing online research to find suitable ideas, designers or retailers. Next, there could be telephone conversations or emails to gather further information or book an appointment to view a collection, sessions to select fabric and develop a personal design, followed by several fittings, the final fitting, taking delivery of the dress and then the wedding itself. Each step in the process is a moment where the consumer and company providing the service interact. Every interaction provides an opportunity for the business to differentiate itself from competitors, create value and ensure a positive experience for the customer.

Process expands the marketing viewpoint beyond the product itself and recognizes the value of smooth interactions and good service. In combination with great product, process builds trust, loyalty and repeat custom. Hopefully, a wedding dress will be a one-off, once-in-a-lifetime purchase, so positive customer experience is less likely to result in a repeat purchase but it will certainly contribute towards an enhanced reputation and customer recommendations. Conversely, customer irritation with any part of the process could lead to a lost sale, deterioration in trust and erosion of customer goodwill or loyalty. In the case of a wedding dress there may be other people to please along the way – the bride's mother or a best friend or bridesmaid. Process may appear to relate to systems and organization but in reality it is all about people and their potential.

People

'People' in this instance does not just refer to consumers, it has much wider implications and opens up the scope to include all those who add value to the development and delivery of a product or service. People can therefore include employees, partners, stakeholders, collaborators, producers and suppliers. It can be a trap to consider fashion as only a product-based industry; it is just as important to view it as retail and a service experience. People add value along the entire length of the supply chain and are, of course, integral to the service provided by any company. People should therefore be considered as a vital part of the marketing mix.

Think OUTSIDE IN!
In other words imagine being the customer. What kind of service do they require? How can you improve the processes they go through to purchase your products? How can you make the process smoother, more exciting, more engaging, more efficient and memorable for the right reasons?

Now think INSIDE OUT.
Have you made internal processes smooth and efficient? Will internal processes support customer experience – even if employees don't deal directly with customers their internal or interdepartmental processes may cause glitches that indirectly affect results.

Valuing people
Earnest Sewn jeans

Earnest Sewn is an American denim brand designed by Scott Morrison in Los Angeles. The name is central to the brand concept – literally translating as 'product sewn in earnest'. The denim label is underpinned by fundamental core values of quality, integrity and authenticity and the Japanese concept of Wabi-Sabi, an aesthetic system honouring the traditional beauty of imperfection. Traditional Wabi-Sabi products are produced by hand and weathered by time. For these values to have any significant worth or real meaning they must be utilized by Earnest Sewn and be embedded into the company's design and manufacturing processes and integrated into the marketing strategy. In order to achieve this Earnest Sewn has abandoned the normal assembly line approach to production. Wherever possible one person carries out the majority of the sewing for each garment; in this way the company is able to manifest the ideals by which it stands. Each maker is able to focus on an individual pair of jeans, increasing the opportunity for subtle inconsistencies, imperfection and the irregularity of things made by hand. Typically, three people oversee and monitor the jeans' progress from design through to shipping. When the jeans are complete, those involved in their production put their name to their work by signing the pocket lining. This validates the authenticity of the jeans and signals the integrity of the manufacture. The signed pocket lining communicates that the jeans are indeed, 'product sewn in earnest'.

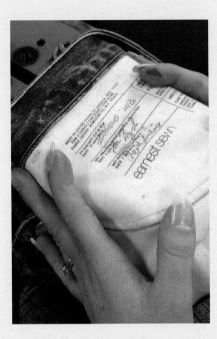

Earnest Sewn jeans are signed by the three people who work on the garment from design through to shipping. One person is responsible for the majority of the sewing on each pair of jeans. This innovative approach changes the dynamic of the manufacture from 'production line' to something closer to 'hand-made'.

Changing the Ps to Cs

The most up-to-date marketing theories, such as **relationship marketing**, recognize the importance of building long-term relationships between a business and its customers, the aim being to attract loyal customers who will spend consistently over time. A model devised by Professor Robert Lauterborn reframes the marketing mix. By changing the Ps into Cs, Lauterborn shifts the emphasis away from product, price, place and promotion onto the customer.

MARKETING MIX – PS	LAUTERBORN MODEL – CS
Product	Customer needs & wants
Price	Cost to the consumer
Place	Convenience
Promotion	Communication

The Lauterborn model may not have been created with fashion specifically in mind, but it is possible to consider its implications. What, for example, might it cost consumers in real terms to satisfy their needs or fashion passions? Factors such as time and convenience have to be integrated into the pricing equation. Consumers may be cash rich but time poor, they might have disposable income but not enough time to shop for clothes. For some, shopping is seen as a social or leisure activity, an experience often shared with friends. A morning perusing the high street or mall might be perceived as time well spent, even if very little was actually purchased. Many women and occasionally some men buy clothing and fashion completely spontaneously, having had no original intention to purchase anything that day. Some consumers could be described as fashion addicts. For them, convenience is not an issue; they might be willing to make special trips or even pilgrimages to ensure they fulfil their fashion dreams or requirements. Others may spend hours monitoring an auction on eBay to ensure that they are the ultimate victor in a bidding war for an exclusive fashion item. There are also, of course, customers with limited interest in fashion and little inclination to spend their time trawling the shops, who nevertheless need to buy clothing for themselves or their family members.

Consumer psychology and communication are the unifying principles that tie this new set of criteria together. There is a need to understand the psychological impulses behind consumer fashion choices and recognize sensitivities to time, costs, value and convenience. By viewing marketing from the consumer's perspective, far more must now be achieved than just delivering the right products at the right price. The way consumers value fashion, style, self-expression and identity should naturally be viewed as part of the marketing equation.

Business processes of marketing

So far we have defined marketing and set out its parameters, explaining that to be effective it should be integrated into the entire fabric of a business. Although strategies and objectives may vary according to the size and goals of the business concerned – a large global corporation, for example, may have a significantly different structure or way of operating compared to a small independent niche company or self-employed fashion designer operating out of a tiny studio – the overall business processes involved in marketing are in fact very similar and can be summarized as:

1. Identifying business opportunity
2. Developing products and services
3. Attracting customers
4. Retaining customers
5. Delivering value
6. Fulfilling orders and business agreements

"Retail is a people business. For sure, customers pay their money for whatever it is that you, the retailer sell to them, but there's so much more to the relationship than this exchange."
Martin Butler

Each process is intimately linked to the others, so the failure of one has the potential to jeopardize the business as a whole and negatively affect customer perception of the company or brand. In order to be successful a business venture must therefore carry out all these processes effectively. This is where the marketing mix comes into play. It is instrumental in supporting a unified approach to the business and marketing.

Relationships in the supply chain

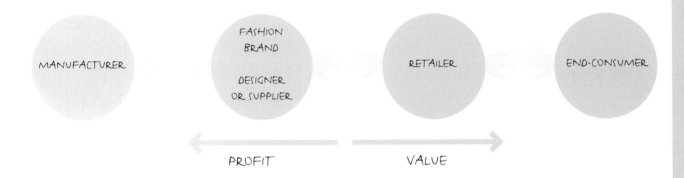

PEOPLE...PRODUCT...PRICE...PLACE...PHYSICAL EVIDENCE...PROMOTION

MANUFACTURER

FASHION BRAND

DESIGNER OR SUPPLIER

RETAILER

END-CONSUMER

PROFIT   VALUE

Marketing strategy

It is an extremely tough challenge for a fashion manufacturer, supplier, designer brand or retailer to appeal equally to all customers or consumers. It makes sense therefore for a business to concentrate its resources and activities and focus on a specific area of the market, fine tuning or 'positioning' the brand, product offer and services so that they appeal more directly to a specified and well-defined target audience. This is the fundamental principle underpinning STP (**segmentation**, **targeting** and **positioning**) marketing strategy.

The framework of the marketing mix and the overall business and marketing processes can be applied to any business throughout the fashion and textile supply chain. Each interaction along the chain should be viewed as a business relationship; this is why it is important to include the criterion of 'people' within the marketing mix. This diagram represents a simplified version of the supply chain but it could be expanded to take into account other businesses, such as agents and distributors.

Segmentation and targeting

Market segmentation is a key function of marketing; its purpose is to divide a market into smaller, more focused sectors. The fashion market can be segmented in several ways, for example by product type or market level. There is a market for couture, the luxury designer market, the accessory market and branded sportswear. The process of segmentation can also be used to cluster consumers into groups that share similar characteristics. Consumer segmentation is the research and analysis technique used to define these groups. It categorizes consumers in terms of their age, attitudes, behaviours or by the type of products and services they might need. (This is described in greater depth in Chapter 4). Segmentation is a means to an end, the tool that facilitates the next step in the process; targeting. This is the process of developing products or services specifically aimed to appeal to a particular customer segment. Companies that offer petite ranges, for example, are targeting smaller-sized customers. A fashion brand targeting older female customers might design, cut and size garments in such a way as to flatter the figure of the older woman.

Positioning

Having segmented the market and selected which sector and consumers to target, a company must now position its brand within the market, so that it will appeal directly to the target market. This is an approach taken by the Arcadia Group, the UK's largest privately owned clothing retailer. The Group operates

Left
Kate Moss appears as a mannequin in the window of Topshop during the launch of her first collection for the retailer. Topshop positions itself as a brand offering cutting-edge fashion at affordable prices; signing Kate Moss was a strategy designed to attract young fashion-conscious customers.

seven well-known high-street retail brands, each positioned to attract a particular type of fashion consumer. Topshop, one of Arcadia's most famous brands, targets young girls and women aged 13–25 and positions itself as a brand offering 'cutting-edge fashion at affordable prices'. Dorothy Perkins (DP) is aimed at a broader range of women aged 25–45. The average DP customer is in her thirties and is a busy mum or working woman; the core value at Dorothy Perkins is 'value for money'.

Positioning, however, is a slightly complicated issue, because it is really a matter of perception. It is about the position a brand occupies in the mind of a consumer or potential consumer. Furthermore this position is relative. Positioning is about where a brand or product is perceived to be within the marketplace relative to the other brands or products operating within the same sector. So for example, consumers may feel that a Prada handbag is inherently more desirable than a bag sold by another luxury brand which they might perceive to be more traditional or staid, or they may consider the garments made by one sports brand to be of a higher quality than another, when in reality both use the same factory to manufacture their apparel.

In order to position itself, its brands or its products effectively a business must develop a positioning strategy. The strategy will be dependent on where competitors position themselves and how the business wants its brands or products to compete. So, taking the example of a luxury accessory brand viewed by consumers as more traditional and less cutting-edge than Prada; this brand could decide to strategically position itself close to Prada – to compete head-to-head and try and beat the competitor brand at its own game. If this were the strategy, then the brand would offer similar products or services at comparable prices. It is of course high risk and costly to compete aggressively with a market leader and there may be no real advantage for consumers in having two virtually identical brands. Another option would be to position the brand within the same market but to offer something distinctly different, or provide extra benefits.

When working on a positioning strategy it is helpful to create a **positioning map**. This can be used to pinpoint the desired position for a brand and give a visual overview of this position relative to that of competitor brands within a market. Given that positioning is actually dependent on the perception of consumers, the company must also attain knowledge of how consumers perceive their brand within the market. Once research has been carried out, a **perceptual map** can be produced. This is very similar to a positioning map but is based solely upon consumers' perceptions of the brand rather than where the company wishes to position it. The map will indicate the consumer perceptions of the brand's current position and identify where shifts are required to align them with the company's desired position. This pursuit of alignment is called repositioning, the process of redefining the identity of an existing brand or product in order to shift the position it holds in consumers' minds relative to that of competitors.

"Positioning is not what you do to a product. Positioning is what you do to the mind of the prospect."
Ries & Trout

Above
The year 2008 heralded the return of the supermodel. In a bid to make their product desirable to a more discerning customer, luxury fashion brands signed up well-known older models like Linda Evangelista who became the face of the Prada Autumn/Winter 2008 campaign.

Positioning or perceptual map

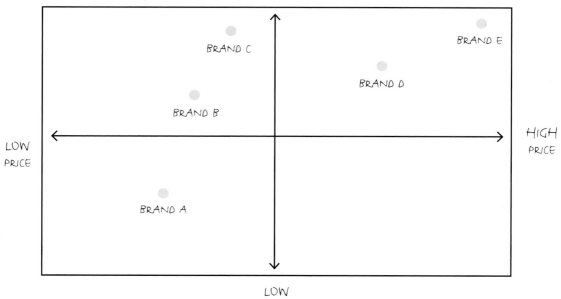

So to summarize the positioning process:

- Define the market in which the brand or product will compete
- Decide where to position within the market
- Determine whether to compete directly against a competitor or how to differentiate and compete by being different
- Understand how consumers perceive the current position
- Determine if repositioning is necessary

Once a clear position for the brand or product has been established, the next step is to ensure that this position is communicated to consumers. All facets of the brand, its image, products, packaging, retail environment, promotion and advertising will convey this position and it is therefore vital that every aspect is congruent and supports the desired positioning. Positioning and repositioning are costly exercises; the most effective positioning should therefore be long-term and remain consistent. Moving a brand's position is not a tactic to be carried out repeatedly. The aim is to establish a strong and recognizable position that is consistent over time and to make sure products and brands are clearly different from those offered by competitors. This is the principle of **differentiation**, closely allied to the concept of positioning it is the next strategic tool to be discussed.

A positioning or perceptual map plots the relative positions of brands or products. Two key criteria are chosen, one for each axis. Normally, price is the criterion chosen for the horizontal axis. The vertical axis may represent quality or fashionability or speed to market. In this instance fashionability has been chosen.

Differentiation

Differentiation is the concept of developing and marketing products or services so that they are different and hopefully superior to those offered by competitors within the same marketplace. It is a fundamental strategic approach that ensures products and services are distinctive and stand out from the crowd.

The ultimate aim of differentiation is to achieve what is known as a **competitive advantage**. A company achieves an advantage if it is able to provide products or services of greater value to consumers than those offered by competitors. As mentioned earlier in the chapter, value is not just an issue of price. Customers might value premium service or luxury quality or the high status of a particular fashion label and they may indeed be willing to pay more for it. Alternatively it might be street credibility that gives a brand a competitive edge or the fact that a world famous sports team endorses the brand. These extra elements augment the basic product, add value and help achieve competitive advantage.

Opportunity to differentiate exists at every stage of the marketing process. Differentiation and competitive advantage can be achieved through design and technology innovation, by strategic management of the supply chain or in the way a brand or product is retailed, distributed or promoted. The Potential for Differentiation table shown opposite uses the 7P marketing mix as a framework for exploring possible areas for differentiation and competitive advantage. Once relevant areas for differentiation have been identified, then practical steps can be planned and strategic actions put into place so as to achieve the desired outcome. The chosen tactics must also contribute towards creating a competitive advantage for the company and, of course, offer clear value and benefit for the consumer.

Competitive advantage

The Potential for Differentiation table should highlight some of the ways a business might differentiate itself and achieve an advantage over competitors. One obvious way to compete in a marketplace is to be the cheapest and gain a cost advantage. In this case the design or quality of products might be comparable but the competitor that offers them at the lowest price might gain the advantage. However this is likely to be a short-lived victory. The problem with this approach is that it soon becomes unsustainable. Competitors will usually reduce prices to match and a vicious cycle of cost reductions will eventually lead to erosion of profits for all concerned. Cost alone no longer provides a strong enough advantage; it needs to be aligned with other beneficial factors such as speed and what is known in the trade as **fashionability**. In other words, companies that manage to get reasonably priced catwalk-inspired styles or the right trends into the market faster than rivals have not only managed to achieve a cost advantage but also a speed advantage and what could be termed a fashion advantage; this of course is the operating principle behind the concept of fast fashion. Zara, one of the

Opposite
This table is designed as a tool to help identify potential areas by which a company can differentiate itself, and its products and services. The marketing mix should be used as a framework. Some initial ideas for differentiation have been given here as an example. Once relevant areas for potential differentiation have been identified, then specific objectives can be set and tactics devised to achieve each particular aspect of differentiation.

2.

Potential for differentiation table

MARKETING MIX VARIABLES	POTENTIAL AREAS FOR DIFFERENTIATION	TACTICS TO ACHIEVE DIFFERENTIATION	COMPETITIVE ADVANTAGE	VALUE FOR CONSUMERS
PRODUCT	• Design & construction of products • Quality of products, fabrics & components • Range of products on offer • Fashion level of merchandise			
PRICE	• Prices in comparison to competitors • Pricing structure and price architecture of a range			
PLACE	• Routes to market • Locations of stores			
PROMOTION	• Designer collaboration • Advertising • Celebrity endorsement • Sales promotions • Limited editions			
PHYSICAL EVIDENCE	• In-store environment – signage, seating, changing rooms etc. • Internet site • Marketing extras – swing ticket and labelling, carrier bag, brochure, in-store magazine			
PROCESS	• In-store and customer service • Website design & ease of use • Aftercare, return of products			
PEOPLE	• Structure of company • Opportunities for staff • Ethics of garment production			

brands owned by the Spanish Inditex Group, has become a famous fashion phenomenon. The international retailer has consistently been able to offer reasonably priced stylish interpretations of catwalk trends at exceptional speed. A tightly controlled production system allows Zara to move swiftly from a design drawing to a finished garment delivered to store in a period of between two to three weeks. The international retailer achieves its speed advantage because the Inditex Group possesses its own manufacturing and distribution capabilities and operates what is termed a **vertical supply chain**. The company has spent more than 30 years perfecting this highly integrated production and distribution model. It is Zara's legendary lead-time (the time between placing an order and the stock arriving in-store) that gives it its competitive advantage.

Asos, the UK online fashion retailer, illustrates the next evolutionary development in the competitive platform in fashion retailing. The web-based company, whose name is an acronym of 'As Seen on Screen', was established in June 2000. By December of the same year it was voted 'Best Trendsetter' by *The Sunday Times* newspaper. In 2008, the company reported profits of £7.3 million and its rapid growth and ability to weather the early stages of the recession has provided a wake-up call to competitors. Aimed at the 'fashion forward' customer between 16–34 years old, Asos has stolen the advantage by bringing must-have fashion ideas straight to the consumer via their computer screen. Asos gains competitive advantage by adding a new dimension to the cost, speed and fashionability dynamic, namely convenience. Not everyone lives close to an urban centre or shopping mall or indeed has time to go shopping. As consumers become ever more comfortable conducting social and commercial activities online, Asos is well placed to take advantage of its position as a fashion e-tail pioneer and capitalize on the ease and interactivity of internet shopping.

The Zara and Asos examples illustrate the standard criteria for competitiveness within a fast-fashion market:

- Cost
- Speed
- Fashionability
- Convenience

When a retail brand competing in this market achieves one or more of the standard measures of competitiveness, it raises the bar for others to match or surpass and eventually new platforms for differentiation and advantage emerge. Companies or brands that find the differentiating element above and beyond the standard will steal the advantage. While Asos certainly gains competitive advantage by throwing convenience into the mix, it also offers something more; shopping online can also be engaging, interactive, informative and dynamic. The company raises the stakes even higher by

taking the competitive game to an emotive level. What this cutting-edge e-tailer is able to do is to tap into the desires and aspirations of the celebrity conscious fashion consumer and satisfy their craving to dress like the rich and famous. Key weapons in the Asos armoury are its online community and magazine style blog; these keep users up to date with the latest fashion news and celebrity sightings. Users who want to dress like their favourite celebrity are directed effortlessly to the appropriate page on the Asos transactional website so the opportunity to dress like a star is only a click away.

Unique selling proposition

Asos has set itself apart, not only because it was one of the first companies in the UK to make the Internet a viable fashion retail destination but also because it provides a unique 'As Seen on Screen' ideology. This is what gives

"Clothes aren't just plonked on plastic mannequins, they are, to use Asos jargon, 'catwalked' – photographed on real models who twirl around to infectious music."
Lisa Armstrong

A timeless signature style
Coco Chanel

Coco Chanel was renowned for her signature personal style, often challenging the dress conventions of her day; she wore black, for example, a colour more traditionally associated with mourning. Accessorizing her quintessential look with copious oversized strings of pearls, Chanel created quite a stir with her dramatic costume style jewellery in an era when the wearing of 'fake' jewels would have been a novelty. The custom at the time would be to embellish outfits with precious or heirloom jewellery so as to indicate wealth and status. Key elements of her signature style are the little black dress, the classic Chanel suit with gilt buttons, costume jewellery and the quilted handbag. These emblems have become the established signifiers of the brand. They are so powerful that they are reinterpreted and used season after season, and not only for the clothes. The set of the Autumn/Winter 2008/9 ready-to-wear show at the Grand Palais in Paris showcased these brand icons. A gigantic central carousel was decorated with colossal strings of pearls, quilted handbags, bows and costume jewellery.

Above
Chanel wearing her signature pearls, photographed by Boris Lipnitzki in 1936.

Left
A colossal Chanel quilted bag adorns the carousel-style catwalk.

Below
Models on the carousel decorated with giant versions of the Chanel signature emblems at the Autumn/Winter 2008/9 ready-to-wear show in Paris.

the Internet brand its distinctive emotional pull and provides its **unique selling proposition (USP)** or unique selling point. A USP represents the fundamental distinguishing proposition being offered to the customer. It is the synthesis of a brand's positioning and differentiation and should encapsulate its overall competitive advantage. The unique selling proposition is a marketing tool that can be used to emphasize and articulate specific points of difference that make a particular product, service or brand unique and therefore distinctive in the marketplace.

Signature style

For many designers or fashion brands it is their unique signature style that helps define their USP. A signature style is a look that is so clear and distinctive that it can easily be attributed to the designer or brand in question. It is also possible for an individual to have a signature style. Karl Lagerfeld, for example, has an instantly recognizable and clearly defined personal style, as has the designer Vivienne Westwood.

For a fashion designer, developing an individual signature style or being able to interpret the style of an existing fashion company is an advantageous and important skill. It is usual for designers to work for several different fashion companies during their career and with each move to a new design label, they will be expected to adapt quickly and produce designs that fit the signature style of the design label or brand. Marco Zanini, for example, was at Dolce & Gabbana and Versace before taking on the role of Creative Director at Halston in 2007 and then moving to Rochas in 2009 to relaunch Rochas fashion. Many designers use their time working for others to hone their skills and experiment with a variety of styles until their own distinctive style emerges and they feel ready to go it alone and launch their own collection.

Above and below
The British designer Orla Kiely has created a contemporary modern brand that includes clothing, accessories, furniture and homeware products. The brand's fresh and joyful style is epitomized by the signature leaf design entitled 'Stem'. This simple and flexible motif represents and embodies the values of the Orla Kiely brand and is used on a diverse assortment of products season after season. The size, colours and application method may vary but the Orla Kiely Stem is instantly recognizable and is fast becoming a modern brand icon.

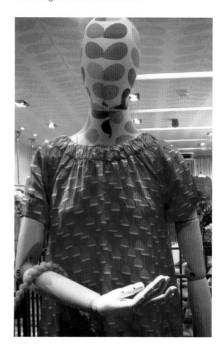

The flow of marketing strategy

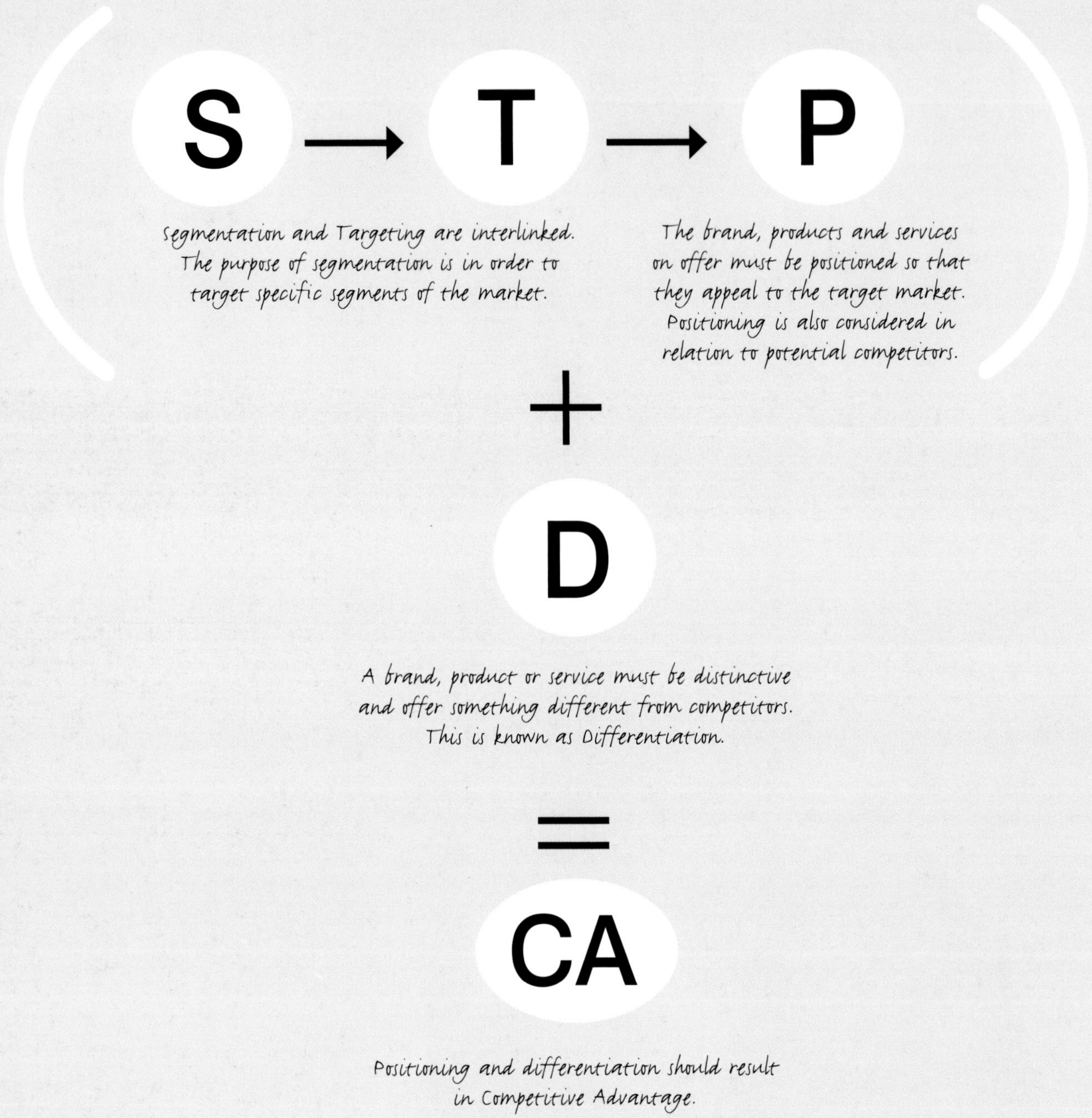

$$(\; S \rightarrow T \rightarrow P \;)$$

Segmentation and Targeting are interlinked.
The purpose of segmentation is in order to
target specific segments of the market.

The brand, products and services
on offer must be positioned so that
they appeal to the target market.
Positioning is also considered in
relation to potential competitors.

$$+$$

$$D$$

A brand, product or service must be distinctive
and offer something different from competitors.
This is known as Differentiation.

$$=$$

$$CA$$

Positioning and differentiation should result
in Competitive Advantage.

This diagram shows the steps involved when applying an STP marketing strategy. The first step is to analyse the market and divide it up into smaller, more focused sectors. This is known as segmentation. This process enables a company to better understand the specifics of a market so that they can develop appropriate product targeted to appeal to a particular group of customers. The next step is to analyse competitors so that the brand or product can be positioned within the market and can be differentiated in some way so that it is clearly distinctive from other brands. The ultimate aim when applying an STP marketing strategy is for a brand to achieve a competitive advantage within the marketplace.

3.

To be effective, marketing needs to be planned consciously, managed strategically, researched continuously and reviewed consistently. This ongoing cycle of endeavour is vital in a highly competitive, fast-paced industry such as fashion. This chapter highlights the importance of research as an adjunct to the business, marketing and planning process and outlines key areas of investigation to consider when carrying out marketing research investigations. Fundamental research and analytical tools, including **PEST** *and* **SWOT analysis***, Porter's five forces analysis and Ansoff's Matrix, will be explained. The value of both primary and secondary research will be highlighted and helpful tips on how to carry out simple but effective primary research and observation of the marketplace are given. The chapter will conclude with information on how to research and write a marketing plan.*

Marketing research

Marketing research is a vital component of both business and marketing. For a fashion company to be able to determine its future business direction and marketing strategy, it will need to continuously gather, analyse and integrate information obtained from a diverse range of business, fashion and market sources. You can see that the criteria of the 7P marketing mix – product, price, place, promotion, people, process and physical evidence – are all valid topics for marketing research. Kotler defines marketing research as:

"Systematic problem analysis, model-building and fact-finding for the purpose of improved decision-making and control in the marketing of goods and services."

Marketing research may take place in order to analyse and resolve a specific problem but it can also take place in order to keep up to date, assess the state of the market, stay proactive in a declining market, anticipate future trends, pursue opportunity or to develop and expand a business.

Research is an essential activity because it can help to eradicate false assumptions, expose potential risks and ensure that decisions are underpinned by relevant and current data. Research needs to be systematic and carefully planned, but it can be a creative and insightful exercise. Getting to know one's subject in depth and investigating a broad spectrum of relevant issues can be a stimulating experience that provides useful insight. The aim of research is not only to find reliable, unbiased answers to questions about the market, substantiate plans, determine production sources, reveal risk factors and determine strategy but also to seek ideas and direction, draw inspiration and foster innovation.

Above
An Indian worker processes raw cotton at the Cotton Corporation of India in Warangal District, 150 km (90 miles) from Hyderabad.

Competition exists at all levels of the supply chain. India is the world's third largest cotton producer after China and the United States. Cotton is India's largest crop, with 5.3 million tonnes harvested in the crop year to September 2008. India competes with the other cotton-producing countries to sell its raw material. Buyers research the market to determine the best cotton source in terms of quality, price and delivery.

The scope of marketing research

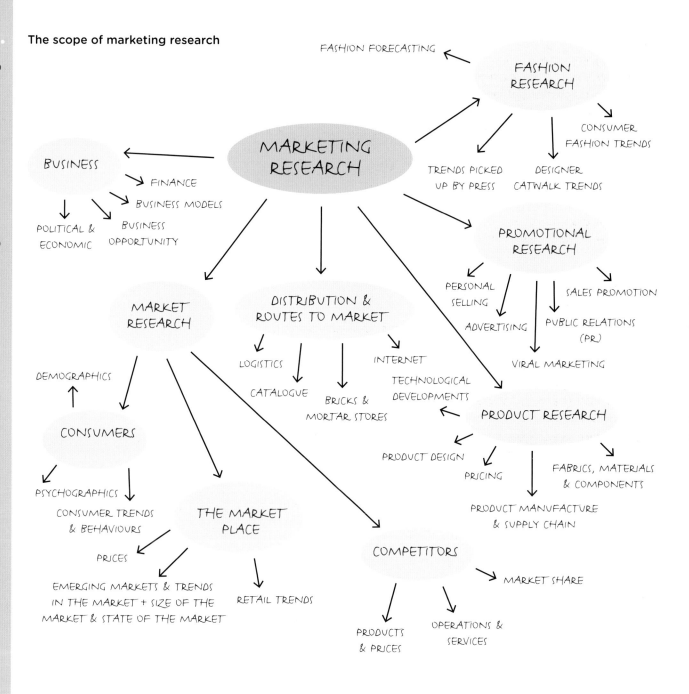

FASHION FORECASTING

FASHION RESEARCH

MARKETING RESEARCH

BUSINESS

FINANCE

BUSINESS MODELS

POLITICAL & ECONOMIC

BUSINESS OPPORTUNITY

CONSUMER FASHION TRENDS

TRENDS PICKED UP BY PRESS

DESIGNER CATWALK TRENDS

PROMOTIONAL RESEARCH

PERSONAL SELLING

ADVERTISING

SALES PROMOTION

PUBLIC RELATIONS (PR)

VIRAL MARKETING

MARKET RESEARCH

DISTRIBUTION & ROUTES TO MARKET

DEMOGRAPHICS

LOGISTICS

CATALOGUE

BRICKS & MORTAR STORES

INTERNET

TECHNOLOGICAL DEVELOPMENTS

PRODUCT RESEARCH

PRODUCT DESIGN

PRICING

FABRICS, MATERIALS & COMPONENTS

PRODUCT MANUFACTURE & SUPPLY CHAIN

CONSUMERS

PSYCHOGRAPHICS

CONSUMER TRENDS & BEHAVIOURS

PRICES

THE MARKET PLACE

EMERGING MARKETS & TRENDS IN THE MARKET + SIZE OF THE MARKET & STATE OF THE MARKET

RETAIL TRENDS

COMPETITORS

MARKET SHARE

PRODUCTS & PRICES

OPERATIONS & SERVICES

It is important to define the difference between marketing research and **market research**. Market research forms a subset of marketing research and refers specifically to investigations of the market itself, comprising the marketplace, competitors and consumers. Marketing research relates to a much wider-ranging set of concerns, which include business, politics, economics, cultural and social trends, fashion trends, developing technologies, logistics, promotion and product research.

This map outlines the wide-ranging topics that must be considered within the remit of marketing research. Marketing and market research will need to be carried out simultaneously; the topics shown in the map should not be viewed in isolation from each other.

Women's jeans

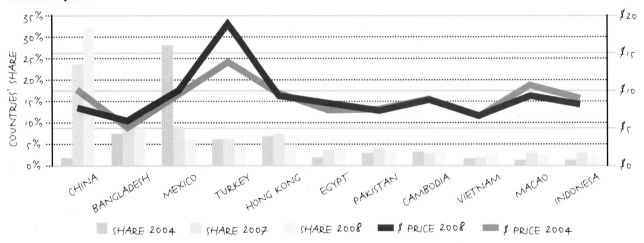

Legend: SHARE 2004 · SHARE 2007 · SHARE 2008 · ƒ PRICE 2008 · ƒ PRICE 2004

Y-axis (left): COUNTRIES' SHARE — 0%, 5%, 10%, 15%, 20%, 25%, 30%, 35%

Y-axis (right): ƒ0, ƒ5, ƒ10, ƒ15, ƒ20

X-axis: CHINA, BANGLADESH, MEXICO, TURKEY, HONG KONG, EGYPT, PAKISTAN, CAMBODIA, VIETNAM, MACAO, INDONESIA

The marketing environment

Marketing research takes place within the **marketing environment**. The modern marketing environment is heavily influenced by an increasing array of factors within what is now a global marketplace. To be fully effective, a business must understand and recognize the impact of these factors at a local, national and possibly multinational market level. The marketing environment is subdivided into three perspectives, the macro marketing environment, micro marketing environment and internal marketing environment. Each of these three areas needs to be explored in turn.

The graph above shows countries that manufacture and supply women's jeans to the EU market. It also indicates how cost prices compare for the years 2004, 2007 and 2008. This kind of information is extremely valuable for those wishing to research the market for jeans manufacture and retail and would form part of the background marketing research for a retailer wishing to produce their own line of jeans. Similar data profiles can be obtained for other product categories, such as outerwear, dresses, blouses, lingerie or socks, can be obtained from Clothesource, an agency providing apparel sourcing information and data for the fashion industry.
(source: Clothesource)

The marketing environment

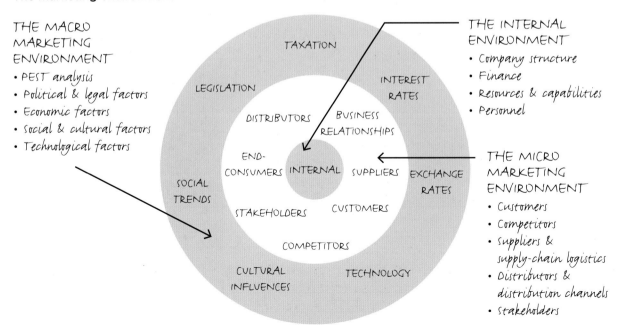

THE MACRO MARKETING ENVIRONMENT
• PEST analysis
• Political & legal factors
• Economic factors
• Social & cultural factors
• Technological factors

THE INTERNAL ENVIRONMENT
• Company structure
• Finance
• Resources & capabilities
• Personnel

THE MICRO MARKETING ENVIRONMENT
• Customers
• Competitors
• Suppliers & supply-chain logistics
• Distributors & distribution channels
• Stakeholders

Diagram labels: TAXATION, LEGISLATION, INTEREST RATES, DISTRIBUTORS, BUSINESS RELATIONSHIPS, END-CONSUMERS, INTERNAL, SUPPLIERS, EXCHANGE RATES, SOCIAL TRENDS, STAKEHOLDERS, CUSTOMERS, COMPETITORS, CULTURAL INFLUENCES, TECHNOLOGY

THE RISK FREE SUIT!

IF YOU LOSE YOUR JOB GET YOUR MONEY BACK!

ask an associate for details

The macro marketing environment

The macro marketing environment refers to the wider situation impacting on all businesses. The macro environment is outside a company's direct control and comprises a complex set of variables that can be simplified into four key areas: **P**olitical and legal factors; **E**conomic factors; **S**ocial and cultural factors; **T**echnological factors.

Research and analysis of these factors is known as a **PEST analysis**, an essential element of marketing research. PEST analysis ensures an organization is responsive to the political, legal, economic, social, cultural and technological situation at any given time.

Political and legal factors These play a significant role in the regulation of business. A company must be conscious of the prevailing political and economic situation at home and abroad (if trading overseas) and keep up to date with relevant legislation, taxation and trade tariffs. They must understand the implications of interest rates, rates of inflation, employment levels, currency exchange rates and fluctuations in prices of raw materials, goods and services. Although the example that follows happened over ten years ago, it illustrates how trade tariffs can affect the supply chain. In 1999, the cashmere industry was threatened by a tit-for-tat trade dispute between the United States and Europe over banana imports. The US, angered by the European Union imposing high tariffs on bananas produced by Latin American growers, announced that it would fight back and levy 100 per cent

Above

In response to the recession, many retailers have cut prices or offered customers special promotions. Jos. A. Bank Clothiers in Chicago launched the 'Risk Free Suit' promotion in March 2009. The business promised both to refund the price of the suit, and let the purchaser keep it, if he lost his job.

The financial crisis has affected fashion in the City of London. Sales of pinstripe suits have plummeted as bankers, too ashamed to be associated with the profession, have opted to wear more discreet styles.

import tariffs on certain European imported goods, including cashmere. The knock-on effects of the 'Banana Wars' were potentially disastrous; the livelihoods of Mongolian goat herders were threatened and thousands of jobs in the Scottish and Italian cashmere garment manufacturing industry were put in jeopardy. Luckily in an eleventh-hour reprieve, cashmere was spared and the US government agreed not to carry out its threat.

Economic factors The economic climate will have significant influence on markets and affect consumer confidence and spending power. In the first half of 2008, the number of clothing, fashion and cosmetic retailers going into administration in the UK rose 21 per cent. As the feared recession became a reality, consumers cut back on discretionary spending, saving their money to combat rising fuel and food costs. Economic factors, such as the weakness of sterling against the dollar, affected many fashion retailers and wholesalers, as raw material and manufacturing purchase prices are usually quoted in US$. The economic downturn did have a positive effect for some high-street fashion brands. The Swedish retailer H&M and its rival Zara both managed to stave off the worst by providing spot-on fashion at prices customers could afford. In the run-up to Christmas, it was the companies trading on the Internet that managed to buck the downward trend in UK high-street sales. The British Retail Consortium reported Christmas online sales up 30 per cent compared with the previous year. An article published in the *Financial Times* in January 2009 reported that British online fashion retailer, Asos, more than doubled its sales prior to Christmas with a 118 per cent year-on-year rise in the nine weeks leading up to 16 January.

Social and cultural factors Recognizing the effect of social and cultural trends is extremely important for those working in fashion design, buying and marketing. Film, television, music and art can all have a significant impact. When Baz Lurhmann's film *Moulin Rouge* hit the screens in 2001, it heralded the revival of the corset, and fashion looks inspired by the film were a key trend on the UK high street for Christmas that year. Another example was the HBO *Sex and the City* television series and movies, all influential in bringing high fashion and designer brands to the attention of a new generation of young women who fell in love with the *SATC* girls' fashion style.

Other social and cultural factors to research include shifts in the demographic of the population, developing lifestyle trends and leisure activities, as well as changes in consumer attitudes and purchasing behaviour. These will be discussed in Chapter 4.

Technological factors Technology has a tremendous importance within the fashion and retail industry. Issues to consider are wide-ranging: EDI (electronic data interchange) and just-in-time product replenishment technologies, developments in communication technology and Web 3.0 will radically change the possibilities for retail via the internet. The latest mobile phone technologies mean it is already possible to scan barcodes with a mobile phone. Body scanning and customization technologies are being used by Levi's and other forward-thinking jeans companies. Computer-aided

Inspired by music and culture
HUMöR

The team behind the young Danish menswear label, HUMöR, are inspired by a rich mix of underground cultural influences such as music, street art, skaters, snowboarders and urban pulse. The HUMöR philosophy is to create an individual and unique style by mixing and sampling the best cultural influences from past and present. This ideology is played out in HUMöR's first collection for Spring/Summer 2009. Heavily influenced by metropolitan underground music and inspired by the Shibuya district in Tokyo, the collection is a pyrotechnic display of happy, strong colours in off-beat combinations. Innovative use of materials, details and colours produces an overall look that is fresh and new but also commercial and wearable. The vibrant ready-to-wear collection of oversized T-shirts, sweats and unique jeans is designed for a fashion-forward consumer who likes to be seen and noticed. The typical HUMöR customer has strong beliefs and is not afraid to make a vivid style statement. The collection is stocked in hip young fashion stores, larger concept stores and sold via Internet dealers. HUMöR also shows at trade fairs such as Modefabrik in Amsterdam, Premium in Berlin and CPH Vision in Copenhagen. The label is marketed and promoted through DJ's, TV shows and other celebrities who are given garments from the HUMöR collection to wear when they perform.

"Music is very important for us as inspiration because it's a very strong media that always moves in different directions, and is always new in both a commercial and edgy way."
**Jan Chul Hansen
Former Creative
Manager HUMöR**

The HUMöR logo symbolizes the Danish menswear brand's connection to underground music culture.

The team behind HUMöR have an innate knowledge of their young male customer and the music and cultural landscape he inhabits. This is reflected in the vivid style, graphics and off-beat colour combinations of the Spring/Summer 2009 collection.

design (CAD) offers designers the opportunity to develop an entire fashion product range on screen. Sophisticated computer software allows greater flexibility for experimentation without having to cut the cloth or waste money sampling products in the early stages of development. Innovation and technological advances in fabric and materials must also be researched. The implications of innovation can be quite dramatic. Take, for example, the invention of nylon in 1939 and the subsequent

The science of fit Bodymetrics

Bodymetrics is a pioneering fashion company that recognized the commercial potential for revolutionary 3D body-scanning technology. Bodymetrics uses a futuristic looking high-tech pod (situated in Selfridges, the prestigious department store in London) to optically scan the body. Hundreds of measurements are captured and used to produce a digital replica of a client's size and shape. This enables Bodymetrics to offer made-to-measure women's jeans, accurately tailored to fit the body as if they were a second skin. The cutting-edge scanning technology was originally utilized for SizeUK, the first national survey since the 1950s analysing the body shape and size of the UK population; a similar programme, SizeUSA, has also been run in the US.

Bodymetrics use this cutting-edge technology to provide customers with three tiers of service:

- Made to Measure Jeans
- Body Shape Jeans
- Online Virtual Try On

The bespoke Made to Measure Jeans service offers clients custom-made jeans. The Body Shape service offers styles specifically designed to fit three key body shapes; straight, semi-curvy and curvy. The Online Virtual Try On service, available to customers who have already had a scan, combines body scanning with virtual-reality technologies. Customers try on different styles and shapes of jeans in a virtual setting. This highly entertaining option allows clients to see on screen if their jeans are too loose, too tight or just right, saving hours of frustration in the changing room.

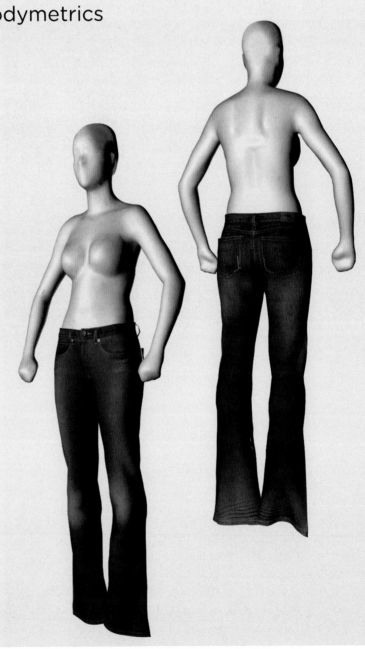

A digital replica of the body is reproduced using the Bodymetrics Online Virtual Try On service. Clients can use their avatar to try on jeans in the virtual world to see how a variety of styles might fit.

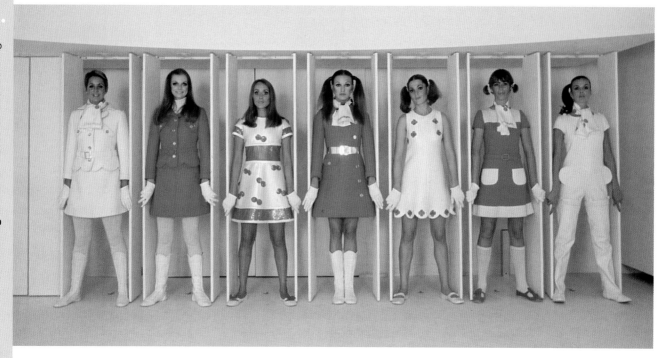

development of Lycra® by DuPont™ in 1958. These two innovations were utilized in the first tights, or 'pantyhose' as they were known when they were created by Allen Gant Senior. This ground-breaking hosiery development paved the way for the 60s mini skirt revolution, a fashion trend that would never have taken off without the benefit of tights.

The micro marketing environment

The micro marketing environment refers to factors that impact more directly on an organization and affect its ability to operate within its specific market. Factors to consider are:

- Customers
- Competitors
- Suppliers and supply-chain logistics
- Distributors and distribution channels
- Stakeholder and partner relationships

Unlike the macro marketing environment, which affects a wide scope of businesses whatever their nature, the micro marketing environment will be determined by the market sector in question and will be unique to each company. The main thrust of the marketing environment is one of impact; the rationale is to investigate and understand factors that might have significant impact on a business or organization, particularly those that influence the relationships a company has with customers, suppliers, distributers, partners and stakeholders.

Above
André Courrèges and Mary Quant revolutionized womenswear in the early 1960s. Both designers are reputed to be the inventor of the mini skirt. Here, models showcase the Courrèges collection of minis worn with thick white tights in 1968. Tights were a relatively new innovation, made possible by the invention of Lycra® in 1958.

Porter's five forces analysis

This is a tool that can be used to assess pressures within a competitive business environment. Porter's model identifies five forces that impact the competitive power and profitability of a business within a particular industry:

1. The bargaining power of suppliers
2. The bargaining power of buyers
3. Rivalry between competitors in the market
4. Threat of new entrants to the market
5. Threat of substitute products or services

The bargaining power of suppliers A supplier or manufacturer will have a strong bargaining position if they provide a unique product or a necessary service. If a particular fashion trend takes off, perhaps one featuring lace or hand embroidery, then a manufacturer in India or China with capability to produce delicate handwork may find that they have a stronger bargaining position on price. Suppliers that have built up a strong relationship with their customers will also be in a stronger position as it can be costly for customers to switch to a new supplier or manufacturer, especially if considerable money, time and energy have gone into product development, creating samples and working on product fittings and specifications. Each season, suppliers and manufacturers put pressure on their business customers by attempting to put their prices up; if customers have driven a hard bargain the previous season, a supplier is likely to try and claw back lost revenue. If a supplier understands that a particular style is on-trend and that there is great demand from end-consumers, then the balance will be tipped in their favour, particularly if they can offer a fast

Above
Manufacturers and apparel suppliers have a difficult balance to achieve. The cost of raw materials, labour or export duties impact upon their pricing and the ultimate profitability of their business. They may be forced to put prices up in response to rising costs or changes to taxation or duties. There is, however, always pressure from customers to keep prices down and the risk is that they will take their business elsewhere and purchase from a cheaper source.

Sustainable pioneers
The North Face

Sustainable design is a growing area of technological advancement within fashion and is an issue taken very seriously by a number of high-performance outdoor sports apparel brands. The North Face is committed to pushing the boundaries of innovation and the company continually explores ways to minimize their impact on the environment. Many of their high-performance outdoor garments are designed using recycled materials such as PrimaLoft Eco insulation, made from a combination of post-consumer products and post-industrial plastic waste. The North Face also uses innovative sustainable technology when designing and building their retail stores.

In November 2008, they opened a sustainably designed 805-m^2 (8,665-ft^2) store in downtown Boise, Idaho. The ambitious project was accomplished using the talents of Minnesota-based design firm JGA, a leader in retail architecture. A wide range of high-efficiency and energy-conserving technologies were utilized throughout the building for lighting, heating and air-filtering systems. Materials were recycled, kept to a minimum and chosen for optimum energy use. Exciting new organic and sustainable materials such as Plyboo renewable bamboo plywood and SkyBlend, a wood particleboard material manufactured from 100 per cent pre-consumer recycled wood fibre, were used for store fixtures and the cashwrap counter.

The overall objective for the project was to create an exciting retail environment that was both sustainable and commercial; this has been achieved to stunning effect. The sustainable makeover incorporates signature North Face elements including large graphics, wooden surfaces, and red accents.

The North Face sustainably designed store in Boise, Idaho.

Dramatic graphics are used to set the scene for their outdoor performance gear. Photographic images of mountain climbers make a dynamic backdrop for the mannequins in the foreground.

Porter's five forces

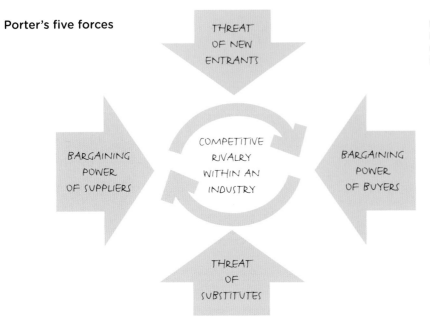

THREAT OF NEW ENTRANTS

BARGAINING POWER OF SUPPLIERS

COMPETITIVE RIVALRY WITHIN AN INDUSTRY

BARGAINING POWER OF BUYERS

THREAT OF SUBSTITUTES

Porter's five forces model highlights key areas of investigation that must be carried out in order to understand the specific nature of the pressures impacting on a business.

lead-time and deliver quickly. In this case the supplier will have stronger bargaining power and may be able to demand a higher price knowing that the buyer needs the stock urgently.

The bargaining power of buyers On the other side of the equation, buyers will naturally want to purchase products or services at the best possible price to ensure that they can remain competitive. Suppliers need to keep their order books filled, so they will be under pressure to meet buyers' demands, particularly in difficult economic times. Buyers from the large retail chains will not only bargain for low prices but will also demand favourable discount terms and usually require suppliers to contribute to markdown costs on stock that does not sell at full price. Fashion retailers that produce their own collections will gain the upper hand in negotiations with manufacturers if they place high-volume orders. Asian clothing exports from countries such as China, Vietnam, India, Bangladesh, Indonesia and Sri Lanka increased during the first half of 2009; successful manufacturers profited from orders from value retailers such as New Look and H&M, whose sales have risen due to customers demanding lower-priced value fashion as a result of the recession.

Rivalry between competitors in the market Competitive rivalry has been touched upon earlier in this book in the section on differentiation and competitive advantage (*see* page 54). Fashion retail is awash with a myriad of available brands and fashion labels, all competing with one another for the end-consumer's custom. Retailers will compete with each other to have exclusivity on certain brands; a boutique generally refuses to carry a particular brand or label if it is stocked by a local rival and suppliers will be competing to ensure they are stocked in the most prestigious stores. Rivalry between competitors does not only relate to retail, it will also be an issue further back along the supply chain. Textile suppliers will compete to gain fabric orders, while manufacturers within a particular country or region are in competition with each other to gain orders from foreign buyers, and will compete on price, quality, lead-time or extra services such as design capability, warehousing and other logistics.

Threat of new entrants to the market New entrants to a market can threaten companies already operating within it. In fashion, it is costly and time consuming to design, develop, produce and sell a collection or product range, so new start-ups may not pose an enormous threat in the first instance. However, an established brand diversifying into a new market could constitute a severe threat. A brand with loyal customers and a solid business might capitalize on their existing resources to extend their operation into a new sector of the fashion market; a successful womenswear retailer deciding to develop a range for men, for example. For retailers there is a constant threat that competitors or new companies will establish their stores just across the road. While this poses a threat, it can also increase footfall, raising the number of customers visiting the area and encouraging healthy competition.

Threat of substitute products or services If customers can find an alternative product or service, they may switch their custom, thus weakening the power of a business to succeed. The threat of substitution applies equally to the end-consumer who may choose from several retailers offering similar fashion styles at comparable prices, and to business customers who could decide to purchase from a competitor if they offer a replacement product or service that could reasonably substitute for the original.

Internal environment

The internal or organizational environment refers to factors inside a company that affect the way it carries out its business and marketing function. These include:

- Company and departmental structure
- Personnel
- Finance
- Resources
- Internal systems
- Technological capabilities

The internal structure and culture of a business organization will impact on the way it operates. In Chapter 2 Seth Godin was quoted as having said that marketing is not a "last minute add-on". To be really effective, marketing should be integrated throughout a business. If this is so, then it follows that marketing will be affected by the allocation of resources, the extent to which responsibility for marketing is shared throughout an organization, and the way internal processes and procedures are set up. A key stage in the process of creating a marketing plan is to carry out an internal audit. The audit provides a company with an opportunity to review its internal procedures, capabilities, resources and marketing strategies.

Market research

So far we have outlined the wider scope of marketing research; now we come to the vitally important subsection of market research. The fashion market in particular is a challenging arena. Designers must come up with fresh new ideas every season and thousands of products must be pumped out from factory to store on a regular basis. At the same time, retailers worry about slowing sales, customers are tightening their wallets and magazines are losing advertisers. It is crucial therefore that organizations, whether large or small, carry out market research investigations to gain an in-depth understanding of the market situation, assess shifts in trends, understand competitors and gain knowledge of consumers and their requirements. The market research process involves gathering, analysing and interpreting information, data and statistics on:

- Market size
- Market trends
- Competitors and their market share
- Consumers

Once research information has been gathered then its relevance can be assessed and the data analysed. The aim is to establish facts that can help with business and marketing decisions.

There are two basic types of market research investigation, classified by the type of information gathered. Research can either be qualitative or quantitative. Added to this, research material can be gathered using a combination of primary and secondary research methods.

Qualitative research Qualitative research investigates the quality of something and provides evidence about how and why the market is the way it is. Qualitative research is exploratory in nature and is useful for gathering facts on what consumers think or feel about particular issues relevant to the investigation. It can be carried out on its own or used as a forerunner to quantitative study. It helps form an overview of a market and assess the need for more in-depth quantitative investigations. Qualitative consumer research usually takes place face-to-face in small **focus groups** or individual interviews. Many fashion retailers or design companies invite a selection of consumers to preview a product range and try on garments prior to the seasonal launch in-store. This helps the company gauge the likely response to the range and to specific products, packaging and marketing materials. Feedback is very useful in working out what could potentially be the best sellers. Buyers can have a better chance to determine appropriate quantities for the buy and work out the ratio of various styles and colours if they receive pre-season information of this nature.

Quantitative research This type of research is numerically orientated. It quantifies the market, and can be used to calculate market share and provide

detailed statistics on consumers. Market research surveys that gather data from a large sample of respondents are quantitative in nature. They can be conducted face-to-face either in the street or home, via questionnaires placed on the internet, by post or via telephone.

Secondary research or desk research   Secondary research investigates and reviews existing data published either on the Internet, in books, magazines, trade journals or via academic, government or industry sources. This kind of research is used to determine the size and make-up of a particular market sector and get background information and more detailed financial data. Much of this type of information will be available for free from libraries, but some sources require payment for access to their research. Companies that supply industry information as a commercial venture usually charge quite substantial sums, but the cost is likely to be considerably less than those incurred if hiring a market research company to conduct extensive primary research.

Primary research or field research   Primary research is the collection of original data gathered directly by going out into the field. Market research surveys, questionnaires, focus groups and individual interviews are examples of primary research. Primary research can also be used to collect data on products in the market and to investigate competitors. Field research does not have to be complicated – visits to the high street or mall, recording information on product, styles, colours, prices, special offers and markdown

Above

It is vital for fashion designers or buyers to get out into the field to visit fashion stores and carry out primary research of the market. It is worth taking a small notebook with you when you go so that you can take note of important information and pricing details. Above, Topshop in New York.

and generally keeping an eye on fashion, all constitute primary, or field, research. Research excursions to the high street are relatively quick and provide a simple way to gather current information first hand. If research is conducted on a regular basis then it should be possible to notice both subtle and dramatic changes that occur in the marketplace over time.

Market research methods

The approach to primary market research investigations will be dependent on the exact nature of the project and why the research has been commissioned. Before research gets underway, first determine the aims and objectives of the study. Marketing research should be considered when:

- Starting a new business
- Entering a new market
- Launching a new product or product range
- Adding a new service
- Targeting a new customer segment
- Reviewing progress or resetting targets
- Researching how to compete in a market
- Investigating issues of underperformance

Once the purpose of the research is clear and the exact aims have been clarified then the next step is to determine who might be most suitable to carry out the research, analyse the findings and produce a final report. Large-scale market research projects are usually carried out by consultancies or agencies, however it may be possible to farm out some aspects of the project to a number of different specialist companies or carry out parts of the project in-house. A full-service market research agency will be able to help determine the scope of the research and assist with the development of a customized project. They will be able to carry out quantitative research and provide personnel to design and conduct market research surveys, questionnaires and interviews. They will also be able to analyse and evaluate data.

Another option could be to use a trend and market consultancy. They usually concentrate on qualitative research and provide information on consumer types, lifestyle trends and market trends. Condé Nast, for example, the publisher of *Vogue* magazine, commissioned The Future Laboratory in 2007 to carry out consumer research so that they could learn more about the motivations and needs of the modern fashion magazine reader. Consultancy companies are practised in conducting focus groups and running interview panels. They may have viewing facilities where interviews and discussions can be watched or recorded. (It is important to stress that market research is subject to guidelines and laws regarding data protection.) Trend consultancies may use the services of a network of freelance **trend scouts** located in major fashion and trend hot spots across the globe. Consultancies will also commission people to go out into the marketplace as a **mystery shopper** or to carry out an investigative procedure called **comparative shopping**. Consultancies of this type may be able to provide additional quantitative research; they may subcontract this element out to a field-work and tabulation agency specializing in data collection and survey analysis.

Another possible option would be to conduct market investigations in-house or commission one company to carry out field-work and then engage a data preparation and analysis agency to analyse the results; these agencies will have sophisticated software programs suitable for in-depth data analysis. If the plan is to employ an outside agency to conduct research or analysis then it is important to define the task and brief the consultancy or agency. A brief should contain:

- Information on the company and its current market
- The background for the research
- The issues the research should address
- What the research should achieve
- Detailed time-frame for the project
- Deadline for submission of the report
- Available budget and resources

Even if a company wishes to carry out all or part of the investigations themselves, it is important that they are clear on the above points before they get underway with the project. The next section will take you through basic primary research methods. While professional market researchers will be able to carry these out in great depth, most of the methods outlined can be carried out just as effectively by students, designers, buyers or individuals running a small business enterprise.

Trend and forecasting companies usually use freelance trend scouts to take photos and report on street fashions in cities around the world. Blogs are also a great way to keep up to speed with fashion style and hot new looks from the street. One of the better known sites for sharing pictures is www.thesartorialistblogspot.com, which comments on women's and men's fashion, as does www.lookbook.nu, an international invitation-only youth culture and fashion website started in San Francisco.

Far left
Two girls photographed on the streets of Tokyo.

Left
Andreas W, a 17-year-old singer from Gothenburg in Sweden posts pictures of himself wearing his favourite fashion looks on his blog and on lookbook.nu. Here Andreas wears a denim shirt over a limited-edition T-shirt by 5 Preview with a distorted version of the YSL logo.

Observation

A great deal of practical and easy research can be carried out simply and at little cost. One of the most beneficial market research methods for anyone working within the industry is observation of the market. It is fascinating how much valuable knowledge can be gathered by watching people in the street, studying consumer shopping behaviour first hand, or perusing the shops. Constant observation and scrutiny of the fashion retail environment is routine within the industry. Designers, buyers and marketers regularly visit key fashion cities and check out activity in their local fashion stores as part of their working routine. Manufacturing companies and suppliers will also send their personnel out into the marketplace to monitor what is going on. This practice is known as comparative shopping or the comp shop.

Comparative shopping

It is very important to visit the stores of key competitors and monitor what they are up to and review their product offer. Comparative shopping is a simple process that involves observing and recording information on the composition of fashion ranges, colours, fabrics, price points, promotional activity and visual merchandising in competitors' stores. Comp shops are a form of primary research. They are generally carried out by visiting the stores and looking directly at the products, but a great deal of comparative information can also be garnered using the Internet. The internet sites of fashion retailers can themselves be the subject of a comparative exercise; they can be compared in terms of ease of use, technology, service and informational content.

Above left
Louisa Via Roma is a must for any fashionista visiting the historic Italian city of Florence. The store houses an extensive selection of international luxury and contemporary fashion brands. The Rick Owens collection is given a prominent position within the store and promoted using a large-scale photographic backdrop.

Above
Colette is the number one fashion destination to visit when in Paris. This cutting-edge concept store offers a whole universe of fashion, art and design.

Like-for-like product comparison

The **like-for-like (LFL) product comparison** is a more detailed
investigation into a specific product. This is carried out when a company
wishes to investigate in depth how a particular product they currently
produce or are planning to develop compares with similar items offered
by competitors in the market. LFL comparisons are generally carried out
to compare core products or basics. The usual procedure will be to
purchase the item from several retailers. So take, for example, a retailer
such as Gap wanting to compare their men's basic white T-shirt with
those offered by competitors within the market. They may go and
purchase similar product from Uniqlo, American Apparel, Marks &
Spencer and Calvin Klein. The garments will be compared in terms of
price, fabric and make quality, design details and fit, wash care and
performance. It would be normal to send the garments to a testing
laboratory to check on issues such as piling, spirality and shrinkage.
Obviously purchasing garments and sending them to a lab for testing will
incur some costs, but it is possible to carry out LFL comparisons without
purchasing garments. In this case comparisons will be mainly for price,
styling, fabric compositions and available colour options.

Above
Mannequins in Barneys New York display the
Stella McCartney collection. It is common industry
practice for designers and fashion buyers to travel
to cities such as New York, Paris, London and
Milan as part of their fashion research and market
observation. It is not ethical to use a camera while
you are in a store but comp shopping and fashion
research can be a fun way to test your memory!
A good tip is to take a small pocket notebook
with you and record your findings as quickly as
you can before you forget the details.

Like-for-like comparison chart

PRODUCT – MEN'S FIVE POCKET JEANS	PRICE	FABRICATION • FIBRE COMPOSITION • FABRIC WEIGHT • FABRIC FINISH OR WASH	STYLING DETAILS	WASH CARE INSTRUCTIONS & AFTERCARE • GARMENT LABELLING	ADDED VALUE (DETAILS OR SPECIAL OFFERS THAT ADD VALUE)
COMPANY A					
COMPANY B					
COMPANY C					
COMPANY D					

Waistband
distinctive, embroidered 1969 stitching

Pockets
soft clean finished pockets

Belt loops
durable tri-fold with a little give

Hardware
stamped copper rivets

Stitching
heavy-gauge thread and single-needle stitching

Fabric
premium, ring-spun denim

Seams
vintage-inspired, busted-side seams

Selvedge
authentic red selvedge

Above
A simple table can be used as a framework for a LFL product comparison. The criteria along the top should contain price, fabrication, design details, wash care instructions and additional labelling or product information. A column can also be added to indicate how many colour options the item comes in. Products can also be compared with regards to details that might achieve added value – this could be a unique technology utilized to enhance the product or promotional campaign with a special offer.

Left
Designers doing a product LFL comparison will scrutinize every detail of competitors' product. Gap promotes their 1969 premium jeans collection by highlighting all the authentic design features that make the style a classic.

Mystery shopping

Many market research companies employ researchers who are tasked to enter shops in the role of a potential customer. As an undercover observer they are then able to monitor and report back on their experience of customer service and other retail activities. Retailers may commission mystery shopping as part of their overall market research so that they can analyse and compare the service offered by competitors. In light of the growing relevance of 'process' (*see* page 47) as part of the marketing mix and the increasing need for retailers to provide an exciting and engaging shopping experience, mystery shopping should be viewed as a worthy investigative method.

Focus groups

Focus groups and discussion groups run by experienced market researchers help provide information concerning consumer opinions, attitudes and purchase behaviour. Fashion companies often use these groups to gauge reaction to new marketing campaigns or product ranges prior to their launch. A selection of consumers will be invited to view the collection and give their feedback. This information can be extremely helpful for designers, buyers and merchandisers who can use the data to determine which styles and colours will be popular. The downside to research of this nature is that a small sample group may not be representative of consumers as a whole. There can also be a risk of the results being skewed if one person in the group becomes too dominant and sways the opinions and responses of other participants. However, if the sample consumer group is selected by a reputable consultancy and the session steered by a professional moderator, then focus groups can provide insights into consumer attitudes and help negate any assumptions that might have been held by a retailer about the customer or the product.

Above
The Zacarias Bilbao bag designed by Rita Nazareno; the unique shape is inspired by Frank Gehry's Guggenheim Museum in Bilbao.

Left
A small focus group meets in Manila in the Philippines to preview cutting-edge bags designed by Rita Nazareno for the new brand, Zacarias, manufactured by S.C. Vizcarra. The focus group allowed Nazareno to gather important consumer feedback on the prototype designs.

Interviews

Face-to-face interviews are useful for gathering more in-depth consumer information. They can be used to expand on data from questionnaires and to gather qualitative data. Interviews can be run as a semi-structured discussion where respondents can share their opinions and views. This type of interview allows researchers to gather customers' feedback on a particular brand under investigation and on competing products and services. Generally an interview lasts 10–30 minutes and can be conducted on any number of selected individuals within the target market. Interviews can be conducted via telephone but face-to-face is better for more lengthy discussions, or if the research requires the interviewee to look at products. The biggest drawback can be the time it might take to conduct the interview, particularly if it is being carried out on the street. Busy people do not always want to be stopped or devote time to lengthy questions.

Questionnaires

Questionnaires are extremely helpful for collecting quantitative information from a large number of people. It is essential to ensure that questions are not leading or biased in any way and that they are designed to obtain accurate and relevant information. Questionnaires must also be designed so that the data can be analysed systematically once it has been gathered.

It is important to make sure the questionnaire looks professional but also simple and user-friendly; this helps to maximize the response rate. Try to ensure that a questionnaire will not take too long to complete. A short statement explaining the purpose of the study should be included at the beginning – you want to establish a rapport with respondents and engage them with the project. Sometimes the company that commissions the research offers a prize to those that complete the survey. When designing the questions, think carefully about what it is you want to know and why. Make sure to:

- Keep questions short and simple
- Make questions precise
- Avoid ambiguity
- Avoid negatives

Open-ended questions allow respondents to formulate their own answers. Closed-format questions force respondents to choose between several prescribed options. It is possible to use a mixture of these two formats but it is best to keep open-ended questions to a minimum as they are much harder to analyse than closed-format questions. The **Likert scale** can be used to gather consumer attitudes to particular statements. For example; "sustainable fashion should be fashionable as well as ethical". The scale offers five positions set out below:

1. Disagree strongly
2. Disagree
3. Neither agree nor disagree

4. Agree
5. Agree strongly

Responses to questions using the Likert scale can be easily analysed by using a numerical system that equates to each position, so for example, agree strongly = 5, agree = 4, and so on. The format of questions using a five-point system can be adapted, so for example you could ask 'How important is price to you when you shop for clothes?'

1. Of no importance
2. Not very important
3. No opinion
4. Fairly important
5. Very important

It is however not good practice to design a questionnaire using this system alone. Respondents can have a tendency to choose one or two of the five positions and tick them consistently. Another option is to use questions that

Consumer Questionnaire: Fashion Shopping Habits

1. How much do you spend on average each month for clothing?
   ☐ £20-50 ☐ £51-80 ☐ £81-100
   ☐ £101-200 ☐ Over £200

2. Where do you shop for clothes?
   ☐ High street ☐ Independent boutiques ☐ Department stores
   ☐ Vintage stalls ☐ Street markets ☐ Supermarkets ☐ Online

3. What fashion labels or brands are you wearing right now?

4. How often do you normally shop for clothing or accessories?
   ☐ Every week ☐ Twice a month ☐ Every month
   ☐ 4-6 times a year ☐ 2-3 times a year
   ☐ Only when there is a sale on

5. Which sentence most represents when / how you shop?
   ☐ Only when I need something specific
   ☐ Whenever I fancy something new
   ☐ Whenever I go shopping with friends
   ☐ As soon as the new fashion season hits the shops
   ☐ It's always spontaneous, when something catches my eye

6. Are you ever influenced by what celebrities are wearing?
   ☐ Yes ☐ No ☐ Sometimes

7. Age:

8. Gender:

9. Occupation:

10. Salary:

offer a checklist from which respondents can choose. So a questionnaire designed to find out if respondents owned clothing made from sustainable fabrics might offer the following check list. Respondents are asked to tick as many options as applicable:

- Garments made from hemp
- Garments made from organic cotton
- Garments made from bamboo fabric
- Garments made from any other sustainable fabric
- Don't know

Ranking is another option that can be used. Respondents are asked to rank a list of criteria in order of importance or relevance.

"Please rank the following as to how relevant you consider them to be to ethical fashion." (1 = most relevant – 5 = least relevant)

- Fair-trade
- Anti-sweatshop
- Low carbon footprint
- Ethical production
- Sustainable design
- Recycling and re-using

When setting out the order for your questions it is best to start with more general questions about the topic under investigation. Start with the easiest and simplest questions and work through to those that are most particular or complex. If you are going to have a mixture of closed-format and open-ended questions, then start with the closed-format questions. The questionnaire should conclude with questions designed to collect demographic data. You will want to know the age bracket, sex, profession and status of respondents. It is vital to preserve confidentiality and to abide by data protection laws. Make sure it is clear who is carrying out the research and for what purpose.

It is a sensible idea to pre-test or pilot a draft survey on a small sample of respondents before it 'goes live' to a large sample of people. This helps refine questions so they are not leading in any way, eliminate any ambiguity and iron out any other teething problems. A well-designed questionnaire should be easy for respondents to answer by themselves either online, via email, in response to a survey in a magazine or if sent in the post. Questionnaire results should be presented in a report that outlines the purpose of the study, explains the methodology employed to gather data, includes a summary of results and provides conclusions and recommendations based on the analysis. The main body of the report will analyse the data and illustrate results with detailed charts and tables.

'What's your e-motive?' An exhibition of ethical fashion at the London College of Fashion, April 2007. The exhibit provided an opportunity to collect data on consumer attitudes to ethical fashion.

Ethical fashion exhibition and questionnaire
What's your e-motive?

In 2007 the London College of Fashion ran a sustainability week. Industry professionals, lecturers and students attended seminars, debates and conferences to discuss issues surrounding sustainable and ethical fashion. An exhibition and interactive data-gathering exercise entitled, 'What's your e-motive?' was held as part of the week-long activities. The exhibition aimed to raise awareness and inform on sustainable and ethical fashion, engage the audience with the debate and encourage them to share their views. The overall objective was to capture consumer views and understand consumer purchasing decisions and behaviour when it comes to sustainable fashion. The interactive exhibit showcased garments and products from a broad selection of fashion designers and companies. Adili, Amazon Life, Blackspot Shoes, Del Forte jeans, howies, Simple Shoe and Terra Plana were some of the companies whose product was featured. Research was inherent to the exhibition; an online 'eco-wardrobe audit' questionnaire was posted on the university website and computers were situated within the gallery so that visitors could answer the audit. The combined results of the interactive exhibition questions and online eco-wardrobe audit provided the London College of Fashion with over 400 individual responses and almost 200 people

answered the questionnaire. This revealed that 97 per cent of respondents were interested in purchasing and wearing garments that they believed to be ethical and sustainably produced, but that only a third claimed to actually own a garment that was fairly traded or made from sustainable materials. Respondents were asked the importance of the following criteria when making purchasing decisions about clothing.

- Fashion and style
- Price
- Fabric
- Ethics behind the production of the garment

Sixty-three per cent said that fashion and style was very important when choosing clothes, while the ethics behind the production of garments was judged by 55.6 per cent to be only fairly important. Interestingly 56.3 per cent of people said that anti-sweatshop was very important in a separate question that asked respondents to compare the importance of:

- Anti-sweatshop
- Fair-trade
- Sustainable fabrics such as organic cotton
- Recycling and re-using garments

This result highlights the importance of language and context. The emotive and more specific term, 'anti-sweatshop', may have been easier for people to grasp than the idea of ethics.

Monitoring the market

Now that we have looked at some fundamental market research methods, the next step is to review the purpose of market research and outline the aspects of the market that should be monitored. Market research and analysis should be used to:

- Define the size and composition of a market sector
- Determine the state of the market
- Assess trends within the market
- Establish which competitors operate in the market
- Analyse competitor strengths and weaknesses
- Research consumers and understand their requirements

The following section will explain the key aspects of researching and analysing market size, market trends, competitors and market share. Consumer research will be discussed in more detail in Chapter 4.

Market size

The size of a market can be determined in terms of numbers of consumers purchasing within a specific market, or more commonly, as a financial figure expressing the value of a particular market. A 2008 Just-style report, 'US Denim Jeans Market', estimates the figure for the worldwide premium denim market (jeans that retail for over US$100) to be in the region of US$4 billion. Another industry report from 2007 put the US accessory market in the region of US$30 billion. The first figure for premium denim indicates the size of the global market, the second piece of data on accessories indicates the size of a market sector in a specific country, in this case the United States. The fashion and apparel market can be broken down and categorized in a number of ways. Data can be compiled on any of the following:

- **Location of market:** global, international, national
- **Product category:** accessories, apparel, lingerie, perfume, homeware
- **Who the product is for:** women, men, tween market, children and baby
- **Product type:** pro-sport, active wear, casual wear, denim, formal wear, dresses
- **Market level:** couture, premium, mid-market, value or commodity market

Once the size of a particular market has been established, the next important issue to determine is the direction and trend within the market under investigation.

Market trends

Even though information on the size of a market at a specific point in time is extremely helpful, it is even more useful to track market data over a longer time-frame. This helps to reveal prevailing trends, indicating if the market is expanding, stagnant or contracting. If a market is experiencing a period of growth then there is opportunity for those already operating within the market to increase their business. But market potential may also encourage new entrants. This means that even in good times, existing players can not get complacent – they still need to be competitive or they may loose business to newer market participants. If a market is static or contracting (this could be due to cultural, social or demographic changes or as a result of an economic downturn), operators in the market will be fighting to ensure they do not lose business or go out of business all together. However, even in a recession or challenging market situation there can still be opportunity for some businesses to grow. In Japan, for example, a yearly TBS General Consumer Preference Survey showed that in 2008 Uniqlo took the top 'preferred brand' ranking for women in their twenties with 41 per cent stating they actively like the brand. This is a giant hike from 23.1 per cent only a year before. The result is all the more remarkable because previously Louis Vuitton had consistently occupied the top spot. Now in 2008, they were down to just over 27 per cent with the same survey group. The reason for the transfer of loyalty has been attributed in part to the economic downturn, with consumers purchasing cheaper fashion brands such as Uniqlo. But cautious spending is not the only reason for Uniqlo's increase in popularity. The Japanese retail brand has worked hard to raise its profile and become a 'purveyor of trendy fashion rather than generic basics'. What Uniqlo has managed to achieve is a canny transformation of basic garments into desirable fashion staples and this shift has been reflected in their financial results. At the end of 2008, when many apparel chains suffered decline in same-store sales, Uniqlo finished the year

Left
Uniqlo UT T-shirt store in Tokyo. Customers choose a T-shirt design from a selection on the rail. The T-shirts come packaged in a canister and can be picked up for purchase from the shelves behind. Uniqlo is a household name in Japan, with over 700 stores, and has opened in London, New York and Paris. The international retailer is rebranding itself as a purveyor of stylish and hip fashion suitable for a trendy, modern customer.

up 10.3 per cent. In 2009 they announced that Jil Sander would come out of retirement to head up design of its womenswear and menswear on a consultancy basis. This major coup is part of an ongoing strategy to ensure the Japanese retailer hits the spot with both trendy northern European customers and the more quirky Japanese market.

Uniqlo's success and the fact that young Japanese women are shifting their allegiance away from designer brands highlight several very important points. Firstly, it is evidence of a consumer trend in the economic downturn to forgo more expensive labels and shift to cheaper alternatives. Secondly, it illustrates the impact of economics as outlined in the macro marketing environment. Finally, although on the surface Uniqlo and Louis Vuitton are not in the same league and do not occupy a similar sector of the market, the TBS survey highlights how it is possible for both brands to attract the same fashion-loving young woman. This illustrates an extremely important point; competition is not just a matter of comparing like for like. In reality it is about consumer purchasing power. Consumers can choose where, when and with whom they spend their money. They can transfer their loyalty from one direct competitor to another, from Louis Vuitton to Gucci or Hermès for example, but they can also trade up and down the market levels. It is dangerous therefore to view competitors solely as similar types of businesses occupying exactly the same market level; in reality the situation is far more complex.

Fashion forecasting and market intelligence

An essential element of monitoring the market is keeping abreast of changing fashion trends. A watchful eye on developments in global fashion culture, catwalk trends, street style and the market in general is vital. But it is not just about monitoring the present or analysing the recent past; the trick with fashion is to try and predict the future. Designers start planning their collections up to a year in advance of when they will sell in store. Fabric mills develop their ranges at least two years in advance, and fibre manufacturers and colour prediction agencies work even further ahead of the season. This is why fashion can be such a risky business and why so much research must be undertaken. Fashion forecasting, market intelligence and trend reporting are indispensable constituents of the apparel and accessory industry. Retailers, design houses and manufacturers will use market intelligence and forecasting information to help them with important product and strategy decisions. There are several ways for a company to acquire this vital information. They can of course carry out their own market observations and trend research, but this will usually be augmented with material garnered from a selection of other sources. Most designers will visit essential fabric and trade fairs as a key part of their job. They will usually be required to report back on predicted trends for the coming seasons. In addition to this there are a significant number of companies worldwide providing a varied range of forecasting and market intelligence services. Agencies usually provide a spectrum of services ranging from specialist consultancy, tailored to meet the specific requirements of the

Above
Mudpie is an international fashion trend analyst and forecasting company. Mpdclick.com is their online service offering in-depth photographic reports on global fashion and colour trends. Fashion forecasters at Mudpie create concept boards to show key trend and colour predictions for the coming seasons. 'Sobriety' (above) is a trend developed for Spring/Summer 2011. This utilitarian concept, inspired by the Amish lifestyle, rejects the material excesses of the pre-recession society in favour of a humble and wholesome existence. The trend evokes a palette of slate and denim blues coupled with bright American red and hints of clay pink, buttery neutrals, deep burgundy and burnt orange.

commissioning company, to off-the peg forecasting, styling and market intelligence reports that can be purchased by fashion industry professionals. Many of the agencies operate an online subscription service; this makes information easily accessible and facilitates the provision of regular updates on a daily, weekly and monthly basis.

Most fashion forecasting and intelligence agencies will supply:

- Market intelligence
- Consumer insight
- Information on emerging global trends
- Reports on street style
- Catwalk reports
- Key styles and design ideas
- Colour forecasting
- Fabric trend information

Fashion designers, manufacturers, retailer buyers, merchandisers and brand managers will all use a mélange of market and trend information as a basis to predict the future direction for their businesses. Sales forecasting is a key part of the research and analysis process carried out by buyers, merchandisers and product managers. Sales forecasting uses data on historical sales patterns to gauge potential sales for the coming season. This background data must be used in conjunction with trend forecasting information so that a design and buying team can have the best chance of 'getting it right' when stock finally hits the shops. In fashion retail, sales data is usually reviewed on a daily basis and analysed in more depth every week. Major assessment of sales, consumer purchasing patterns and product performance will take place at the end of each season for both retail and wholesale businesses. Designers and product developers will build on this information with research into colour, fabric, design and technical trends so that they can develop appropriate products for the coming seasons.

Above
Thousands of international buyers and designers visit Première Vision in Paris each season. Around 700 textile suppliers from approximately 28 countries exhibit their fabric collections and innovations. Fashion industry professionals use the fair as an opportunity to preview up-and-coming trends and colours, and to place orders for sample fabrics so they can begin the design and development process for the next season.

Life cycle of a fashion trend

An important point about markets and fashion trends is that they change over time; this is why research should be an ongoing discipline.

A fad A fad is short-lived and usually difficult to predict. A fashion fad can be an individual item, look or style that becomes intensely popular almost overnight and then dies out as suddenly as it came in. A fad might be in fashion for one season only and then next season be most definitely out of fashion. A fad generally lasts for a year or less.

A trend The main difference between a fad and a trend is duration. A fashion trend may start slowly with low acceptance in the early stages and then build momentum over time. It will peak and then taper off, either disappearing altogether or flattening out and remaining in fashion long enough to be reclassified as a classic. The woman's trouser suit has become

Left
Poncho by Alexander McQueen for Autumn/Winter 2005/6 ready-to-wear.

The term 'trend' is often used as a catch-all, referring to a hot new fashion trend even if in reality it is a short-lived fad. The poncho is an example of a style that caught hold with sudden tenacity, trickling down from the designer catwalk shows through to the mass market. For a couple of seasons it took the world by storm before losing its appeal and going out of fashion.

Life-cycle of a fashion trend

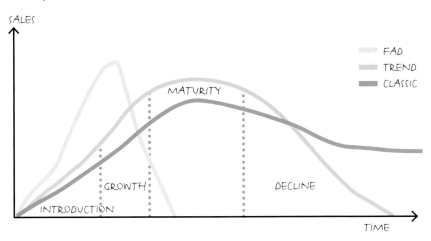

SALES

FAD
TREND
CLASSIC

MATURITY

GROWTH

INTRODUCTION

DECLINE

TIME

The first stage of the trend life cycle is the introduction stage. The next is growth, then comes the maturity stage, and finally the decline, which may tail off to nothing, or remain low and constant in the case of a fashion classic. Sales of a fashion fad might take off suddenly. Growth might be rapid, reach a peak and then drop quickly; the fad will die out once everyone who wants the particular fashion has it. Fashion buyers need to be sharp when it comes to fads – while they obviously have great potential if you get it right, there is a risk of getting on the bandwagon too late and being caught with stock no one wants. When a fashion trend reaches maturity, sales will flatten out. This is the indication that the market is saturated and sales will start to go into decline. Declining sales for a specific retailer or supplier could also result when a trend is established, and other competitors offer something similar that consumers prefer.

a classic. The seed of this trend was sewn in 1966 when Yves Saint Laurent introduced 'Le Smoking', a tuxedo trouser suit for women. This illustrates how a trend may be initiated at couture or designer level and then work its way down through the market levels to be sold in high-street stores; this is known as the trickle-down effect. Trends can also move in the other direction, they can start on the street and bubble up through the fashion hierarchy to be reinterpreted by designers on the catwalks of Paris, London, Milan and New York.

Megatrend A megatrend is a large social, cultural, economic, political or technological change that is slow to form but will influence a market over an extended time-frame. Denim jeans could be described as a megatrend.

Pop-up stores

Pop-up stores and guerrilla projects are one of the latest ongoing trends to hit fashion retail. This particular development really hits the spot in terms of satisfying customers' appetite for the buzz of newness while at the same time protecting businesses from the costs of long-term investment. Pop-ups increase consumer interest and desire as they know the project will only last a short while and there is an element of being in the loop, which is de rigueur in the information age. Rei Kawakubo opened a Comme des Garçons guerrilla store in Berlin for one year – rather long in pop-up terms. The Comme store has popped up since in several cities, including Reykjavik, Helsinki, Los Angeles and Glasgow.

Identifying competitors

It is important for a business to monitor its competitors, keep an eye on what they are up to and scrutinize the products and services they offer. The first step is to identify competitors and determine who to research. As we have just seen this is not always straightforward. A twenty-year-old Japanese fashion consumer may choose to purchase in Uniqlo and Louis Vuitton. A forty-five-

Above
Temporary pop-up stores have become a recognized feature of fashion marketing. A pink pop-up store in Times Square, New York, was set up by the fashion retailer, Target. All profits went to support the Breast Cancer Research Foundation.

year-old woman with an artistic sensibility and creative sense of style may purchase designer labels such as Crea Concept, Shirin Guild, Eileen Fisher or Oska but may also shop in Zara, Uniqlo and Gap. Within the manufacturing market, an apparel manufacturer in China might find that they are in competition not only with other Chinese manufacturers but also with countries in the Asia region such as Vietnam that may have lower labour costs, or other global producers in Turkey or Eastern Europe that are closer to the European fashion markets.

The most basic way of categorizing competitors is to define those that offer and supply similar types of products and services at the same level of the market. So one could say that Gucci and Prada, or Nike and adidas, are brands that are in direct competition. But this is a very simplistic way to view the competitive landscape, especially for fashion.

Competition is not so much an issue of brand against brand; it is more a case of:

- Product type and usage
- Consumer psychology
- Product and brand positioning
- Shopping location

Let's take a man who wants to buy a well-made classic but *contemporary* suit from an upmarket designer brand. He wants to purchase a respected label because he feels that a designer suit will last, be well tailored and of *good quality*. This shopper lives out of town but plans a trip into the city to look for the suit. Prior to the visit, he goes online to gather information, compare prices and check store locations. Once in town he starts with a visit to Armani. He likes the brand's *classic simplicity* and knows it has a great reputation for men's tailoring. On the basis of classic simplicity, Calvin Klein might be considered a direct competitor, so our potential customer heads for a department store to continue his search. Once there he notices a suit by Paul Smith and is intrigued by the fusion of *classic style* with quirky designer details; the suit most certainly is contemporary. So now this brand also enters his consideration. This short scenario should help to illustrate how competition is dependent upon the interplay of several factors: the type of product, the positioning of brands under consideration, the requirements, needs and psychology of the consumer as well as the options actually available to our potential purchaser in the locale at the time of his shopping expedition. Throughout this description certain words have been highlighted in italics. They have been used to indicate the qualities the man expects; he wants a suit that is classic yet contemporary, simple yet stylish and good quality. Also of importance is that it should be a designer brand. However, he may not adhere to these particular criteria for other products. Imagine he also wishes to purchase two or three basic white cotton shirts and some T-shirts to wear with the suit. He might not consider Armani, Paul Smith or Calvin Klein for these but

Competing for retail space
Product stocked in a boutique or department store is not just competing for the end-consumer's custom but also the store buyer's. Labels that perform well are more likely to be bought season after season by the buyer and may be given more floor space and a better profile within the store. Brands that don't sell so well risk being positioned in a less prominent location, having their floor space diminished or being dropped by the buyer.

head straight to Gap, Uniqlo or Zara to buy what he considers a commodity product at a more reasonable price.

Pushing the idea further, if a consumer goes to a shopping centre with the aim of purchasing, then any one of the shops in the mall or brands in a department store housed in the mall has the potential to be in competition for the shopper's custom on that particular shopping trip. This leads us to the concept of indirect competition. The best way to view this is to think of it as everything that might compete for a consumer's discretionary expenditure. A woman who wants to splash out and treat herself may decide to spend her money on make-up or beauty products rather fashion, or she may purchase a new iPod or iPhone rather than an item of clothing or fashion accessory. The trick in determining who competitors could be is to try and consider the topic from the consumer's perspective. This is why understanding the consumer is so important. Constant monitoring of the market will also help to reveal what is going on and ascertain which competitors to examine.

Competitor analysis

Once competitors have been identified, the next step is to analyse their business. The aim is to evaluate how they are performing and investigate their operation in terms of size, **market share**, capabilities and resources, product offer, services, routes to market and number of retail outlets, if this is applicable. The purpose is to assess their strengths and weaknesses and determine how best to compete. Background research using published industry and trade data should help to reveal the competitor's overall financial situation, share of the market and operational activities. Market share is expressed as a percentage. It is used to indicate the composition of the market and highlight the value of key competitors relative to each other, thus helping to gauge their importance and power. This links to Porter's five forces, as powerful companies may have a stronger negotiating position with suppliers.

Market share

	2007	2008
BANGLADESH	8.8%	8.0%
CHINA	35.7%	35.6%
HONG KONG	1.5%	0.9%
INDIA	4.4%	4.5%
SRI LANKA	3.2%	3.5%
VIETNAM	1.7%	1.8%

Source: Clothesource

Left
The table shows the share Asian countries had of world apparel manufacture in 2007 and 2008.

Market share figures are expressed as a percentage and can be calculated by dividing the total market value by the sales revenue of each business operating in the market, or by dividing the total volume of units sold in the overall market by the number of units sold by each market participant. It is possible for a market leader to maintain a steady market share over a long period, but their share may not necessarily remain stable, so it is important to monitor the market and market share over time.

Utilizing marketing research

Market research must be used in combination with more extensive marketing research to monitor the state of the market, gauge the viability of projects, assess their feasibility, work out how to implement projects and support the writing of business and **marketing plans**. Wide-ranging research is crucial for those planning to start a venture, introduce new product lines, or enter a new market. Research may also be needed so as to re-confirm existing plans and direction, respond to changing situations within the market, or address issues surrounding underperformance of a business or product. In order to determine the remit for a research project and navigate through the research process, it can help if you ask questions about what it is you need to know. To review this and look at how market and marketing research blend together, let's take a luxury fashion brand planning to expand into the Chinese market. In order for the company to invest in such an initiative and follow through with their plans, they would need to carry out wide-ranging research to assess the potential for retailing foreign luxury goods in the Chinese market. So the first question to ask would be:

What size is the Chinese market and is there potential for expansion into this market?

To answer this, investigations will need to review market trends and data from the recent past and gauge the current market situation. In addition, forecasting and analysis will need to be employed to determine and predict future developments within the market. Certainly, up to 2008 the prognosis was very good, with business analysts posting figures of 20 per cent annual growth for the Chinese luxury market, with apparel accounting for a third of this value. A report released by Ernst & Young in 2005 predicted the market would grow by 20 per cent a year until 2008 and would then expand at the lesser rate of 10 per cent annually until 2015. Even this reduced rate of growth is predicted to be greater than the 5–7 per cent growth rate predicted for Europe and the United States for the same period. Results from luxury brands already trading in China such as Louis Vuitton, Gucci, Dior, Versace, Prada and Fendi showed a steady upwards trend from 2005 to 2008. This positive outlook was backed up by a report issued by the World Luxury Association which stated that in 2007 Chinese people spent US$8 billion on luxury accessories, apparel, leather products and perfume. It would seem that entering the Chinese market might be profitable for our fictitious luxury fashion brand, even within the current economic climate, and it may help to mitigate the slowdown in the European and US markets.

Market research into the size and trends within a market does not provide enough information on which to base decisions. Broader marketing research should also be carried out to assess how best to

Opposite
The 2007 Fendi fashion show on the Great Wall of China. The extraordinary catwalk extravaganza showcased the Spring/Summer 2008 collection as well as an additional mini-collection created specifically for the occasion. The entire production was said to have cost in the region of US$10 million. This enormous investment gives a clear indication of the importance of the Chinese market for luxury brands.

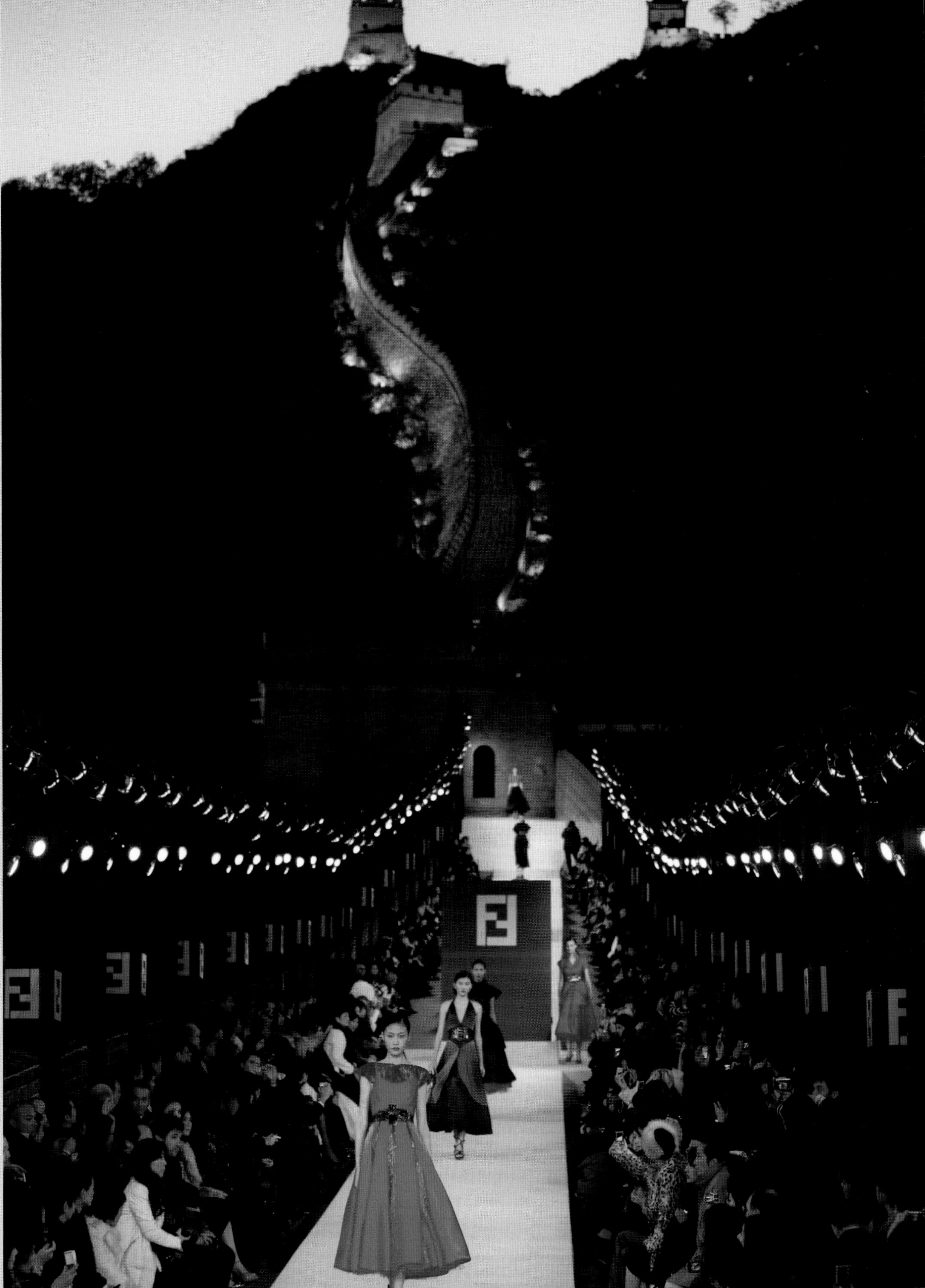

operate in the new market. The process of importing, distributing and selling European manufactured luxury goods in China is challenging; information on local taxes, import duties and supply-chain logistics will need to be researched. There will be political, economic, cultural, technological and logistical implications to consider, so PEST analysis will be required (*see* page 65). The next question should therefore be:

What issues will the PEST analysis reveal, what resources will be needed and are there local business partners or agencies that could help?

It will be necessary to establish and understand the impact of cultural differences, both in the way business is conducted and as reflected in consumer preferences and purchasing behaviour. The luxury brand will require this information so they can determine how they might adapt their operation or modify their product offer to ensure it is suitable for the Chinese market. There may be subtle differences from one city to the next. Marks & Spencer discovered this when they opened a store in Shanghai at the end of 2008. The company made assumptions based on their understanding of the Hong Kong market, where they already had ten stores. Unfortunately this did not equate to the realities of mainland China, where different consumer behaviour and needs applied. One of the problems was that Marks & Spencer had miscalculated the correct sizing for their clothes ranges – all the smaller sizes rapidly sold out. Sir Stuart Rose stated in an interview with the *Financial Times*, "We need to get the A to Z of sizing right and we need better market research."

China is a renowned global manufacturing market. Many of the major European luxury fashion brands that retail in the Far East have shifted part of their production to the region in order to service the market more effectively. In 2007 the World Luxury Association predicted that 60 per cent of the world's luxury brands would be manufactured in China. By 2009, China had overtaken the US to become the world's second-largest luxury market. There are, of course, market research companies that specialize in providing intelligence on different sectors of the Chinese market and there are also many auxiliary businesses to the apparel manufacturing industry such as trading agents, sourcing agents and supply-chain and logistic experts. These companies understand the intricacies of the local market and can help foreign companies wishing to navigate these complexities. Hong Kong sourcing giant Li & Fung Limited manages the sourcing and supply chain for many global fashion brands and retailers. In February 2007 Li & Fung acquired the sourcing operation for Liz Claiborne Inc in a deal worth US$83 million. The Claiborne stable includes brands such as Kate Spade, Juicy Couture, Lucky Brand and Isaac Mizrahi. Many of the major foreign luxury brands now trading in China and Asia have formed similar alliances, negotiated business partnerships or entered into **licensing** deals with local Hong Kong and Chinese trading companies.

Research questions
Posing a question helps focus the direction for research and makes it easier to determine where to look for answers.

What is the purpose for the research? Who is the current customer? Is there a new customer to target? What potential is there to expand into a new market? Do customers like our products? Is there a new service we could provide?

Planning and strategy

Analysis of data and information gathered from marketing research is essential in underpinning the planning process and for the creation of a marketing plan. In essence the planning process aims to clarify an organization's current marketing position, define what the business is aiming to achieve and determine the most effective strategies to use. Strategic planning makes use of key marketing tools such as the marketing mix, and strategies such as segmentation, targeting, positioning and differentiation. The culmination of the process is to create and write a marketing plan.

The marketing plan

The marketing plan is where the two indispensable disciplines of research and analysis come into play. The purpose of the plan is to review and assess the existing circumstances of both the business and the market, to determine marketing objectives and strategies, and establish the actions an organization intends to take in order to achieve its marketing and business goals. Although the marketing plan is a separate entity to the business plan, they are linked – the marketing plan will ultimately become a key component of the total business plan. The marketing plan should be created first and it should then be further developed into a more comprehensive business plan. The marketing plan is of ultimate use as a document that represents the results of systematic research and planning. It should contain the following elements:

- **Situation analysis**
  Where are we now?
  What is the current state of the market?
  Utilizes SWOT and PEST analysis
- **Objectives**
  Where do we want to go?
  What are the market opportunities?
- **Strategy and tactics**
  How do we get there?
  What actions do we need to take?
  Who will carry them out?
- **Sales forecasts, predicted costs and budgets**
  How much will it cost?
  What is the predicted return on investment?

The first step in creating a marketing plan involves an internal marketing audit and a review of the external market situation. This research is known as **situation analysis**. In order to move forward a company must first establish exactly where it stands and determine what has been working effectively so far and what has been less successful. This is covered by an internal audit used to examine the strengths and weaknesses of the organization and assess the efficacy of its current marketing strategy. The audit should include a review of the following:

- Marketing mix
- Target customers
- Positioning strategy
- Differentiation strategy and USP
- Competitive advantage

Situation analysis also includes an investigation of the current state of the relevant market sector; consumer research, analysis of competitors and a review of their products, prices and market positions. Situation analysis utilizes the PEST analysis (*see* page 65) as well as what is known as **SWOT analysis**.

SWOT analysis

A SWOT analysis provides a framework to collate and review investigative information. It is used to audit the internal strengths and weaknesses of a business enterprise and identify external factors that might provide potential opportunities within the marketplace and business environment. A SWOT is also used to determine and assess external issues that could pose threats to the enterprise or its brands. Once the strengths, weaknesses, opportunities and threats have been established they can be presented in a simple overview table. It is important to stress that the SWOT analysis is not merely a list or the chart itself but an analytical tool that corresponds to four key strategic positions detailed below.

1. **Strength + Opportunity**
   Utilizes internal strengths to capitalize external opportunity and potential
2. **Strength + Threat**
   Utilizes internal strengths to overcome external threats
3. **Weakness + Opportunity**
   Works to addresses or minimize internal weaknesses to ensure opportunity is not jeopardized
4. **Weakness + Threat**
   In this position a company is exposed and at risk. The strategy would be to mitigate weakness and ward off threats

The real purpose of the SWOT is to use the information to determine how to capitalize upon a company's internal strengths, using them to create opportunity and potential or to determine how strengths could be best employed in order to overcome threats in the market. It is not always easy to assess internal weakness but facing up to issues that might be holding a business back is vitally important. Again the idea is to address weaknesses in order to ensure that opportunity is not being missed.

Opposite
A summary of the results of a SWOT analysis can be recorded in a simple table. The example here gives an overview of the possible issues to consider for each area of investigation.

3.

SWOT analysis

STRENGTHS

- Reputation of the company, brand or fashion label
- Distinctive signature style and USP
- Strength of the creative and technical team working to support designer
- Strong relationships with suppliers
- Loyal core customer base
- Strong management and excellent ability to integrate business and design functions
- Contract with very good PR company
- Good credit facilities with suppliers

WEAKNESSES

- No clear USP – undifferentiated products that look similar to other fashion labels
- Lack of creative and technical support. Designer has to do everything themselves and is overstretched
- Weak relationships with suppliers
- Not yet built a reputation with buyers and customer base not yet established
- Cash flow or financing problems
- Lack of business or marketing expertise
- Do not have a website or has one that customers find difficult to use

OPPORTUNITIES

- Potential to take on an agent or PR company
- Relaxation of import duties, opening up of new markets
- Potential to diversify into subsidiary products such as stationery, homeware or beauty products
- Strategic alliances or opportunity to partner with others with complementary skills
- Rise of social marketing – opportunity to raise awareness and promote products
- New fabric or manufacturing technology
- New supply sources become available
- Government trade incentives

THREATS

- Changes in fashion trends, signature look of product goes out of style or becomes wrong for the market
- New competitor enters market
- Changes in import or export laws that affect pricing or supply sources
- Changes to exchange rates or interest rates
- Rise in operating costs
- Changes to trade laws
- Economic downturn – difficulty in gaining credit
- Key buyer drops the range

Market opportunity – Ansoff's Matrix

Ansoff's Matrix is a tool that offers four potential scenarios for opportunity that could be used by a company that has an objective to achieve growth.

1. Market penetration
2. Market development
3. Product development
4. Diversification

Market penetration means continuing to sell existing product within an existing market with the aim of capitalizing and improving upon the profitability of the current market proposition. Essentially this presents several key strategies:

- Increase number of customers
- Increase average spend
- Increase margin (raise prices and buy in at lower cost price)
- Improve product mix and range plan

This first scenario equates to the general situation within fashion. Although in many respects fashion product could be considered new each season, many designers and retailers producing their own collections stick to a recognized formula and it is usual for ranges to include signature or carry-over styles that customers have come to expect.

    Market development is the second proposition for achieving growth. This is also common within fashion when brands expand their business by taking an existing product to a new market. Topshop did this by expanding into the US market when they opened a 2,790-sq-m (30,000-sq-ft) flagship store in New York. Versace has invested more than US$56 million in developing its Asian market, and opening several stores across the region.

Above
British fashion chain, Topshop, expands its operations into a new geographic market, opening in New York in 2009.

Ansoff's Matrix

	EXISTING PRODUCTS	NEW PRODUCTS
EXISTING MARKETS	CONSOLIDATION OR MARKET PENETRATION	PRODUCT DEVELOPMENT
NEW MARKETS	MARKET DEVELOPMENT	DIVERSIFICATION

Product development, the third option for opportunity, relates to developing new product for an existing market. This allows for growth by capitalizing on a brand name to launch a new individual product or branded product range such as a diffusion line.

Diversification means developing new product for a completely new market, such as homeware or fragrance. This is the most risky of the four options. It usually requires solid strategic partnerships and is most likely to be achieved by licensing the brand name. Licensing is discussed further in Chapter 5.

The planning process

Once the current market situation has been established and an internal audit carried out, the next step is to use the information in order to set marketing objectives and strategy. The Potential for Differentiation table shown in Chapter 2 (*see* page 55) can be used as a framework to set objectives and determine necessary strategies and tactics. The key is to ensure that objectives are SMART, in other words: **S**pecific, **M**easurable, **A**chievable, **R**ealistic, **T**ime-based.

It is important to establish how each objective will be achieved, who will carry it out, and to set a planned schedule for key activities with interim staging posts for monitoring and review. The key to creating a plan is to keep it simple and realistic; the overall vision should be easily understood by everyone engaged in bringing the plan to fruition. Expenditure will need to be carefully researched and calculated; the proposed strategies and tactics will all have a cost. It is important to set a budget and determine time-frames to ensure the best use of resources. However, even with a solid plan in place, it is unlikely that everything will go according to plan. It is not always possible to predict with accuracy how markets will behave, what customers want or what competitors will do.

If things do not go to plan, it may not be the strategy that needs amending but how it is achieved; tactics might need to be reassessed and budgets trimmed. It is always useful to consider, 'could we do more with less?'!

Structure of a marketing plan

A clear, well-written marketing plan helps communicate the company vision and objectives to internal staff as well as strategic partners, investors and stakeholders. It is useful to have a plan so that progress can be monitored and results gauged against targets. The basic structure of the plan should include:

- A cover page with overall title, date, name of author or company
- A contents page listing sections covered with relevant page numbers
- A brief introduction setting the context and purpose of the plan. For example, it might be part of an overall business and marketing planning process, or required because of a new venture, brand repositioning exercise or to resolve a current marketing problem.

Above
Prada launched its cheaper Miu Miu line in 1992. The strategic aim of this development was to extend the Prada brand by appealing to a more youthful customer.

- A one-page executive summary that summarizes key points from the overall document, gives key financial data and an overview of objectives, strategy and recommendations
- The main marketing plan
- Relevant references and appendices

The main body of the marketing plan brings everything together. The actual structure for the main body is open to interpretation; it should be tailored so it is relevant to the type and size of business concerned. The key is to analyse and utilize the marketing research and internal audit information to produce a cohesive document that outlines the following:

- The market sector – giving figures to show size and financial trends
- PEST analysis
- Information on the company's current position within the market
- Information on targeted customers
- Internal audit including SWOT analysis
- Current products, services and USP
- Current marketing mix including routes to market, distribution and promotion
- Current positioning, differentiation and competitive advantage
- Information on key competitors
- Conclusions and recommendations
- Key marketing objectives, proposed strategies, actions and anticipated outcome
- Timescales, costs, budget and anticipated return on investment
- Resources, strategic partners and stakeholders, relevant staff skills and capabilities

The planning process

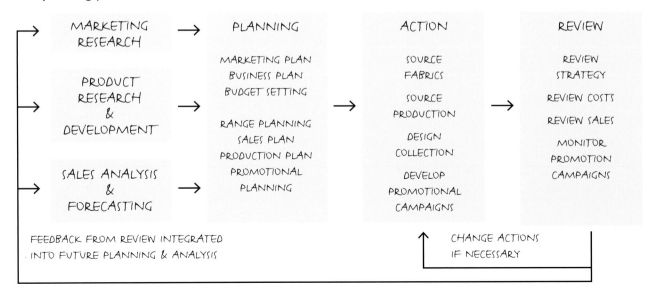

4.

Researching and understanding the customer is central to marketing. Indeed, recognizing the requirements and needs of the customer is essential for those tasked with creating and selling fashion products. This issue concerns business at every point in the supply chain from manufacturer to retailer – without customers there is no business, so detailed knowledge of their preferences, motivations and purchasing behaviour is crucial. This knowledge better equips designers, manufacturers and retailers to design, produce and sell products and services that fulfil or exceed consumer requirements.

Not all consumers are the same – each individual will have their own complex set of motivations and shopping behaviour – however it is possible to group consumers into clusters of broadly similar characteristics, needs or fashion traits. This process is known as **customer segmentation** and is a key feature of STP (segmentation, targeting and positioning) marketing strategy (*see* page 50). Basic customer analysis can be carried out effectively by a small start-up with limited budget; an example appears later in the chapter showing the type of research carried out by someone setting up their own fashion boutique. A national brand wishing to expand into a new global market may require more in-depth and detailed analysis; for this the services of a professional market research consultancy may be necessary. This chapter explains the basics behind consumer research and analysis and explains the various criteria, or **segmentation variables**, used to classify and profile existing or potential new fashion consumers. The process of creating a **consumer profile** will be explained with details on how to write a **customer pen portrait**. The chapter concludes with information on simple ways to analyse business customers.

Understanding customers

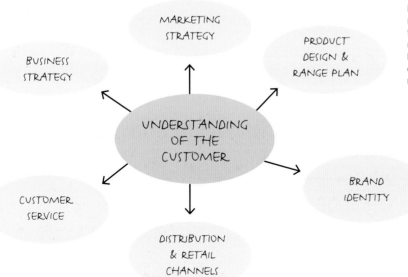

Understanding of the customer is central to all aspects of effective marketing. Many businesses become so focused on internal processes or monitoring the activities of their competitors that they fail to recognize the needs or changing requirements of their customers. Solid background knowledge and understanding of customers is essential and should underpin key business and marketing decisions.

Before going any further, it is important to establish the difference between the often interchangeable terms of consumer and customer. The consumer, or **end-consumer**, is the eventual wearer of the product and will generally be the customer who purchases the garment or accessory. However in the case of a baby or small child, while they would be the end-consumer, they would not be the purchasing customer. In this case, a baby- or childrenswear retailer needs to understand not only the special requirements of a baby or child but also the motivations and expectations of the person who purchases the clothes, most generally the mother.

'Customer' is a broader term. It can be used to refer to the end-consumer who will be a customer of a particular fashion retailer or it can be used to describe a business customer, which could be a business or organization operating within the fashion supply chain. In the first instance the relationship described is **B2C** (business-to-consumer). When a business is the customer of another business, it is termed as **B2B** (business-to-business). A boutique owner, for example, who purchases collections from a wholesale design company is a B2B customer. Companies supplying this boutique must not only have a good knowledge and understanding of the boutique owner as their business customer but also a thorough understanding of the end-consumers or customers who purchase from the boutique.

Customer segmentation

Customer segmentation is one of the key functions of marketing. It aims to divide a large customer base into smaller subgroups that share similar needs and characteristics. Typical criteria for classification are age, gender, occupation, financial situation, lifestyle, life stage, residential location, purchasing behaviour and spending habits. Segmentation helps enhance a company's understanding of its customers so that it can position its brand and offer products and services designed to appeal to the targeted customers. Lifestyle plays a crucial role in segmenting fashion consumers; clothing needs and style preferences will be highly influenced by a person's type of work, peer group, and their sporting or leisure activities. Attitudes and opinions on a variety of issues, such as politics, art and culture or environmental issues, might also impact someone's choice of clothing. When analysing a consumer's lifestyle and determining what type of customer they might be, the aim is to gain insight about what they buy, why they buy, which companies they purchase from, and how and when they purchase.

Segmentation variables

At the beginning of any consumer analysis it is important to determine the segmentation variables that will be used to classify and characterize consumers. It is normal to use a combination of criteria; the exact mix will be dependent on the objectives of the research project and the specifics of the company and its market. Traditional segmentation falls into the following main categories – **demographic**, geographic or a combination of the two known as

"I dress everyone from students to superstars. The end user is what I am, what I do."
John Rocha

Above
Fashion customers will have a variety of clothing needs dependent on their lifestyle and personality. The person illustrated here may be required to wear a traditional suit to work. Outside the workplace they might wish to dress less formally and adopt a more flamboyant or relaxed style.

geo-demographic, all of which focus on identifying who customers are and where they live; behavioural and **psychographic segmentation** look at the psychology behind consumer purchasing behaviour. Here the idea is to decipher what consumers think, how they behave, why they purchase and what product benefits they require.

Segmentation variables

DEMOGRAPHIC VARIABLES
- Gender
- Age
- Generation
- Ethnicity
- Marital status
- Life-stage
- Occupation
- Education
- Income
- Social grade classification

PSYCHOGRAPHIC &
BEHAVIOURAL VARIABLES
- Lifestyle
- Social aspirations
- Self-image
- Value perceptions
- Purchasing motives & behaviour
- Interests & hobbies
- Attitude & opinions

GEOGRAPHIC VARIABLES
- Region
- Urban / suburban / rural
- Residential location
- Housing type
- Size of city or town
- Climate

USAGE & BENEFIT VARIABLES
- Benefits sought from products
- Usage rates
- Volume of purchases
- Price sensitivity
- Brand loyalty
- End-use of product

Demographic segmentation

Demographic segmentation is one of the most widely used methods of classification. It uses key variables such as age, gender, generation, occupation, income, life stage and socio-economic status. Each of these factors is extremely important in its own right, but should not be considered in isolation – for example, age. A woman may spend heavily on lounge-wear or exercise clothing for yoga or Pilates; she may work from home and require only casual clothing. Another woman of exactly the same age and stage in her life might be employed in a professional office and need an extensive wardrobe suitable for work. In general men spend less on fashion than women but this is not always the case. Male consumers can be extremely fashion conscious and spend a significant proportion of their disposable income on clothing or accessories. Some young male consumers are addicted to purchasing branded sportswear, trainers or jeans. An article in *The Times* newspaper on trainer and sportswear addicts by Laura Lovett describes a twenty-one-year-old male who gains kudos by wearing Y-3, the

fashion/sportswear fusion brand created by Yohji Yamamoto in collaboration with adidas. This customer explains that while some people collect stamps, he collects Y-3. Gooey Wooey, an avid trainer collector living in southwest England, has a collection of nearly 200 pairs. Gooey trades trainers online, often buying a pair a week or selling some of his prized limited-edition retro sneakers to other enthusiasts.

Demographics also consider the life stage of a consumer; they may still be living with their parents or be single, in a partnership or married, with or without children, or they could have children who have left home. As a person passes through the various phases of life, their priorities are likely to shift and their income and discretionary spend will also be affected. Key stages in the life cycle are:

- **Dependent –** children living at home, dependent on parents
- **Pre-family –** independent adults who don't yet have children
- **Family –** adults with children
- **Late stage or empty nesters –** parents with children who have left home, or older people with no children

Market research companies often attribute names or acronyms to different consumer groups as a way to signify stage in life. Examples of this are:

DINKYs – Double Income No Kids Yet

HEIDIs – Highly Educated Independent Individuals

SINDIs – Single Independent Newly Divorced Individuals

NEETs – Not in Employment, Education or Training

YADs – Young And Determined Savers

TIREDs – Thirtysomething Independent Radical Educated Dropouts

KIPPERS – Kids In Parents' Pockets Eroding Retirement Savings

Above

Gooey Wooey, an avid 36-year-old sneaker collector living in the southwest region of England has a collection of nearly 200 pairs. Gooey trades online, often buying a pair a week or selling some of his prized limited-edition retro sneakers to other enthusiasts. In this image, Gooey shows off one of his most expensive acquisitions, a pair of Nike Dunk Low Pro SB 'Paris' sneakers featuring artwork by Bernard Buffet. Only 202 pairs of this limited edition were produced, so they exchange hands for prices in the region of US$4,000.

Above left

Nike sneakers on display at the Niketown store in New York.

Consumer generations

Another form of demographic segmentation is to classify consumers by generation. This considers the effect of the exisiting political, economic, social and cultural situation someone is born into. More specifically, it takes into account the period when a consumer comes of age as a teenager or young adult, as this will play an important part in shaping their opinions and attitudes on fashion, style, consumerism, branding, advertising and technology. Generational traits can impact the way consumers shop, how they spend money, the types of items on which they spend it and their allegiance and loyalty to certain brands. The following section provides a snapshot of the key consumer generations from baby boomers to Generation Z.

Generation timetable

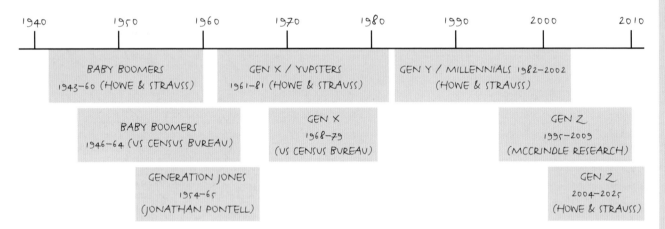

1940   1950   1960   1970   1980   1990   2000   2010

BABY BOOMERS
1943–60 (HOWE & STRAUSS)

GEN X / YUPSTERS
1961–81 (HOWE & STRAUSS)

GEN Y / MILLENNIALS 1982–2002
(HOWE & STRAUSS)

BABY BOOMERS
1946–64 (US CENSUS BUREAU)

GEN X
1968–79
(US CENSUS BUREAU)

GEN Z
1995–2009
(MCCRINDLE RESEARCH)

GENERATION JONES
1954–65
(JONATHAN PONTELL)

GEN Z
2004–2025
(HOWE & STRAUSS)

Leading edge baby boomers

Baby boomers were originally defined as those born between 1946 and 1964. However this 20-year generation span was later broken down into two groups – leading edge baby boomers (1946–1954) and trailing edge baby boomers (1954–1964). The name 'boomer' alludes to the birth rate explosion that occurred during the period of economic stability following the Second World War. As they came of age, baby boomers challenged traditions and adopted styles of dress guaranteed to upset the establishment – long hair for men, the shortest of mini skirts for women. Ironically, baby boomers are now part of the establishment and relatively wealthy in comparison to other generations. However they are increasingly being left out in the cold by fashion companies keen to reposition their brands in order to attract young professionals or the youth market. The boomer generation should not be forgotten – in their heads they are still young, and they still want to look current and fashionable. The trick with this group is to provide good service, better quality and offer stylish clothing with excellent cut and fit.

Trailing edge baby boomers (aka Generation Jones)

The name 'Generation Jones' was coined by American sociologist Jonathan Pontell. Derived from the slang 'jonesin', the name relates to feelings of craving, fuelled by unfulfilled expectations. Pontell identified a generation born in 1954–65 that had mistakenly been lumped in with the boomers, but which was actually a separate group with distinct characteristics. Douglas Coupland wrote

"Jonathan has it right. My book Generation X *was about the fringe of Generation Jones which became the mainstream of Generation X. There is a generation between the Boomers and Xers, and 'Generation Jones' – what a great name for it!"*

Generation Jones is a powerful demographic representing 26 per cent of the US population, with almost a third of the spending power, according to the U.S. Department of Commerce's Bureau of the Census. Research carried out by Carat identified that they represent 20 per cent of the UK adult population (www.projectbritain.co.uk 2009). Barack Obama is Gen Jones and many political commentators believe that it was the Joneser vote that brought him to power (www.huffingtonpost.com 2009). Generation Jones' attitudes and tastes were shaped by the political, social and cultural events of the 1970s and early 1980s. Financially they have been affected by negative equity in 1990s and the current breakdown of the pension system.

Generation X

Generation X was the title of a book written by journalist Jane Deverson and Charles Hamblett in the 1960s, but the term came to prominence many years later when Douglas Coupland published his novel, *Generation X, Tales for an*

Above

Each week *The Guardian* newspaper runs an 'All Ages' fashion feature in its Saturday magazine, championing diversity and challenging perceived notions of fashion. Though an important demographic variable, age is not always the best indicator of a consumer's style or what they might purchase. A fashion retailer might stock thousands of units of a particular garment and quite often two women, one thirty-five and another fifty, will purchase the same item. Mary Portas, Creative Director of Yellowdoor communications, calls this important customer segment 'The Forever 40s'. The customer may be in her forties but could also be fifty, sixty or even older. This customer group is connected not by age bracket but by fashion attitude, style and purchasing choices.

"I don't have an ideal, just someone who genuinely likes my clothes, between 18 and 81."
Erdem Moralioglu

Accelerated Culture, in 1991. Described as a lost generation, this demographic came of age in the 1980s and early 1990s, shaped by the Thatcher and Reagan years. Affected by escalating rates of divorce, fear of AIDS, recession, job insecurity and the potential of employment in a menial 'McJob', this disaffected generation, also termed as 'slackers', sought comfort by creating their own self-sufficient culture and alternative tribal family unit of close-knit friends, as illustrated by the television shows *Friends* in the United States and the British drama *This Life*. As Gen X has grown up and matured, they have cast off their more juvenile slacker habits and morphed into 'yupsters', creative urban professionals who endeavour to balance the personal with wider social concerns of family, community and work. Yupsters manage to maintain an intricate set of contradictions; they are corporate but have hip individual fashion style, business minded but independent and entrepreneurial in spirit. They value family time and aim to work smarter not harder.

Generation Y

Generation Y, also known as Millennials, are according to Howe & Strauss, those born after 1982, although others have classified them as born between the late 1970s and the mid-1990s. This generation are the children of Gen Jones; they have experienced pressure from parents to succeed and overachieve, money has been spent on their education and those with a college education are likely to start their working lives paying off sizable student loans. For this reason Gen Y have also been given the rather depressing title of the IPOD generation; Insecure, Pressurized, Over-taxed and Debt-ridden, a name coined by Bosanquet & Gibbs in the report *Class of 2005: The IPOD Generation*. This generation also includes the post-1980s children born in China during the one-child policy. Millennials have grown up with technology and increasingly live their lives online; they are plugged-in and globally connected. They understand branding and are media and marketing savvy, they communicate using social media, form online communities and are happy to create their own online content. A study carried out by Robert Half International in association with Yahoo! Hotjobs in the US (2007) found that 41 per cent of Gen Y workers surveyed want to dress in business casual, 27 per cent prefer jeans and sneakers, 26 per cent prefer a mix depending on the situation and only 4 per cent stated they preferred business attire.

Generation Z

There is still much debate as to the dates and characteristics that define this generation. Some say the generation consists of those born after the mid-1990s; others such as Howe and Strauss believe it is those born from 2004 onwards. What can be said is that they are the offspring of Gen X and Y and their grandparents will be baby boomer or Gen Jones. This generation will take the Internet for granted and have no knowledge of a time before World Wide Web. They will be the Web 2.0 generation and beyond.

Above
Celeste, a hip hop tap dancer living in New York belongs to Generation Y. Communicating online and belonging to an online community is normal for this media-savvy generation. Celeste is a member of lookbook.nu, an invite-only community sharing fashion inspiration from real people around the world.

Celeste wears a ripped-up, mended T-shirt and skinny jeans, both hand-me-downs from an ex-boyfriend. The beautiful bag and shoes are finds from a vintage store in Brooklyn.

Table of 20th- & 21st-century generations

BORN	GENERATION COHORT NAMES	DECADE OF INFLUENCE	AGE IN 2010
1912–27	DEPRESSION ERA & WORLD WAR II	1930S & EARLY 1940S	83–98
1926–45	THE POST-WAR GENERATION	1950S	65–84
1946–54	LEADING EDGE BABY BOOMERS	1960S	56–64
1954–65	TRAILING EDGE BABY BOOMERS GENERATION JONES	1970S & EARLY 1980S	46–56
1961–81	GEN X YUPSTERS	1980S & EARLY 1990S	29–49
1982–2002	GEN Y MILLENNIALS ECHO BOOMERS NET GENERATION IPOD GENERATION	1990S, 2000S, 2010S	8–28
AFTER 2000	GENERATION Z	2010 & BEYOND	UP TO 10

Generational cohort of fashion designers

GENERATION	FASHION DESIGNERS
DEPRESSION ERA & WORLD WAR II	PIERRE CARDIN ANDRÉ COURRÈGES
POST-WAR GENERATION	VIVIENNE WESTWOOD REI KAWAKUBO KARL LAGERFELD YVES SAINT LAURENT GIORGIO ARMANI CALVIN KLEIN
BABY BOOMERS	JEAN PAUL GAULTIER PAUL SMITH MIUCCIA PRADA DONNA KARAN
GENERATION JONES	JOHN GALLIANO MARC JACOBS TOM FORD DRIES VAN NOTEN MARTIN MARGIELA JOHN ROCHA
GENERATION X	STELLA MCCARTNEY PHILLIP LIM NICOLAS GHESQUIÈRE MARCUS LUPFER
GENERATION Y	CHRISTOPHER KANE ZAC POSEN

Geographic segmentation

Geographic segmentation analyses customers by region, continent, state, county or neighbourhood. This type of information is important to consider, particularly as fashion markets become ever more global and retailers and brand managers are required to understand the particular needs of customers in each of the countries or regions where they do business. The product offering, marketing and promotional approach may need to be adjusted in order to address differences of climate, culture or religion. It is also important to consider whether someone lives in a city, large town or the countryside, as this will affect the types of shops accessible to the customer.

Geo-demographic segmentation

Geo-demographic segmentation makes use of a combination of geographic and demographic analysis – this can be far more effective for understanding the social, economic and geographic make-up of a population. Geo-demographic analysis divides a country up and then analyses each geographic subdivision demographically. It is particularly useful for helping

The table of 20th- and 21st-century generations gives guideline dates for generational cohorts. The table also indicates the decade of influence affecting each cohort as they come of age as teenagers or young adults, which is when they are most likely to form their attitudes, opinions and approach to life.

retailers determine which locations might be the most profitable or how best to adapt stores to fit with the geo-demographic of a location. Research shows that consumers can show strong attachment to their local area, carrying out shopping and leisure activities 5–23 km (3–14 miles) from their home or place of work. Matches is a boutique fashion retailer with a small chain of high-class womenswear and menswear stores situated within London. The owners of Matches recognize that London consists of many small 'villages' and customers prefer to shop close to home or work. Each store has its own fashion profile designed to cater specifically to the unique style characteristics of the local customer. The boutique in Marylebone High Street, central London, is situated in a locale that is both residential and work-based. There are cafés, boutiques and hip art galleries, so in a bid to attract the art-loving demographic who live and work nearby, the store has been transformed into an innovative retail/gallery space where fashion and art can coexist. The Wimbledon shop, by contrast, has a more intimate style better suited to the village atmosphere of its local residential area.

Geo-demographic analysis and consumer profiling can be carried out using the services of a market research and analysis consultancy, which will have access to sophisticated database profiling systems. However a small business can carry out simple but effective research using basic census data, free online postcode analysis, statistics from the local council, and fashion industry information on market trends. The example on pp.114–15 describes the basic geo-demographic background research carried out by a boutique owner as she prepared to launch her business.

Geo-demographic analysis tools

There are several proprietary geo-demographic neighbourhood classification systems, such as ACORN (A Classification Of Residential Neighbourhoods), Mosaic and Super Profiles. These database analysis tools use government census data, postcode or zip code analysis and a complicated array of demographic and lifestyle variables to segment populations by neighbourhood and social status. The ACORN Classification Map, created by CACI Ltd, divides the UK population into five categories: Wealthy Achievers, Urban Prosperity, Comfortably Off, Moderate Means and Hard Pressed. These are then divided into 17 subgroups, some examples being: Affluent Greys, Flourishing Families, Blue Collar Roots, Settled Suburbia and Aspiring Singles. These groups are then further subdivided into 56 consumer types.

The Mosaic Global system devised by Experian is available in Europe, North America and the Asia-Pacific region. The population is divided into ten neighbourhood types, US examples being: Affluent Suburbia, Upscale America, Metro Fringe, Urban Essence or Remote America. These groups are then further broken down into 60 subgroups.

The Super Profiles Geodemographic Typology was developed by Batey and Brown in 1994 in collaboration with CDMS Ltd, part of the Littlewoods home-shopping organization. The Super Profiles system features three levels.

The first has ten lifestyle profiles, some examples being: Affluent Achievers, Thriving Greys, Settled Suburbans, Nest Builders, Hard Pressed Families and the Have-Nots. This level is divided into 40 target market clusters which are then subdivided into 160 specific profiles.

Psychographic and behavioural segmentation

Psychographic and behavioural segmentation analyses consumers based on their lifestyle and personality type. The purpose is to determine the underlying motivations that drive a person's attitude or behaviour as a consumer. It is possible for consumers to have similar demographic profiles but entirely different attitudes to clothing and appearance. One person, for example, might believe that they must look crisp, smart and well turned-out for all occasions, whereas someone else might choose to wear expensive branded fashion that looks worn and battered even when new, giving the impression they don't care how they look. Psychographic, behavioural and lifestyle studies aim to gain further insight into consumer attitudes, interests and opinions (AIOs) and understand how these influence a person's fashion needs, desires and purchasing choices. This is a complex topic, especially when it comes to attitudes to fashion. If you remember, the aim of marketing is to satisfy consumer needs and wants and, while it is fair to say that we may want or desire new clothes, most western consumers certainly do not need more clothes, accessories or shoes. The reality is that many of us have brand new items in our wardrobes that remain unworn; we give copious amounts of unwanted clothes away to charity shops (although the amount has decreased since the recession) and we cast an alarming amount of surplus clothes into landfill. So what is it that motivates us to continue purchasing even if we do not theoretically need anymore or can ill afford it? The answer lies in psychology and the theories of human motivation.

Consumer motivation and behaviour

What motivates us to buy into fashion, what influences our purchasing behaviour, how do our attitudes, interests and opinions affect our purchasing choices? At a simplistic level it could be said that the motivating force to purchase a garment, handbag or pair of shoes is a real physical need; in other words we do not have a receptacle in which to carry our keys, money and mobile phone, or a pair of winter boots to protect us from the cold and wet, so in order to satisfy this need we must purchase the required item.

The reality is that in most cases the motivation is more akin to desire and the need is psychological. Danish brand guru and futurologist Martin Lindstrom argues in his book *Buyology: How Everything We Believe About What We Buy Is Wrong* that the motivation is neurological and University of New Mexico evolutionary psychologist, Geoffrey Miller, contends in his book *Spent: Sex, Evolution and the Secrets of Consumerism* that evolutionary biology is behind our need to purchase and display conspicuous consumption. Miller's theory of 'display signalling' proposes that we wear

Above

Psychographic and behavioural analysis aims to gain insight into consumer attitudes, opinions, interests and purchasing behaviours, which in turn will influence the way a person chooses to dress. A person who believes they must look stylish, appropriate for the occasion and well turned-out may spend a great deal on clothes and take great care with their appearance.

Researching your target market
Starburst Boutique

Starburst Boutique is an independent retailer situated in the beautiful and historic coastal town of Dartmouth in southwest England. The boutique offers a unique blend of womenswear and accessories from a host of international designers including Day Birger et Mikkelsen and Rützou from Denmark, Armor Lux and Petit Bateau from France as well as UK labels, Marilyn Moore, Pyrus, Queen and Country and Saltwater. Running alongside the contemporary womenswear collections are one-off vintage pieces, bespoke jewellery and luxurious lifestyle products. The boutique is situated in Dartmouth's most exclusive shopping street and its stylish and relaxed in-store atmosphere is reflective of its coastal setting. It is designed to attract affluent second-home owners, weekenders and tourists, but also to provide local clientele with a chic destination in which to buy exclusive and desirable fashion brands.

Background market research

Starburst Boutique owner and buyer, Hannah Jennings, carried out detailed research in order to set up her business. Investigation of the current status, trends and predicted future of the independent retailing sector and the UK womenswear market was carried out; relevant data was obtained from trade magazines such as *Drapers* and *Retail Week*, industry analysts such as Mintel, WGSN, Fashion Monitor and the British Retail Consortium, as well as a range of relevant websites, magazines and newspaper articles. Information on the demographic of the local area and tourism were sourced from the local and county councils. Jennings also carried out an extensive investigation of existing independent retailers within the locale, including the nearest city, 40 km (25 miles) away. She also travelled to other cities such as London, Edinburgh, Winchester, Bath and Brighton to visit similar stylish independent boutiques.

Research findings and information

Tourism makes a significant contribution to the local economy. Research revealed that Dartmouth attracts 400,000 visitors a year plus an additional 100,000 during a festive regatta week held in August. Sixty per cent of those visiting the area can be economically grouped as ABC1. More UK residents are choosing to take vacations within Great Britain and a resurgence in popularity of seaside towns is highlighted by data released in 2008 that shows footfall in seaside towns grew 4.9 per cent compared to 1.3 per cent in all towns and cities. The local area also boasts the third highest percentage of second-home owners in the UK, and has experienced a net population increase of 441,000 since 1996 – a result of people migrating to the area in search of a better quality of life. Jennings found market data published in *Drapers* which revealed the UK womenswear market to be worth in excess of £17 billion in 2008, with the independent retailers' market share at just under 7 per cent. Data from a 2007 British Retail Consortium survey identified a growing proportion of UK consumers who preferred not to shop at high-street multiple retailers, and retail expert Mary Portas backed this up with a prediction that customers in their thirties will spend less on fast fashion and transfer their allegiance to local shops where they can invest in quality product and receive a higher quality of personal service. Research also indicates that female shoppers stay 'younger for longer' and that once they have defined their personal style in their thirties they will want to continue purchasing chic, contemporary and stylish clothing through to their sixties and beyond.

4.

Conclusions – the Starburst Boutique customer

Hannah Jennings recognizes how important her background research has been in helping her understand the Starburst Boutique customer and the potential of the market.

"The customer profiling I did turned out to be very accurate with regards to my core customers. It is fundamental for my business and I now buy with that segment in mind."
Hannah Jennings

The Starburst Boutique target market can be split into two customer profiles. The first represents the core customer to the business, namely women aged 30–45 who are married with small children. They either have a second home in the area or are weekender or tourist visitors who aspire to coastal living. The second customer profile is represented by slightly older, locally based women, aged 45–60 or over, probably with grown-up children and possibly grandchildren. The 60+ market is important to the boutique as this customer might bring along daughters or even granddaughters. They too may love the chance to shop in the store's chic and laidback environment and snap up something desirable to wear on their holiday or to take back home.

"Independent retailers offer a personal service and cultural understanding of the local market."
Mary Portas

certain fashion styles or brands labels in order to signal specific qualities of character to others. Someone wearing an ethical or eco-fashion brand, for example, is at some level trying to communicate that they are conscientious. A person wearing conspicuously branded designer labels is advertising qualities of wealth and desirability, while someone with an active and sporty style is trying to signal their health and fitness.

Consumer purchase decision process

It is evident that fashion purchasing decisions are rarely based on logical criteria alone. The motivations behind our purchasing behaviour are driven by a complex interplay of demographic, geographic, psychological, neurological, economic, social, cultural and personal factors. Research indicates that consumers go through a decision-making process when they purchase a product. The basic steps are as follows:

- Recognition of need
- Information search and identification of options
- Evaluation of options
- Decision

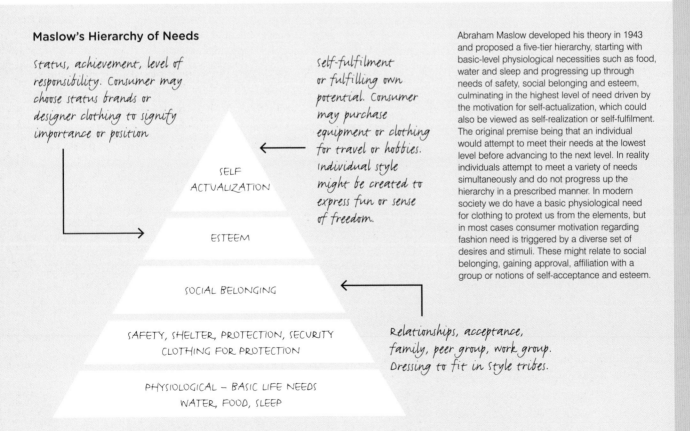

Maslow's Hierarchy of Needs

status, achievement, level of responsibility. Consumer may choose status brands or designer clothing to signify importance or position

self-fulfilment or fulfilling own potential. Consumer may purchase equipment or clothing for travel or hobbies. Individual style might be created to express fun or sense of freedom.

SELF ACTUALIZATION

ESTEEM

SOCIAL BELONGING

SAFETY, SHELTER, PROTECTION, SECURITY
CLOTHING FOR PROTECTION

PHYSIOLOGICAL — BASIC LIFE NEEDS
WATER, FOOD, SLEEP

Relationships, acceptance, family, peer group, work group. Dressing to fit in style tribes.

Abraham Maslow developed his theory in 1943 and proposed a five-tier hierarchy, starting with basic-level physiological necessities such as food, water and sleep and progressing up through needs of safety, social belonging and esteem, culminating in the highest level of need driven by the motivation for self-actualization, which could also be viewed as self-realization or self-fulfilment. The original premise being that an individual would attempt to meet their needs at the lowest level before advancing to the next level. In reality individuals attempt to meet a variety of needs simultaneously and do not progress up the hierarchy in a prescribed manner. In modern society we do have a basic physiological need for clothing to protext us from the elements, but in most cases consumer motivation regarding fashion need is triggered by a diverse set of desires and stimuli. These might relate to social belonging, gaining approval, affiliation with a group or notions of self-acceptance and esteem.

Customer motivation and behaviours

GETTING A BARGAIN
- shops in sales
- Attracted to promotional offers
- Buys second hand or vintage
- Goes to designer outlets, warehouse sales
- Sources good deals on the internet
- Collects vouchers or coupons

TRYING TO AVOID CLOTHES SHOPPING
- shops infrequently for clothes
- Purchases mainly for replacement items
- shops from catalogues or internet
- Does not browse – heads straight for required item
- Abandons store if queue to pay is too long

STANDING OUT FROM THE CROWD
- Buys from independent stores and boutiques
- Makes an effort to seek out new trends and ideas
- Makes own clothes or customizes
- shops in street markets

LOOKING LIKE A CELEBRITY
- Avid reader of celebrity gossip magazines
- Attracted to stores that are current with celebrity fashion trends
- Would queue to purchase special celebrity or designer fashion collections

FITTING IN AND BELONGING
- Buys similar style to friends
- Asks peers where they shop
- Personal style fits with chosen tribe

The decision process starts with the recognition that there is a need. This might be a valid physical need; a person may gain or lose a significant amount of weight and need to purchase new clothes to fit. A couple may be planning a traditional wedding and therefore need to purchase or hire appropriate outfits and accessories. The need could be cultural – a person travelling to a country where the convention is to dress more modestly may need to acquire a long skirt or a top with sleeves and a high neckline. It is more likely, however, that the need will arise at a sub-conscious level. If a person thinks, "I look old and frumpy, no one will find me attractive", deep down they believe they lack something. The belief sets up what could be termed as a false deficit in their mind, the discrepancy between what they believe is lacking and what they desire creates the sensation of need; "I need a fresh look. I'd better buy some new clothes." This thought becomes the motivation, leading towards action and a potential decision to purchase.

Once a need has been established, the next stages are to search for information and check out and evaluate options. This could occur by visiting shops, going online, reading magazines or gathering opinions from friends. However, these steps are very much dependent on the situation and the person in question. Some people may devote a great deal of time and energy to research and evaluation; others might be less cautious, less willing to spend time and generally more spontaneous. Research and evaluation are perhaps

A consumer's attitudes, preferences and motivations will influence their purchasing behaviour. This table presents possible purchasing behaviours associated with a variety of potential motivations. If someone's motivation is to get a bargain, for example, then this will drive certain behaviours, such as shopping during the sales, signing up to a discount website like Vente-privee, or scouring vintage stores for that special bargain.

Shopping mission: buying a pair of jeans in GAP

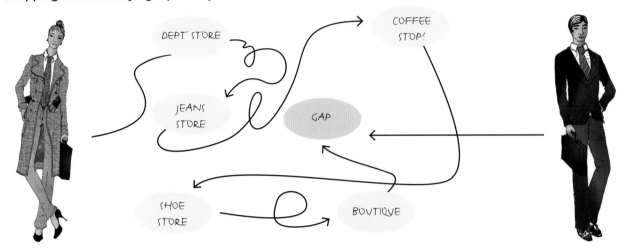

less relevant for fashion purchases compared to buying a car or expensive piece of furniture. Nonetheless there are those who enjoy the process of checking out what is available, browsing, trying on clothes or hunting down a bargain. A potential purchaser may decide upon a selection of brands from which to choose; the brands in serious contention for the consumer's purchase are known as the **consideration set**.

Fashion purchases are often unplanned, impulse buys usually being the result of spontaneity combined with opportunity. Impulsive purchasing may occur as a result of a shopper experiencing what could be termed a 'shopping high' or 'buying buzz'. It has been proven that shopping can produce a surge of excitement generated by the brain as it releases dopamine, a chemical involved in the experience of feeling pleasure. Habitual shopping patterns could also be linked to this phenomenon – someone might always go shopping on the day they get their pay cheque, the heady combination of money and shopping producing an elevation in mood.

Other factors may also affect the consumer's choice, such as the country of origin of a product or brand. Consumers may have a positive perception of particular goods from certain countries: Italian leather, French lace, Scottish cashmere and tweed or British tailoring are examples. This is known as the **country of origin effect** (**COO** or **COOE**). It is not only the country of manufacture that can affect perception but also the country of design (COD). In this instance the product may be designed in a country renowned for a particular design skill but manufactured elsewhere – Swedish-designed furniture, for example. There are strict trade laws concerning country of origin so it would be illegal to label garments incorrectly. However it is possible to create and market a brand with an identity that is suggestive of a particular country. The UK fashion brand, Super Dry Japan, was set up after an inspirational trip to Japan. Garments are embroidered with Japanese-style writing and given names like the 'Osaka' T-shirt.

Above
This cartoon puts a humorous spin on the different behaviour of women compared to men when shopping for fashion. The man heads straight to Gap and purchases a pair of selvedge jeans for around US$89, taking about 20 minutes to complete the mission. The woman on the other hand completes a more circuitous journey, she visits several shops, takes more than two hours to complete the mission and spends more than US$300, purchasing designer jeans, a pair of shoes and some make up!
Source: Adapted from Tom Peters (2005)

Below
A highly skilled artisan makes a pair of finely crafted leather shoes for Italian brand Tod's.

Adoption of innovation and trends

Consumers will vary in their response to new trends and ideas. Those who are more conservative or reticent might take some time before they feel ready to buy into a new or developing trend. They might want to feel safe, fit in or not look out of place. Others might feel that a new innovation or style is too expensive. They might wait till the trend hits the mass market and the price comes down; their motivation is to be cautious and spend wisely. There are others who like to be on the cutting edge of style. They may purchase the new season collections at the earliest opportunity; they want to be the first, be noticed or stand out from the crowd. The way in which an innovation, new idea or trend is taken up by consumers and moves through a population can be explained using Everett Rogers' diffusion theory. Rogers identified five types of individual classified by their propensity to adopt innovation.

Innovators – a small percentage of adventurous people who initiate trends or adopt innovations before others. They are risk-takers and visionaries. Designers such as Vivienne Westwood, or John Galliano for Dior Couture, would fit into this category, along with those that innovate and instigate subculture and street trends.

Early Adopters – people who take up a trend in the early stages, often cultural opinion leaders or those that disseminate fashion, style or artistic ideas. This group accepts and embraces change and enjoys new ideas. They will have the confidence to follow or adapt the trend, mix styles and create the desired look from designer, boutique, high-street and vintage.

Rogers' Diffusion of Innovations

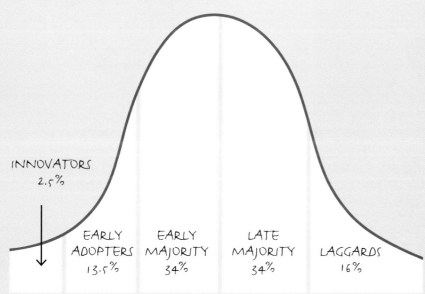

INNOVATORS
2.5%

EARLY
ADOPTERS
13.5%

EARLY
MAJORITY
34%

LATE
MAJORITY
34%

LAGGARDS
16%

A trend will originate within the innovator group of individuals, adventurous types who are cutting edge in their ideas. As the trend takes hold a **tipping point** will be reached. This is the moment when the trend or idea crosses a significant threshold; the adoption rate increases exponentially and the trend spreads rapidly and reaches the mass market. Eventually the trend will peak and begin its decline. The late majority purchase the trend just as its fashionability and mass market appeal begin to dwindle. Laggards are those at the tail-end who just manage to cotton on to the idea when it is already too late and the trend is over.

Source: Everett Rogers' Diffusion of Innovations (1995)

Early majority – represents the main bulk of people who adopt a trend as it gathers momentum and begins to penetrate the mass market. This group is likely to take up a trend after they have seen it worn by others or in fashion and gossip magazines or recommended on blogs or websites.

Late majority – those who buy into a trend when it is already very well established and reaching its peak or beginning to decline.

Laggards – these people do not take fashion risks, and are the last people to catch on to a trend, usually when it is already too late.

Rogers proposed a five-stage Mechanism of Diffusion model to explain the decision process that an individual follows in order to progress from first knowledge or awareness of a new trend or product innovation through to adoption of the trend or purchase and evaluating their decision.

Purchasing a new innovation
The FitFlop shoe

The stages described in Rogers' Mechanism of Diffusion can be seen in action in this example, which relates the actual steps a purchaser went through from first awareness and knowledge of an innovative new product (FitFlop shoes), to final decision to purchase – a process that took well over a year. The example demonstrates not only the way in which a new product innovation is accepted and purchased by a consumer, but also the integrated nature of marketing. It wasn't just press articles or advertising that persuaded this person to buy, but a complex combination of factors including publicity, information on the benefits of the new technology, the design and look of the FitFlop, its pricing comparative to other shoes in both the fashion and tech-shoe markets, the recommendation of a friend, and seeing the distinctive footwear worn by others of a similar tribe.

1. The product is brought to the attention of the consumer in early spring 2007 when they read a promotional article in the press.
2. The potential consumer, who has gained awareness of the product is further reminded of the FitFlop when they see another press article later in the year. They become curious about the product and their interest is raised.
3. The potential consumer continues to see adverts and press articles during spring 2008. They observe people wearing the distinctive FitFlop. Tempted by the price – cheaper than shoes of another brand using similar technology – the consumer begins to persuade themselves that FitFlops might be just what they need.
4. They encounter a friend who owns a pair of FitFlops; the friend communicates positively about the shoes. The consumer is further persuaded and decides they want a pair too.
5. Finally, in summer 2008, the consumer sees the FitFlops in a store window and decides to purchase. They wear the FitFlops and find them extremely comfortable. The purchaser is very happy with product.
6. The purchaser tells friends about FitFlop shoes. The process now moves to a new stage of word-of-mouth recommendation. Knowledge and awareness of the innovative product is transmitted to new people following Rogers' Diffusion of Innovations model.

The Walkstar FitFlop. The shoe's USP is the innovative technology used for its patent-pending sole, made of multi-density material that supports and exercises leg and buttock muscles as the wearer walks. The sole's 'wobble board' effect creates extra tension in the muscles, causing them to work harder. The shoe quickly made the transition from fitness product to 'fashion must-have' with new, more fashionable designs such as the Liberty Print Obi FitFlop, or the Electra sequinned version for Summer 2009.

1. **Knowledge –** the particular product or trend must come to the attention of the potential consumer. They gain initial knowledge of uses, benefits or key ideas behind an innovation or trend. This could be because they read about it in the press or see others wearing or using the product.
2. **Persuasion –** the person forms an opinion about the product. They may be persuaded by the opinions of others. If it is of interest to them, they might begin to desire the product and persuade themselves that it is suitable, useful, a good investment etc.
3. **Decision –** the person makes a decision to adopt the innovation or trend; in other words they take action and purchase.
4. **Implementation –** the person uses the product.
5. **Confirmation –** the person evaluates the results of their decision and compares actual usage of the product with original perceptions.

Consumer trends

Identifying and understanding consumer trends is a vital element of fashion market research. Observing consumers and gathering information from markets around the globe keeps you up to date. The trick is to keep an eye out for innovators and early adopters; they are likely to be ahead of the curve. Trend watching helps you to develop intuition, spot new ideas and gain inspiration. Remember consumer needs will change in response to political, economic and social change. Trends come and go but here are some things to think about…

Frugal cocooning – The American futurist Faith Popcorn came up with the concept of cocooning way back in the 1990s. The trend has re-emerged in response to the recession. Frugal cocooning is all about staying in and hunkering down. Think cosy knits, comfy lounge-wear and slipper socks.

Generation G – G for generosity, people reacting against greed. Growing online culture allows them to share, give, engage, create and collaborate. Think clothes swapping, skill sharing, freecycling or random acts of kindness (RAK).

Sellsumers – Consumers no longer just consume, they sell creative output to corporations or fellow consumers. The global recession combined with online democratization means more consumer participation in the world of demand and supply.

Cosy childhood memories – Nostalgic items remind us of childhood days – 50s florals, tea-time cup-cakes, board games, storage tins with 60s and 70s branding. Baby boomers and Gen Jones desire to feel cosy and secure in tough times.

The lipstick effect – Tough times mean consumers go for 'trade-down' spending; they forego extravagant purchases and opt for small feelgood treats like lipstick.

"If you knew everything about tomorrow what would you do differently today?"
Faith Popcorn

Perfect pieces – Fed up with product overload, consumers want well-considered fashion items. Perfect basics that offer more, beautifully crafted quality pieces designed to last; classic fashion emblems such as the perfect trench, the little black dress, a striped French matelot T-shirt or sweater or Japanese selvedge jeans.

Addicted to niche – Consumers want to find an intricate balance between being one-of-a-kind and fitting in. This is 'niche', just enough to form a tribe but not too many, not a crowd; this is about being one of the few. Niche brands come with a story – niche is knowledge, niche is the kudos of being in the know.

Fashion online – An increasing number of consumers are purchasing fashion online. The web has democratized fashion, making it available to a much wider group of consumers. Not everyone lives near a major shopping centre, and some shoppers feel intimidated entering certain types of fashion store, or they feel embarrassed when clothing does not fit or suit. Fashion e-tailers are experiencing phenomenal growth; Vente-privee, the membership-only e-tailer, achieved sales of £545 million in 2008. The French-owned company, with members across France, Germany, the UK, Italy and Spain, holds online sales events, with luxury fashion and designer brands selling for 50–70 per cent below normal retail price. The British online retailer, Asos, reported sales up 104 per cent, reaching a figure of £165 million for the year ending March 2009.

Above
Cocooning and frugal cocooning are trends that emerged in response to the recession. The idea is to stay at home, spend less and wrap up in comfy clothes and cosy knits.

"Online fashion has changed everything. It's made fashion accessible physically and psychologically."
Jackie Naghten

4.

Creating a customer profile

Once consumer research and analysis is complete, the next step is to create a consumer profile report to describe the consumer groups being targeted. The report should give background demographic, geo-demographic and psychographic data, information on current or emerging consumer trends, current sales statistics and relevant observational data. It is normal practice for personnel such as buyers, marketing or brand managers, or designers to give presentations summarizing the consumer report to other staff members or to suppliers, partners and stakeholders. A technique used to précis the research and describe the customer is known as a **customer pen portrait**. This written description can be enhanced by the addition of a customer image and lifestyle visual shown on a display board or using PowerPoint or Flash presentation.

Writing a customer pen portrait

A pen portrait is a short, written profile that describes the characteristics and traits of a **core customer**, representative of the target market. The portrait provides a composite picture of the target consumer, which should be built up using information gathered from primary and secondary market research. The portrait should present a realistic and factual description of the consumer demographic, age or age bracket, lifestyle, fashion style, brand preferences, purchasing motivation and attitudes towards purchasing fashion.

Make sure you define their age and gender, describe their lifestyle, social status and stage of life. You can list the clothing brands that they wear or aspire to wear and indicate how much they spend on clothing. The problem with pen portraits is the tendency to describe a fantasy life or the aspirational life of the consumer rather than the reality; it is important therefore to reiterate that the portrait must be based upon researched information and data. Information can be obtained from government demographic statistics, articles in the fashion media, fashion trend publications and websites, blogs and by carrying out a customer questionnaire.

A visual depiction of the customer and their lifestyle is a useful addition to the written portrait. This can be created using a collage of images taken from magazines as well as your own illustrations. Consider magazines that cover interiors, lifestyle, food, gardening, sport, gadgets or technology. When creating a visual profile, it is important to ensure that images reflect the consumer's lifestyle and activities and not just their approach to fashion. Try to use pictures that typify the product or brand choices for that consumer type such as their car, watch, scent, accessories and clothing. The images chosen should reflect accurately the market level and status level of the customer.

Questions for a pen portait

Try to visualize the person, get inside their head and imagine who they are. What influences are there in his or her life? What are their key concerns, opinions or interests?

Think about their routine as they go through the day. Do they have specific clothes or outfits for work, sport or leisure? What non-clothing brands are important to them and why?

Building a customer profile
The niche denim market

Sliced Bread is a fresh new denim brand created by James Hayes while still a student studying fashion at Plymouth College of Art in the UK. The idea was developed in response to increasing consumer demand for authentic, stylish and nostalgic product. The Sliced Bread concept is simple; to make quality jeans and T-shirts that people will remember. Each piece is hand-made in England using the finest ingredients and production methods. Sliced Bread products are transeasonal and 100 per cent fresh!

Researching the customer

James carried out face-to-face, telephone and Internet interviews with young men in their early twenties who might be potential customers for Sliced Bread jeans and T-shirts. He wanted to gather more information on their lifestyles, the type of brands they currently wore and find out more about which brands they aspired to wear. James discovered how much they spent on clothes, what they did for a living and how they spent their leisure time. After conducting a number of interviews, James noticed commonalities in terms of purchasing behaviour, attitudes and brand preferences that appeared to typify the traits of the sample group. James used this information to compile a customer pen portrait for a character he named 'Jason Powell', who would be representative of the target audience for the proposed Sliced Bread brand.

Images of James Hayes' Sliced Bread jeans and T-shirt collection.

Pen portrait of a Sliced Bread customer

Jason Powell is a twenty-one-year-old student studying architecture at Manchester University. Now in his second year of study, he has rented a student flat with three friends. In the holidays he lives with his parents in Windsor, about 50 km (30 miles) outside of London. Jason is entrepreneurial and aspires to set up his own design business. He already communicates online with other young architects and designers around the world and has set up a blog with thoughts, sketches and ideas for his dream city. Jason says that his blog is "Like an ever-changing profile of who I am; it's where people can see what I am like and follow my interests." Jason loves T-shirts, particularly those from 5Preview in Italy – "they sell cool, one-off printed Ts, and British brands, To-orist and Tom Wolfe." Jason's passion for architecture translates into a respect for product that is well designed but understated, like a good pair of jeans from Prps, Flat Head, Dr. Denim, Acne or Levi's Red – BUT he can't always afford them unless they are on sale, so sometimes it's down to the charity shop to find something quirky, or a trip to Primark if he is feeling cheap. Jason always pays in cash when he goes shopping for clothes, "If you haven't got it [money], don't buy it." He uses his credit card only when purchasing online. Jason's money goes on his car, rent, going to gigs and clubs, and topping up his mobile phone. At the start of term he spent £180 on a bus pass and £150 on gym membership. Rent is £70 per week and food about £40. Jason spends more on clothes than he used to because now he constantly goes out to clubs in Manchester. "With club culture you have to wear something different every time. I'll go out and spend £300 on clothes in one go and then won't shop again for three months or so – unless something catches my eye."

Photographs showing three of the young men interviewed by James Hayes during his customer research investigations. James discovered there was a gap between the brands his target group aspired to wear and those that they actually bought. Aspirational brands were Paul Smith, Comme des Garçons, Diesel Black Gold and Dsquared[2]. Labels actually worn were Zara men, Primark, charity shop clothes, Topman, Levi's and Jack Wills. It is important to point out that although James focused on young men aged 20 or 21, the potential market for the Sliced Bread concept is likely to extend to customers aged 30, so extra research into customers of this age bracket should also be carried out.

AARON WATTS
Age: 20
Student

Wears:
Adidas Originals and
charity shop

Aspires to wear: None

SAM PHILLIPS
Age: 20
DJ

Wears:
Levi's, Adidas, Wood Wood,
Religion and Bantum

Aspires to wear: Paul
Smith, Diesel Black Gold
and Vivienne Westwood

ALEX PUGH
Age: 21
Student

Wears:
Jack Wills, Topman
University Gear,
Crew Clothing

Aspires to wear: Paul Smith

Understanding business customers

Understanding business customers is also extremely important. In B2B situations it is normal procedure for a business to analyse its customer base. This is done for two main reasons – firstly to determine how valuable each customer is to the business, and secondly to understand how best to meet customer needs and service them effectively. In order to fully understand the needs of business customers, it also makes sense to have good knowledge of their end-consumers as well.

Take, for example, an independent designer with their own fashion label who supplies their collection to approximately 40 stores worldwide. They could analyse and classify their customers by country or region, such as Europe, Asia and North America, particularly if end-consumers in each region have differing requirements. The designer may supply independent boutiques that order small quantities from a limited selection of the range, or much larger retailers that take a greater proportion of the collection; so they might want to analyse these customers by the amount they order or by the type of product they order. They may have customers that require little effort to service whereas other customers may have input into the design process, specifying particular colours, styles or fabrics suitable for their end-consumers, and they may require exclusivity, requesting certain styles be made available only to them. These customers might be of great value to the business even though they require a higher level of service.

B2B customers might be assessed by their financial contribution, but there are other assets of value to consider, such as status and reputation of the customer, publicity potential, partnership or networking possibilities, or their ability to provide access to other organizations. In reverse, large high-street retailers usually analyse their supply base so that they can determine which suppliers provide the best service, quality and prices. A large business like a textile manufacturer, for example, might segment its customers by the type of market they represent; separating the companies that purchase for the high-street multiples from other clients who might be at couture or designer level. Below is a summary of criteria to consider when analysing business customers:

- **Location –** local, national, international or global
- **Financial contribution –** how much they contribute to turnover and profit
- **Reputation –** the value attached to their name, type of end-consumer they attract and publicity potential
- **Status –** new start-up or well established, length of business relationship. Loyalty of custom. Financial security.
- **Type of company –** department store, independent boutique, retail chain. Or manufacturer, producer or designer.
- **Market level –** a fabric supplier, for example, may have customers at couture and designer level, as well as retailers that develop own-brand collections.

5.

Branding is becoming an ever more important tool for marketing fashion. As companies manage to match each other with their ability to deliver appropriately priced, quality fashionable product, so something extra needs to come into play, something emotional and connecting. This is where the brand comes in. There is no doubt that marketing fashion has evolved. It is no longer just about the products themselves or ensuring that the right products are in the right place at the right time; now it is brand experience that differentiates. Lori Rosenwasser, Global Director of Brand Engagement at Landor Associates, suggests that, "We are now in the age of the experience brand" (2008). In a highly competitive marketplace, brand managers and marketers must find ways to augment products and services with emotional meaning and experiential dimensions. Allen Adamson, Managing Director at Landor Associates, describes branding as, "The process by which brand images get into your head" (2007). Branding is the mechanism by which a company creates and manages a brand and conveys the messages and values that underpin the brand to its customers. Branding is therefore a significant strategic activity for companies wishing to differentiate their products and services. This chapter introduces the key branding concepts, illustrating how these may be viewed within the context of fashion.

"A brand is the sum of the tangible and intangible benefits provided by a product or service and encompasses the entire customer experience."
How Brands Work Chartered Institute of Marketing

Defining a brand

The concrete features of a brand are its logo, strapline, slogan, actual products and physical retail environment. But a brand is more than the sum of its parts – most of what constitutes a brand is intangible. In many ways the brand is a paradox, a composite shaped internally by company strategy and externally by consumer perception and experience. Formed from a unique mix of tangible and intangible elements, a brand is created out of a total package including not only garments, retail environment, packaging and advertising but also the meanings, values and associations that consumers ascribe to the brand. Walter Landor, a pioneer of branding, famously said, "Products are made in the factory, but brands are created in the mind." Adamson defines a brand as, "something that exists in your head. It's an image or a feeling. It's based on associations that get stirred up when a brand's name is mentioned" (2007). Influential and successful brands manage to engender positive or constructive associations in the minds of consumers, triggering emotions and feelings that can be extremely potent and affirmative. However, each consumer forms their own opinions so there is the possibility that they may develop negative perceptions and beliefs. It is therefore important for those who manage brands to consider carefully the associations that a brand conveys, making sure wherever possible that messages are transmitted by design rather than default. A brand must have clear points of difference, not only in the products and services but also at an experiential level. Consumers need to be aware of the brand's existence, connect with its ethos and value

what it has to offer – and of course the brand offering should be relevant to the needs, aspirations and desires of customers.

The values, messages and ideas that underpin a brand will be expressed through:

- The brand name and logo
- The product
- Packaging and display
- The environment in which it is sold
- Advertising and promotion
- Company reputation and behaviour

The brand name and logo

The brand name and logo are tangible features that can be controlled from within the company. The logo provides the most fundamental visible element of the brand; the style of this unique identifier should capture and represent the essence or core idea behind the brand. Intelligent or ingenious use of colour, typeface and symbol can help to achieve a distinguishing logo that hopefully will stand as an iconic and trusted visual agent of the brand. Luxury fashion brands such as Gucci, Prada, Fendi or Chanel use fonts in upper case to create an aura of authority and tradition. Some brands add a crest or cartouche to enhance the logo and bestow an air of grandeur or heritage. Sports brands design their logos with the aim of generating a sensation of movement, speed or direction. Brands that wish to convey elegance or femininity tend to use lower-case script with flourishes and tails.

Above
Chanel trademark quilted handbag with iconic interlocking C logo on the clasp.

Above left
Flags display the brand names of luxury fashion, accessory and jewellery retailers on London's Old Bond Street. The style and design of a logo and the colour of a flag form a significant manifestation of brand identity.

A well-designed and powerfully recognized logo is a great asset to a brand. The logo can be formed using the brand name, i.e. Gucci or Prada; Paul Smith uses his signature as the brand logo. Initials and letters can be exploited to construct a brand name such as DKNY (Donna Karan New York) or used to form a secondary logo, examples being the interlocking letters of Fendi, Chanel or Gucci. There are, of course, legendary brands such as Nike with its iconic Swoosh symbol, so powerful that it instantly identifies the brand without the need for any accompanying name or words. Similarly, the Fred Perry laurel leaf and the Lacoste crocodile also act as iconic emblems for their respective brands.

Trademarks

Brand logos, symbols, slogans and straplines can be registered. It is also possible to register elements of a design that are specific signifiers of a brand. Levi's, for example, has registered the marketing slogan, 'Quality never goes out of style'® and the Burberry iconic camel, black and red check became a registered trademark in 1924 when it was used as a lining for the Burberry trenchcoat. A registered **trademark** gives the brand company exclusive rights over usage of the registered article. This helps to protect the brand from piracy or unauthorized use of the trademark. Once a mark is registered it can be indentified by the ® or ™ symbol.

A small business intending to trade in their home market can register their mark for exclusive use in their national market. But to ensure more comprehensive protection, it is sensible to be internationally registered.

Left top
Logos for adidas Performance and adidas Originals. A logo should represent the essential nature of a brand in a simple and easily recognizable format.

The international sports brand adidas has an instantly recognizable logo featuring its quintessential three-stripes motif. The classic adidas emblem has been modified to create logos for the adidas sub-brands.

Left bottom
When creating logos it is important to consider the underlying message and choose a typeface accordingly. The stretched font and forward direction of the sport logo below creates a feeling of momentum. An uppercase copperplate Gothic Light typeface communicates the timeless authority of heritage and luxury. The italicized Edwardian Script adds a feminine touch to a logo. A contemporary modern look with a retro feel is created using the Bauhaus 93 typeface.

Brand canvas

Fashion product provides a fantastic canvas for branding. Logos can be emblazoned boldly on T-shirts or used more subtly in placement embroideries. Denim brands use trademark stitching on back pockets to identify their jeans or use labels, like the iconic Levi's red tab. When designing branded product, think about how to incorporate brand insignia. Clasps, clips, buckles and zips can all be developed so as to include recognizable and identifying symbols or emblems, and fabrics can be woven or printed with trademark stripes, checks and patterns.

Left and top
Burberry's distinctive check is utilized by the brand for many of its products. Here it is used for the menswear collection. The scale of the check has been enlarged significantly but it is still instantly recognizable as a signifier of the brand.

Above
The Fred Perry tennis sweater is branded with an embroidered laurel leaf – the signature trademark of the brand.

The adidas Originals by Originals (ObyO) limited-edition collection created by adidas in collaboration with New York fashion designer Jeremy Scott exemplifies how a logo can be integrated within a garment design to creative effective branding. Scott takes an inventive approach by partly concealing an oversized adidas Originals emblem with layers of fringing.

Above
Jeremy Scott's fringed hooded top for the adidas ObyO collection.

Types of brands

Brands exist at every level of the fashion industry. There are branded fibres, branded textiles, sports brands, designer brands such as Armani or Donna Karan, luxury brands like Louis Vuitton or Hermès, iconic couture brands like Dior, fashion retail brands, and even department stores that have achieved brand status. Defining types of brand can be complicated, however they can be categorized as explained below.

Corporate brand This is where an organization has one name and one visual identity across its brands. The corporation is the brand.

The Sri Lankan manufacturing corporation, MAS Holdings, has this kind of structure: MAS Intimates produces lingerie and intimate apparel for global customers such as Marks & Spencer, Gap and Victoria's Secret; MAS Active is a supplier of active sports and casual wear to Nike, Adidas, Reebok, Gap and Speedo; and MAS Fabric develops fabrics, elastics, lace and other garment components.

Manufacturer brands These are created and marketed by producer companies who will choose a name for their branded product. Manufacturer brands are prevalent within the fibre and textile industry where chemical manufacturers brand their fibres. The science-based company DuPont™ for example manages the well-known fibre brand, Lycra®. Another DuPont™ brand is Kevlar®, utilized in garments worn by workers exposed to a variety of hazards including abrasion and high levels of heat. NatureWorks LLC, a joint venture between Cargill and Teijin of Japan, produce Ingeo™, a branded fibre made from renewable plant resources derived from corn. The avant-garde French fashion label Marithé + François Girbaud selected Ingeo™ to use in their first eco-inspired designs, launched in 2008.

Private brands Private brands are also known as own brands, store brands, retailer brands or **own label**. The US department store, Nordstrom, offers its own brand, Classiques Entier, and Macy's offers a wide portfolio of private label brands, including I.N.C. and Tasso Elba. Private brands raise the profile of a retailer, differentiate its offering and add value for customers. Retailers tend to favour them because they offer opportunity for higher margin than selling designer-branded merchandise.

Endorsed brand This is when a parent brand gives its name or endorses one of its own sub-brands. The names of the parent and sub-brand are linked. Examples would be Polo by Ralph Lauren or the perfume Obsession by Calvin Klein. The endorsement gives credibility to the sub-brand while also capitalizing on the status and reputation of the existing main brand.

Co-brands or partnership brands A **co-brand** is created when two brands join together to develop a new brand. The Japanese designer Yohji Yamamoto has two co-brands – Y's Mandarina, a bag and accessory collection for men and women created in conjunction with the luggage and accessory brand Mandarina Duck, and adidas Y-3 (also known as Y-3), a collaborative brand project with adidas. Y-3 takes its name from the 'Y' from Yamamoto and the three stripes of the adidas logo.

Above
Swing tickets developed to promote Woolmark sub-brands, Cool Wool and Merino Extrafine. Each sub-brand has its own specially developed logo and is endorsed with the universally accepted Woolmark symbol. Each swing ticket is further branded with the Woolmark strapline, 'Take Comfort In Wool'.

Brand portfolio When a company has a brand portfolio the aim is to maximize coverage of the market without the individual brands within the portfolio competing with each other. The multiple brands within the company will be designed to address specific needs across different key segments within the market. The Gucci Group's brand portfolio includes prestigious and clearly defined luxury brands, including Gucci, Alexander McQueen, Stella McCartney, Balenciaga, Bottega Veneta and Yves Saint Laurent. The Adidas Group has a brand portfolio that includes Reebok, Rockport, the shoe company, and TaylorMade, which is a golf brand.

The purpose of branding

The purpose of branding is to establish a clear and distinctive identity for a product, service or organization. The aim is to ensure that the brand is differentiated and that it offers something distinguishable from competitor brands. Branding should also add value or increase the perceived value of a product, allowing a company to charge a premium for its branded merchandise. On a more complex level, branding works to create emotional connection between customers and the brand. It raises not only the consumer's potential financial outlay but it can also affect their emotional investment in the brand. A pair of Nike trainers, for example, is not just a pair of running shoes but 'my Nikes', imbued with additional associations and meaning. In a pair of Nikes 'I can do it'. This is why a brand can be so powerful and influential – the Nike wearer might feel more committed and better able to get up early and run, they might believe themselves to be more sporty, active and alive when they wear this particular brand. Consumers are therefore more likely to engage constructively with a brand and purchase its products if the brand satisfies several criteria. The brand's products and services must have relevance to their life and needs, the consumer should identify closely with the brand ideology and style, and their association with the brand should trigger positive or affirmative feelings and emotions.

Branding should generate reassurance and a sense of security and trust for customers. If they have connected emotionally with a brand and want what it has to offer then the hope is that they will remain loyal. It is important therefore that the brand remains consistent and continues to deliver the values and promises that customers expect.

The issue of brand continuity is an extremely important factor within the fashion industry. This is because two contrasting factors – newness and consistency – need to be integrated season after season. Customers will naturally demand choice and want to be tempted with fresh merchandise each season, but they also require some sense of stability when engaging with a brand. This presents a challenge to designers who must create and develop new product collections on a regular basis. They must ensure the

> "Brands help businesses cross geographic and cultural borders. Global brands are an enormous asset to their home country. They aid exports of products and services to foreign markets."
> **Clamor Gieske, FutureBrand**

Above
Levi's trademark red tab outside their flagship store in San Francisco.

integrity of the brand remains intact and create the sensation of permanence
for customers, even when the products in-store change on a frequent basis.
Even though the theme, concepts, colours and fabrics might be different for
each seasonal collection, the overarching branding, **brand message** and
values need to remain consistent.

Branding is essentially about building a relationship between consumer
and brand. This is why a thorough knowledge and understanding of
consumers is so vital and why companies invest so much time and money
in consumer and market research. The more intimately a company
understands its customers, the better able it is to develop products,
services, retail environments and marketing strategies that encourage
consumer engagement, promote loyalty and foster trust in its brand.

So to summarize; the aim and purpose of branding is to:

- Tap into values and beliefs
- Create connection
- Generate emotional response
- Provide reassurance
- Ensure consistency
- Build loyalty
- Add value and charge a premium

An important element of branding is to develop and establish what is
known as a **brand identity**. This is one of the foremost tactics for achieving
the emotional connection with a target audience that is so vital to the
concept of branding.

Brand identity

Brand identity is controlled from within an organization and should relate to
how the company wishes consumers to perceive and engage with the brand.
People use brands, and fashion in particular, to make statements about

themselves – the meanings and associations consumers have with brands will be closely connected with how they want to feel, how they want to be seen and how they wish to be perceived by others. Consumers are more likely to connect positively with a brand if they associate closely with its overall identity and ethos. It is extremely important therefore for an organization to develop a compelling and engaging identity for its brand. The identity will be built up using the following:

- The logo
- The product and services
- Packaging
- Retail environment
- Windows and visual merchandising
- Promotion, advertising and PR
- Website

Each outward expression of the brand as listed above will work towards building up the brand identity. One simple way for a fashion designer to strengthen their brand identity and connect with a fashion audience is to bestow garments with names to captivate the imagination. Erdem gives luscious and evocative names to all the garments in his collection. The 'Felicitas' jewelled dress, the 'Invidia' silk blouse and the 'Laverna' skirt all featured in the Erdem Autumn/Winter 2008 Collection. Isaac Mizrahi adds a splash of humour to his collections with colour names such as 'Lorne Green', 'Burlapse' and 'James Brown'. Subtle details such as these set an emotional tone and help make a brand and its products memorable.

It is important to point out, however, that consumers will interpret all of a brand's signifiers and form their own impression of the identity. It is vital therefore, that each and every manifestation of the brand upholds the identity coherently and consistently. The image of the brand from a consumer perspective is known as the **brand image**.

Brand image

The image of a brand will differ depending on whether it is formed by a brand-user or non-user or someone who has a business association with the brand such as a supplier or stakeholder. Someone who is a devoted customer of a brand would compose their image based on actual experience. Take someone who regularly purchases from Ralph Lauren. They may visit the same flagship store frequently, be consistently served by a specific staff member and build up a very personal relationship with the brand and its products. Another person may aspire to the Ralph Lauren lifestyle, but believe the designer clothes to be expensive or extravagant. They might buy into the brand on a rare occasion by purchasing sunglasses, perfume or homeware from a department store

Above
Eloise Grey's 'Toklas' checked wool jacket, named after the American writer Alice B. Toklas. Inspired by a love of literature, the British designer has named the jackets and coats in her collection after writers such as de Beauvoir, Waugh and Beckett, evoking the tweedy world of twentieth-century authors.

- ■ Reproductive red
- ■ Dark pollen
- ■ Green sap
- ■ Green mystery
- ■ Luscious lily

Above
A lily provides inspiration for a colour palette and for the name given to each of the colours.

such as Bloomingdales or Selfridges. A fashion-aware non-user would generally construct their brand image from magazines; looking at the adverts, fashion spreads and reading the editorial content.

They may also form judgements by absorbing the opinions of others. The power of a brand rests in its relationship with consumers, so every interaction a customer or potential customer has with a brand is important as it will contribute to their brand experience, either positively or negatively.

The company behind a brand needs to ensure that there is a close match between the identity they control and the brand image as perceived by outsiders and consumers. A large gap between identity and image can result in catastrophic problems for a brand. There have been cases where companies have lost control of their identity. This happened to Burberry when consumers it had not intended to attract started purchasing both legitimate Burberry product and counterfeit products. The skewed image of the brand affected its identity, which no longer related to the strategic intentions within the company.

Brand identity and image

There is a strong correlation between brand and consumer identity. Consumers are likely to connect with brands that affirm their personal viewpoint and ideals.

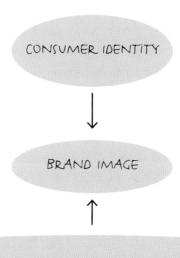

CONSUMER IDENTITY

BRAND IMAGE

Consumers will use the external expressions of the brand to form their own perception and opinion of the brand. This is known as the brand image.

LOGO + PRODUCTS + PACKAGING + DISPLAY + PROMOTION + WEBSITE

BRAND IDENTITY

Brand Identity is controlled internally from within a company. It is reflected externally through every outward expression of the brand. Each aspect of the brand must be consistent and congruent in order to build a strong and coherent brand identity.

Identity and ideology
Davidelfin

The Spanish fashion label Davidelfin was launched in Barcelona in 2002 by a multidisciplinary group of artistic individuals that included a professional model, a journalist, an architect, a film director and musician, and the figurehead, David Delfin, a self-taught designer. In 2003 David Delfin won the Marie Claire Prix de la Mode for best new designer of the year.

In an interview with Mariona Vivar Mompel for cafebabel.com in 2006, Delfin commented that young designers starting out faced difficulties because the market is at saturation point. "This means that in order to stand out in the fashion industry you need two things: your own identity and ideology." Delfin believes that to succeed it is necessary to be something more than mere fashion designers. "Nowadays you have to be able to awaken emotions." This point is well illustrated by the name and ideology behind the new davidelfin sub-brand, Da Davidelfin, aimed at the younger customer. The word 'Da' comes from the Spanish verb 'to give' and the collection is marketed with the statement, 'Understanding fashion is an act of generosity. Made with love' and signed 'davidelfin'. Launched in 2007 at the European fashion tradeshow Bread & Butter in Barcelona, the new davidelfin second line is defined as a 'sports couture' concept and consists of T-shirts and casual clothes aimed at men, women and children.

Right and below: Da Davidelfin garments printed with the text using the same distinctive left-handed script as the brand logo.

davidelfin
MADRID

Developing and managing brand identity

Developing and managing the brand identity is an extremely important aspect of **brand management**. A brand is a precious commodity and a valuable asset for a company – a powerful brand name, brand logo and brand identity as well as the accumulated goodwill that exists towards the brand all contribute to the **brand equity** or total worth of the brand as an asset. A brand with high equity and a strong identity can command a price-premium for its product, which is one of the main purposes of branding. Those managing a brand need to ensure that there is a close match between the brand identity created and managed from within the company and the brand image held by consumers and others outside the company. In order to develop and manage an identity effectively it is important to understand that it is formulated from three key constituents:

- Brand essence
- Brand values
- Brand personality

The brand essence, values and personality govern the overall character and feel of the brand; they give the brand its meaning and uniqueness and serve to differentiate the brand from others in the marketplace. These are vital components of the identity and should be reflected in the outward manifestations of the brand – its symbol or logo, product, packaging, display, promotion and website.

Brand essence

The first step in defining brand identity is to determine and establish the **brand essence**. A brand's essence describes the essential nature or core of a brand. It could be described as the brand's heart, spirit or soul. It is extremely important to understand what lies at the heart of a brand and to be able to articulate it concisely. Edun, for example, launched by Ali Hewson and Bono of U2, describes itself as "A socially conscious clothing company with a mission to create beautiful clothing while fostering sustainable employment in developing areas of the world, particularly Africa." (www.edunonline.com). This short statement identifies the fundamental aim of the brand, marks out its central proposition and sums up its essence. Writing a statement such as this is important as a clearly defined essence forms the key building block upon which all other aspects of the brand are built.

Closely allied to the brand essence is the **brand proposition**, which is a succinct expression of what the brand intends to offer or promise its customers. The Edun statement above clarifies the Edun brand essence but it also explains the Edun brand proposition as shown overleaf.

Edun brand essence – a socially conscious clothing company
Edun brand proposition – to offer beautiful clothing while fostering sustainable employment in developing areas of the world

As you can see from the example above, the essence and proposition (or promise) explains the raison d'etre behind the brand and clarifies the motivation for the business. A genuine brand essence in combination with an achievable and deliverable proposition will contribute to creating a well-defined brand identity which in turn can act as a potent force for marketing and set the tone for communication and promotion. If essence is considered to be the heart of a brand then **brand values** (sometimes referred to as core values) are its foundation stones.

Building brand loyalty

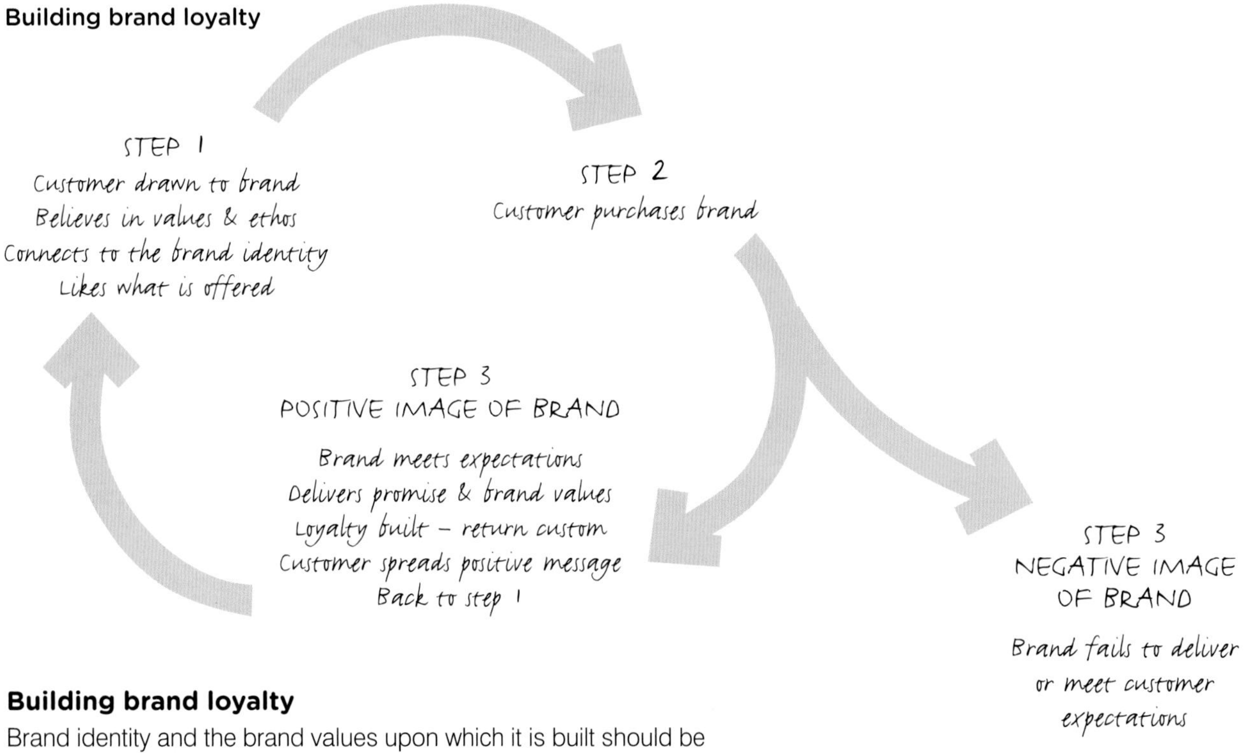

STEP 1
Customer drawn to brand
Believes in values & ethos
Connects to the brand identity
Likes what is offered

STEP 2
Customer purchases brand

STEP 3
POSITIVE IMAGE OF BRAND

Brand meets expectations
Delivers promise & brand values
Loyalty built – return custom
Customer spreads positive message
Back to step 1

STEP 3
NEGATIVE IMAGE
OF BRAND

Brand fails to deliver
or meet customer
expectations

Building brand loyalty
Brand identity and the brand values upon which it is built should be considered important tools for establishing **brand loyalty**. Authentic brand values and an engaging brand identity are powerful communication tools, but if consumers engage with a brand because they respect what it stands for they will want to feel confident that the values will be upheld over time. A company managing a brand must ensure that customers' loyalty and trust are honoured and that the brand identity and values are maintained and remain consistent. The diagram above shows the impact on consumer loyalty of both a positive and negative brand image. If a consumer forms a positive image, they are likely to remain loyal and become advocates of the brand. If the brand fails to deliver, they will be disappointed and form a negative image.

Brand values

Brand values build upon and expand the central theme of the brand essence. They are the core values that set the code by which a brand organization operates. The values should inform all aspects of how the company runs its business, designs and develops its products, delivers its services, and markets and promotes its brand. Consumers are more likely to engage with a brand when they respect or connect with its values, as the title of Martin Butler's book testifies, *People don't buy what you sell: They buy what you stand for.*

Comptoir des Cotonniers, created in 1995, is an upmarket French fashion retail brand owned by Japanese parent company Fast Retailing – the company that also owns Uniqlo. Comptoir's central value is to appeal to women of all ages and to create a close connection with its customers. To that end they do not use professional models but showcase their collections using "real mother and daughter pairs, who over the passing years and seasons, embody and affirm the brand values with ever more naturalness, enthusiasm and pleasure." (www.comptoirdescotonniers.com). The Comptoir brand values are to be accessible, contemporary and to promote sharing and what they term proximity – meaning close and authentic relationships as demonstrated in mother and daughter relationships.

Connecting company and customer

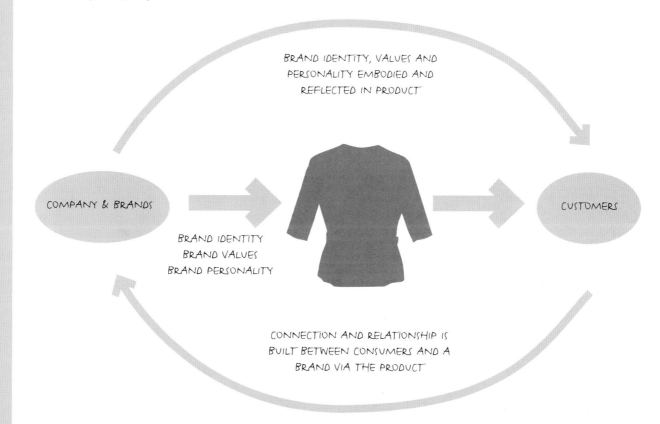

BRAND IDENTITY, VALUES AND
PERSONALITY EMBODIED AND
REFLECTED IN PRODUCT

COMPANY & BRANDS

BRAND IDENTITY
BRAND VALUES
BRAND PERSONALITY

CUSTOMERS

CONNECTION AND RELATIONSHIP IS
BUILT BETWEEN CONSUMERS AND A
BRAND VIA THE PRODUCT

A small clothing company with big brand values
Nau

Nau is a US company selling its own design range of sustainable fashion and performance wear. The team behind the Nau label describe the company as "a small clothing company with big ideas"; they understand the potential of building a brand up from its core values and are committed to the power of business as a force for change. As a business Nau seeks to balance the **triple bottom line**: people, planet and profit. The triple bottom line is an ethical system that measures a company's success in terms of economic, social and environmental criteria. The ethical stance taken by Nau leads the company to pose the question: "Does the world really need another outdoor clothing company?" Only if its products and practices contribute to "positive, lasting and substantive change", they reason.

The Nau website also explains the company design philosophy is: "Built on the balance of three criteria: beauty, performance and sustainability." From these statements it is possible to extrapolate the Nau core brand values:

- To contribute to positive, lasting and substantive change
- To produce and sell clothes that balance beauty, performance and sustainability

Brand values should be more than just a list of impressive sounding words. They should be a call to action. The idea is to create values that inspire and drive a business forward. The values should be understandable and deliverable; those that manage a brand will need to instigate strategic actions to ensure the values are manifested throughout the company. Valid and authentic brand values strengthen the brand identity, give a business direction and provide motivation for management, stakeholders, partners and employees. Brand values are important not only in terms of their potential for guiding the internal business operation but also for building relationship and communicating with consumers. Websites provide an obvious advantage for businesses wishing to communicate their ethos and brand values. The Nau site explains the philosophy behind the company and details how this is reflected in the product design and manufacture.

Below
The Profile Fleece jacket made from recycled polyester fabric developed from post-consumer and post-industrial polyester waste.

Above
The Nau team at work. Valid and authentic brand values strengthen the brand identity, give a business direction and provide motivation for the team.

Brand personality

Brand personality works on the premise that brands can have personalities in much the same way as people. Professor Kotler, when describing the differences between the computer brands IBM and Apple, suggested that Apple has the personality of someone in their twenties and that IBM has the character of someone in their sixties!

When related to fashion, the issue of brand personality needs some careful thought. It is all too easy to say that a brand is fashionable, stylish, modern or luxurious. But do those characteristics really capture the flavour of its personality or distinguish the brand clearly from any other? Probably not! The Vivienne Westwood label could be described as British fashion with a twist, so could that of Paul Smith, so it is vital to take some time to delve deeply and define other more descriptive qualities that capture the uniqueness of a brand's persona. Vivienne Westwood is also anarchic, irreverent and perhaps a little subversive, whereas the Paul Smith brand augments its British style with quirky elements of the unexpected.

When a brand is built around the distinctive personality of an individual designer, the brand personality is likely to resemble closely that of the designer in question. New York fashion designer Betsey Johnson has variously been described as exuberant, whimsical, over the top and fearlessly eccentric. Betsey's dramatic personality is reflected throughout her fashion empire. Her collections are known to be colourful and capricious with sexy silhouettes and whimsical embellished details. The Betsey Johnson retail stores (there are over 50 worldwide) amplify her singular creative vision with an iconic rock-n-roll meets Victoriana style defined by bright colour, abundant floral wallpapers and bursts of ornamental decoration. As Betsey says on her website:

Above

Beauté Prestige International (BPI) creates, develops and markets fragrances for Jean Paul Gaultier, Issey Miyake and Narciso Rodriguez. The Jean Paul Gaultier perfume, Ma Dame, was launched in 2008; BPI worked with branding consultancy Interbrand to define the personality for the perfume, inspired by Gaultier's vision of the perfect woman. Ma Dame's personality is described by Interbrand as a "trendy tomboy with classy sex appeal".

"My products wake up and brighten and bring the wearer to life…drawing attention to her beauty and specialness… her moods and movements… her dreams and fantasies."
Betsey Johnson

In comparison to Betsey Johnson it could be said that the Martin Margiela brand sits at the opposite end of the personality spectrum, particularly in terms of colour. Whereas Betsey Johnson draws attention by use of bold bright colour, Margiela creates drama by the use of white. White is the signature for all Margiela boutiques. Sales personnel are styled in lab-assistant white coats – the uniform traditionally worn by workers in a Parisian couture atelier. The signature use of non-colour could be described as self-effacing, like the Belgian designer himself. Famous for keeping a low profile, he has been described by journalist Sarah Mower as "fashion's mystery man". This desire for secrecy exudes from many aspects of the brand personality and identity. A noticeable example of inscrutability is evidenced in the garment label for the women's collection. It is not woven or printed with the Maison Martin Margiela brand name but is left blank. For the other collections, the label is constructed from a simple piece of white cloth printed with a series of numbers 0–23. The specific collection is indicated by encircling the appropriate number on the label. The key to the numbers and the collections is represented below.

0   Garments reworked by hand for women
010   Garments reworked by hand for men
1*   The collection for women
10   The collection for men
4   A wardrobe for women
14   A wardrobe for men
11   A collection of accessories for women and men
22   A collection of shoes for women and men
13   Objects and publications
MM6   Garments for ♀
* The original white label

Basia Szkutnicka is a fashion lecturer and Maison Martin Margiela devotee. She has been wearing and collecting Margiela clothes and accessories since the label launched in 1988. In a conversation with the author in 2009, Basia explained why she connects to the Margiela brand.

"I love the irreverence and the intelligence… I feel I connect with the ethos of the label… I love the attention to detail, the garments flatter me, they are an extension of me… I love the tradition, craftsmanship and the values of the product. I feel really well dressed – it's like a second skin to me."

This connection to the ethos behind the Margiela brand is mirrored in an interview with a fashion journalist conducted by Mark Tungate. In his book *Fashion Brands* Tungate relates how this well-known journalist had two jackets with them for a trip to the Paris collections; one from Margiela, the other was from Zara. The Margiela jacket cost around five times the price of the Zara garment but the journalist did not mind paying this premium because as they explained,

"I like what Margiela stands for. I'm paying for the person, not the article."
(Tungate, 2005)

This illustrates the potential of brand personality as a tool for building relationships between a brand and its customers. The product is the visible symbol of the personality and a physical manifestation of the brand values. On the company website, the design aesthetic of the Edun collection (*see* pp.139–40) is described as being edgy with a modern approach and drawing inspiration from intellectual ideas behind poetry and art. The Edun brand personality could therefore be described as edgy, modern, intellectual, brainy, beautiful, ethically conscientious and socially aware. It is likely therefore that the brand will appeal to consumers who connect with these personality traits; they are likely to be socially aware ethical customers who might wish to feel edgy and intellectual or modern and beautiful.

Top
Each Maison Martin Margiela collection is given a number rather than a name. MM6 is a line for women that is more casual and edgy than the main line, MM1.

Above
Maison Martin Margiela store signage features no name, just the numbers 0–23.

Carrying the brand

The carrier bag is a highly visual symbol of a brand. This simple item is often overlooked as a marketing tool but just think about it – every time a customer leaves a store carrying their purchases in a distinctive and recognizable carrier bag, they become a walking advertisement for the brand. For many customers, the bag is considered to be an important element of the shopping experience and deemed just as much of a status symbol as the garments or product contained within it. It is an amazingly democratic device, available to all who purchase irrespective of the amount of money they spend.

Brand touchpoints

Fashion product is one of the most important vehicles through which a brand transmits its message, values and identity to customers. The product can be described as a **brand touchpoint**, which is a point of interaction between a brand and consumers, employees or stakeholders. The concept of brand touchpoints was first published in 2002 by Davis & Dunn. A brand has between 30 and 100 potential touchpoints and each touchpoint has the potential to make either a positive or negative impression (Davis & Longoria 2003). Touchpoints affecting consumers can be categorized into those that occur pre-purchase, during purchase and post-purchase. Think about all the possible interactions a consumer could have with a brand. Each touchpoint offers the potential for someone to be converted either for or against the brand. Take, for example, the pre-purchase stage. A person who is not aware of the brand may be converted to become conscious of it. Someone who is

Above
The carrier bag is a highly visual symbol of a brand. This simple item is often overlooked as a marketing tool.

The touchpoints that affect a consumer when they interact with a retail fashion brand during the pre-purchase, purchase and post-purchase stages. There can be between 30–100 touchpoints, but it would be impossible for a company to focus on all of these effectively. A limited selection of key touchpoints must be identified. For an internet-based retailer, the website would be an extremely important touchpoint.
Source: Adapted from Davis & Dunn (2002).

Brand touchpoints

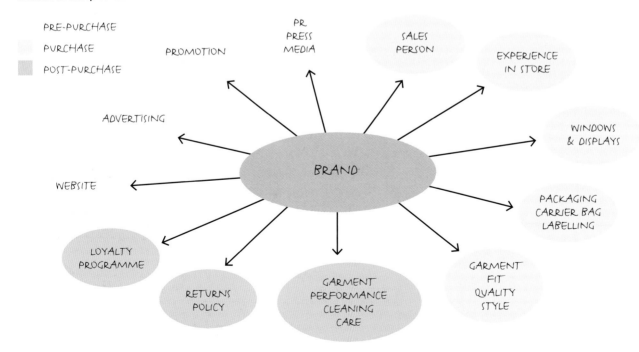

PRE-PURCHASE
PURCHASE
POST-PURCHASE

PROMOTION
PR PRESS MEDIA
SALES PERSON
EXPERIENCE IN STORE
ADVERTISING
WINDOWS & DISPLAYS
WEBSITE
BRAND
PACKAGING CARRIER BAG LABELLING
LOYALTY PROGRAMME
RETURNS POLICY
GARMENT PERFORMANCE CLEANING CARE
GARMENT FIT QUALITY STYLE

brand-aware may be converted and take the next step towards actually purchasing. During the purchase stage a potential customer may be converted and make a purchase, or they may be put off in some way by their experience and decide not to buy and not to interact with the brand again.

Analysing brand identity

Brand touchpoints represent a point of interaction between a consumer or potential consumer and a brand. These touchpoints could also be considered as the brand in action, or in other words, the way in which a brand expresses its ethos and identity in actual strategic actions. This takes us on to a tool used in brand management known as a brand onion.

A brand onion is used to analyse and map the brand identity and show it in diagrammatic form. The brand onion represents the layers of a brand from its inner essence, or core, through to the outer personality layer and brand in action at the surface. The object of the exercise is to summarize the brand identity, capturing the essence, values and personality traits that differentiate the brand from competitors. The real benefit of the tool is its use in establishing how the identity should be made manifest in reality, represented by the 'brand in action' section of the diagram. So, for example, Comptoir des Cotonniers (*see* page 141) aims to be accessible; how exactly will this accessibility be realized? As we saw earlier, one way Comptoir reflect this value is to use real people to model their clothes. They also want to promote authentic relationships, so they use mother and daughter pairs to express this aspect of the brand.

Creating a brand onion
When analysing a brand and developing a brand onion, it is often easiest to start with the personality layer first. Look at websites, in-store promotional material, carrier bags, labelling, window displays, in-store ambiance or advertising – what kind of personality do you think they convey? How do you feel when you connect to the brand or how do you think customers feel when they wear the brand?

Work inwards through the brand onion and determine the brand values and the essence. Finally, don't forget the brand in action section. Try to determine how the brand essence, values and personality are put into action and record findings in the outer ring of the onion.

Brand onion diagram

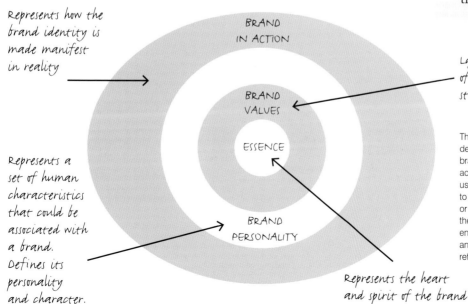

Represents how the brand identity is made manifest in reality

BRAND IN ACTION

BRAND VALUES

ESSENCE

BRAND PERSONALITY

Lays the foundation of what a brand stands for

Represents a set of human characteristics that could be associated with a brand. Defines its personality and character.

Represents the heart and spirit of the brand

The brand onion is a popular and effective device for showing a concise overview of a brand identity and how it is expressed in actual strategic actions. Brand onions are usually created by branding consultancies to show the results of a brand investigation or re-branding exercise. Once completed, the onion can be used as a guide to ensure that all aspects of the business and key brand touchpoints accurately reflect the brand values.

A new fashion brand and collection
Grandma's Trunk

The brand proposal showcased here forms part of a project undertaken by a student studying fashion at Plymouth College of Art in the UK. The student has set the scene and outlined the concept for the brand, Grandma's Trunk.

Grandma has a hidden trunk full of secret treasures. Dresses, brooches, old ribbons, buttons and scented love letters have remained preserved and undisturbed for decades. It's a girl's dream to rummage through this treasure trove and unearth vintage gems that could inspire new ideas or spark off a trend. Grandma's Trunk transforms faded treasures into delightful, edgy new garments with a surprising, vintage, rock-chic feel. The girl who wears this quirky new brand is adventurous, eclectic and confident. She radiates happiness, is admired as a trendsetter and experiments with creating her own special style by mixing vintage with raw classics.

INCORPORATE A HIDDEN GEM IN EVERY GARMENT

FOCUS ON EMBELLISHMENT & ANTIQUE TRIMS

CREATIVE

INNOVATIVE

CONFIDENT

QUIRKY

CREATE FRESH STYLES FOR THE INNOVATIVE CUSTOMER

MIX ODD ELEMENTS OF VINTAGE WITH NEW, EDGY DESIGN

MODERN DOWDY

OFFER AN EXTRA SPECIAL TOUCH

QUIRKY RE-MADE MODERN VINTAGE

OFFER INTIMATE CONNECTION

ROCK CHIC

REWORK VINTAGE CLOTHES & ACCESSORIES

ADMIRED

BE EXCLUSIVE & AFFORDABLE

EDGY

STYLE CONSCIOUS

INDEPENDENT

ADVENTUROUS

MAKE PRICES AFFORDABLE £30–230

SELL IN QUIRKY INDEPENDENT BOUTIQUES

Below
The concept board for Grandma's Trunk. The imagery gives a visual feel for the brand and the customer.

A brand onion showing how the personality of the Grandma's Trunk brand matches closely the personality of the targeted customer. The brand onion also shows how the potential customers might feel when they connect with its quirky mix of vintage and modern.

The Brand Identity Prism

Another model for analysing brand identity is Jean-Noël Kapferer's Brand Identity Prism, first introduced in 1992. Kapferer's six-sided model aims to capture the complexity of brand identity and the concepts behind it are perhaps harder to pin down than those of the simpler brand onion.

Brand Identity Prism

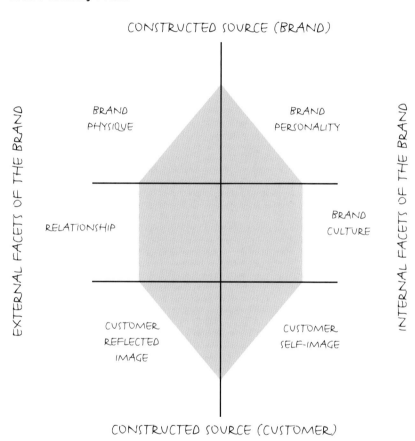

Both systems of analysis attempt to depict the internal and external aspects of brand identity. Kapferer's model does this by dividing the diagram by a vertical axis, whereas in the brand onion the internal elements are placed towards the centre and external aspects, such as 'the brand in action' are situated on the outer layer of the onion.

Source: Kapferer and Bastien, *The Luxury Strategy* 2009.

- **Physique –** this equates to the essence of the brand as well as its physical features, symbols and attributes. At a symbolic level Nike is signified by the Swoosh, Levi's by a red tab while Ralph Lauren is epitomized by Polo. The physical facet also comprises iconic products like Levi's 501 jeans or Yves Saint Laurent's 'Le Smoking' dinner jacket.

- **Personality –** the character, attitude or personality of the brand. Kapferer believes a brand should have a unique personality. In his book, *Strategic Brand Management* (1992), Kapferer modifies the definition of USP, changing it to become 'unique selling personality'.
- **Culture –** a brand has its own distinctive culture and brand values. At Hermès the culture is built around luxury, craftsmanship and exceptional quality, at Ralph Lauren it is formed from a unique blend of preppy American, rugged outdoorsy casual and classic English tweed.
- **Relationship –** this relates to beliefs and associations connected with a brand. What does the brand promise? How is the brand perceived in the outside world? What does wearing a particular brand say about someone? It concerns social communication and the idea of using brands to belong to a style tribe or group.
- **Reflection –** this is the idealized image of the consumer as reflected in brand advertising. Kapferer describes this facet as the 'external mirror' of the brand. In the short film advertising Chanel N° 5, Nicole Kidman reflects the allure, sophistication, elegance and mystery of the Chanel brand.
- **Self-image –** corresponds to the mental image consumers have of themselves when wearing the brand. Kapferer refers to this as the consumer's 'internal mirror'. Someone who wears Ralph Lauren might aspire to live the American dream or a person wearing Chanel may wish to feel independent and classy.

Branding: emotion and feeling

Branding aims to create connection by generating an emotional response. Brand personality and brand values are instrumental in achieving this. Teri Agins says in her book, *The End of Fashion*: "Fashion happens to be a relevant and powerful force in our lives. At every level of society, people care greatly about the way they look, which affects both their self-esteem and the way other people interact with them"(2000).Kapferer's brand prism takes this into account by including relationship and self-image among its six dimensions. The brand onion positions the personality layer as the interface between the brand and consumer, both models can be used to analyse why consumers might connect with a particular brand and how they might feel when they do. Bernd H. Schmitt includes a chapter entitled 'Feel' in his book, *Experiential Marketing*. Schmitt explains that the aim behind the marketing and promotion of fashion and fragrance is to evoke certain types of emotions or feelings likely to make a customer want the brand; this is what Schmitt calls 'sense marketing'. The naming convention for fragrances illustrates this concept; for example, Joy by Patou, Happy by Clinique, Pretty by Elizabeth Arden or Beautiful by Estée Lauder.

5.

Brand strategy and management

Establishing a brand is a long-term and costly process and companies do not take on this risky task lightly. Creating a brand with a clear identity takes time – it usually takes several years or decades to achieve brand status. Orla Kiely, for example, started her business in a small way working from home. It took approximately ten years for the company to expand and morph into the modern fashion lifestyle brand so loved today. Luxury brands like Fendi, Gucci and Prada started out as small family businesses. Fendi was a furrier, Gucci a handbag manufacturer and Prada designed and sold handbags, shoes and luggage. It was not until Mario Prada's granddaughter Miuccia took the helm in 1978 that Prada started its journey to becoming a global fashion brand. Once a brand is recognized and valued by consumers then opportunity arises to capitalize on the power of the brand name and leverage the brand identity in order to take the brand forward. While it could be argued that a brand is formed in the mind and hearts of consumers, it is a valuable business asset that must be managed effectively from within the brand organization. Two of the most widely used strategies utilized in brand management are **brand extension** and **brand licensing**.

> "Branding connects corporate strategy with consumer psychology."
> **Pamela N. Danziger**

Core and peripheral fashion markets

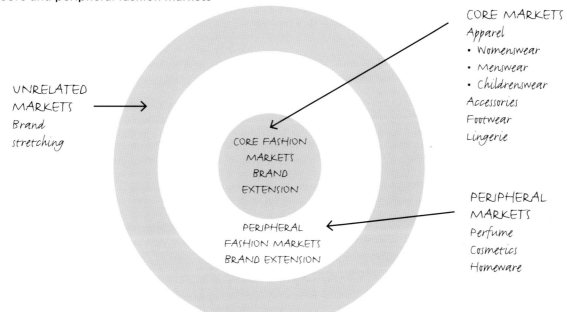

CORE MARKETS
Apparel
• Womenswear
• Menswear
• Childrenswear
Accessories
Footwear
Lingerie

UNRELATED MARKETS
Brand stretching

CORE FASHION MARKETS BRAND EXTENSION

PERIPHERAL FASHION MARKETS BRAND EXTENSION

PERIPHERAL MARKETS
Perfume
Cosmetics
Homeware

Brand extension and stretching

Brand extension and brand stretching relate to Ansoff's matrix for growth discussed in Chapter 3 (*see* page 100). Brand extension allows a brand company to capitalize on the power of an existing band's equity and value to launch new products in a broadly similar market. This relates to product development in Ansoff's Matrix. Brand extension exploits a brand's identity, associating the meanings and values behind it with new products. So an apparel supplier who manufactures a branded range of men's performance and outdoor apparel would be extending their brand into another area of the apparel market if they launched a similarly branded womenswear collection. The benefit of brand extension in this case is that distributers and buyers are likely to perceive less risk when taking on the women's version of the brand if they have had success selling the menswear, and end-consumers will have existing **brand awareness**.

If the company decided to utilize their established brand name in a completely different and unrelated market such as adventure travel then this would be termed brand stretching ('diversification' in Ansoff's Matrix). Missoni have done this by creating the Missoni Home Collection as well as opening the Missoni Hotel in Edinburgh. When considering a brand stretching strategy it is important that there is a strong conceptual fit between the original brand and the new market. Missoni, for example, is a brand built around luxurious mixes of colour, texture and pattern which translates well into the arena of interior design.

Brand licensing

A brand is a business asset that should lead to higher profit levels for the operating company. One strategy utilized to achieve increased revenue and profit is licensing and this has increasingly become a favoured strategy for fashion brands wishing to achieve growth. According to the International Licensing Industry Merchandisers' Association (LIMA), fashion licensing was worth US$ 775 million, equating to 14 per cent of the licensing industry revenue in 2008.

Licensing is a business arrangement where a brand company sells the right to use their name to another company who can then develop, manufacture and market specified branded merchandise under licence. The manufacturing company (the **licensee**) will pay a royalty fee to the brand owner (the **licensor**). Royalty rates vary. The exact percentage is dependent on the time-frame of the agreement, the type of product involved, the financial investment, the time it takes to develop the product, and the volumes of merchandise predicted to sell. For women's ready-to-wear, the standard rate will be between 3–8 per cent of the wholesale volume. According to Chevalier and Mazzalovo in their book *Luxury Brand Management*, perfume royalties are slightly less, usually 3–5 per cent of wholesale and export volume. This is because perfume licensing deals stipulate a high advertising-to-sales ratio (around 15 per cent), thus ensuring a high level of exposure for the product. By comparison, fashion ready-to-wear operates at a 2–4 per cent ratio. This is why perfume advertising is so prevalent and takes up so many more pages in a fashion magazine than adverts for clothing.

Licensing provides a means of diversification for a fashion brand, allowing it to expand into other markets and reach a broader audience. There is less

"Successful brand licensing can have a very positive effect on the overall perception and value of the brand... However, it is not an easy proposition and failure to manage licensing effectively might weaken or permanently damage the brand."
Sean Chiles

risk attached to licensing compared to brand stretching because the brand company is not responsible for the capital investment or the costs involved in producing, distributing or marketing the licensed product.

It is important therefore that licensing agreements are signed with companies with the correct expertise in manufacturing and marketing specific products. Avon has agreements to manufacture fragrances for Finnish brand Marimekko and French designers Emmanuel Ungaro and Christian Lacroix. Luxury footwear retailer Kurt Geiger signed a seven-year licence agreement in 2009 to distribute and sell Nine West women's footwear, handbags and small leather goods in the UK and Ireland. Licensing allows the brand company to expand into fresh geographical market territories that it might not otherwise be able to enter. The Japanese company, Onward Kashiyama, holds the licence to manufacture and distribute Paul Smith womenswear as well as Calvin Klein, Jean Paul Gaultier and Sonia Rykiel. The Japanese market is extremely important for sales of global luxury and designer brands. Sales of British brands such as Paul Smith, Liberty and Hackett rose during 2008, even though clothing sales overall were down in Japan. Japanese consumers appreciate fashion with a British feel and these brands are perceived to have a classic and timeless image.

Brand repositioning

Repositioning is the process of redefining the identity of an existing brand or product in order to shift the position it holds in consumers' minds relative to that of competitors. A brand organization may decide to alter its strategic direction and reposition a brand if the current positioning is no longer relevant or effective. The decision to do this might be required as a response to:

- A brand losing market share
- Changes in the macro or micro marketing environment
- New brands entering the market
- Repositioning of competitor brands
- Shifts in consumer demand

Repositioning does not usually entail a change of brand name but might include updating and modernizing the existing logo. Rebranding refers to not only a potential repositioning of a brand but also to a complete change of brand name and logo. This usually occurs in response to a company takeover and could also include radical internal restructuring. Total rebranding is rare within fashion; it generally occurs in industries such as banking and insurance, although it could occur within garment manufacturing or in the chemical fibre industry.

The following section gives two examples of repositioning. The first illustrates how a brand was repositioned by changing the fashion level of its product and altering the structure of the product ranges. The second example shows how a brand updated its visual identity by modernizing its logo, store **fascia**, in-store design and packaging.

Brand repositioning

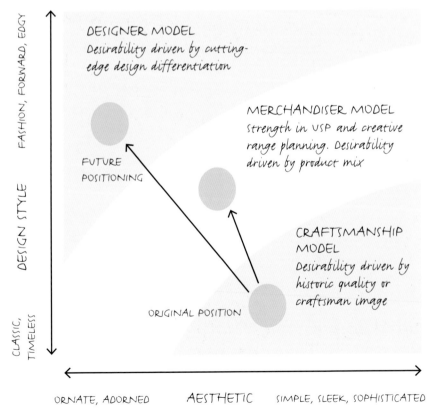

This repositioning map was created by brand management at MCM in order to visualize potential new positions for their accessory brand. The map shows the original position of the luxury accessory brand and two proposed positions for its future. The original positioning is based on MCM's historic image and craftsmanship. The first new position, based on what MCM term the 'Merchandiser model', aims to retain the craftsman quality but drive desirability by creative merchandising and range planning. The second proposed position, the 'Designer model', is driven by cutting-edge design, potentially with a high-profile designer name as figurehead.

Source: MCM (2008)

Creating a contemporary luxury brand
Repositioning MCM

MCM (Mode Creation Munich) is a modern accessory and clothing brand that manufactures and sells quality leather travel goods, handbags and fashion apparel for both women and men. Sold by high-status retailers in the United States, the UK, Europe, Russia, Dubai and Asia as well as in MCM's own boutiques in London, Berlin, Athens and Beijing, the brand is accessible in more than 260 points of sale worldwide. The company is run by Sung-Joo Kim, the Chairperson and CEO of the MCM Group. Kim is a business woman of great integrity and foresight. Predicting a likely economic downturn in 2008, she took strategic action to modernize and reposition the brand within the lucrative luxury accessories market. Sung-Joo Kim believes that the recession will necessitate change and that consumer tastes will shift in favour of a growing demand for what Kim terms "responsible luxury". A key component of the strategy has been to revive and update a classic from the past. MCM reintroduced its signature Cognac Visetos collection for Spring/Summer 2009. In an article by Ann Hynek for FoxBusiness, Sung-Joo Kim explained the rationale behind this decision, "Going back to the brand's traditional roots is a safe bet in uncertain times."

The MCM repositioning strategy aims to modernize the brand, making it more fashionable and cutting-edge while at the same time maintaining the brand heritage and traditional values of quality, luxury and craftsmanship.

Bottom left
An MCM advertising image shows the original 1980s Cognac Visetos range.

Below
Bag from the updated and revitalized Vintage Visetos collection, Spring 2009. The logo-embossed, soft cognac-coloured leather is finished with brown trim and satin gold hardware. The introduction of sleek modern shapes and innovative detailing helps to give the product a more contemporary aesthetic and make it relevant for the twenty-first-century consumer.

Bottom
Bag designed by Michael Michalsky for the MCM Cognac Visetos range.

A fresh visual identity for an established business
Greenwoods

Greenwoods are a menswear specialist retailer and suit hire business established in 1860 by Willie Greenwood. The company, which has generations of experience in the menswear business, was family owned up until 2009 when it was bought by a Chinese company, Harvest Fancy Hong Kong Ltd., a unit of Bosideng International Fashion Ltd. Greenwoods trades from approximately 100 stores, situated mainly in the northern regions of the UK. It also has a website (www.1860.com) which focuses on the suit hire side of the business, specializing in traditional men's eveningwear, morningwear and Highlandwear for formal occasions and weddings.

In 2009 an independent graphic design consultancy, Studio Ten and a Half, were commissioned to revitalize and update the Greenwood brand identity. Footfall had gone down and Greenwoods were loosing existing customers to competitors on the UK high street. The Greenwoods retail environment no longer looked fresh, the brand identity and message had become unclear and the brand personality was tired. There was a lack of coherence between the visual identity, the product on offer, the pricing strategy and the overall look of the retail environment. The bottom line was being affected and Greenwoods were struggling to compete. Research revealed that consumers valued Greenwoods for its heritage and specialist menswear knowledge, and they valued the individual attention and service offered by staff. They also thought of the brand as masculine and trustworthy. The new visual identity created by Studio Ten and a Half was designed to ensure that Greenwoods could capitalize on the tradition, heritage and trust that consumers so valued. The rebranding package included an updated design for the logo, a new store fit, a refresh of the fascia, new swing tickets, in-store signage, stationery and carrier bags.

The makeover of Greenwoods achieved by design consultancy Studio Ten and a Half illustrates the importance of having the right visual style for a brand. The new logo, signage and fascia build upon the original heritage of the brand. Traditional elements such as the gold lettering were retained, but the introduction of a more refined and modern typeface brought the overall look and feel of the brand up to date. The clean but traditional typeface creates a fresh and contemporary brand identity, and a simple palette using Greenwoods' trademark green, gold, cream and grey ensures a balance between classic and modern. The brand's long-standing heritage is communicated clearly by the use of the statement, 'Menswear since 1860'.

6.

Fashion promotion is a key element of the marketing mix. The task of promotion is to communicate with customers and publicize products and services. Promotional activities such as advertising, public relations and sales promotions are used to build a brand's status, enhance perception of a brand, increase desire for products, raise awareness of what's on offer and inform consumers about benefits or services. The ultimate aim of promotion is of course is to support sales and persuade consumers to purchase.

The promotional mix

The promotional mix refers to the combination of promotional tools used by a company to promote products and services and communicate their message to consumers. The four standard elements of the mix are advertising, sales promotion, public relations or PR, and personal selling.

Similar to the concept of the marketing mix, the promotional mix simplifies a vast array of potential promotional possibilities into four overarching headings. However, the fashion industry's approach to promotion is somewhat different to that of other market sectors, so this simplification masks the full range of promotional opportunities that might be employed. Additional promotional tools essential to fashion marketing are the fashion press, seasonal catwalk shows, window displays, visual merchandising and signage.

The fashion press

The press plays an important role in fashion promotion. Fashion magazines are vital cogs in the machinery of fashion promotion in terms of advertising and editorial. They report on designer shows at London, Paris, New York, and Milan Fashion Week; premier new season collections in their fashion editorial; give details of key fashion trends; profile hot looks for the season; and report on trends in art and culture. Important to fashion promotion is the press obsession with celebrity. Acres of print are devoted to celebrity goings-on. Weekly celebrity gossip magazines keep readers updated with the latest celebrity news, fashion trends and must-have items available in-store. National newspapers also cover celebrities, the designer catwalk shows and report on seasonal and day-to-day developments within the industry.

Fashion shows

Fashion shows are an integral part of the industry and provide significant PR and publicity for designers. The major international designer catwalk shows take place twice a year during London, Paris, Milan and New York Fashion Week when design houses, designers and luxury fashion brands show their ready-to-wear collections for the forthcoming season. A catwalk show at London Fashion Week can cost upwards of £50,000 and only a selection of designers will be invited to join the schedule, but for those who show it is an important opportunity to garner press coverage, raise awareness and build

Below
Vogue Editor-in-chief, Anna Wintour, sits fourth from the right in the front row for the Ralph Lauren Autumn 2009 show. Wintour is a powerful force in fashion; if she decides to feature a designer's work in the magazine, it will provide vital free publicity and marketing for the designer and their brand.

the reputation of the brand. The fashion press and buyers, as well as a select number of celebrities, flock to these four prestigious fashion capitals to view the spectacle. The press will report on the latest fashion ideas and start gathering inspiration for fashion stories and photo shoots; buyers will begin planning their buy for the coming season. There are also fashion weeks in India, Sri Lanka, Australia, Hong Kong and China and, while these might not be as well known, they are equally important for the relevant regions' designers, press and buyers. Fashion shows also take place at trade fairs like CPD womenswear and accessories in Düsseldorf, Pure in London, Prêt à Porter Paris® and Bread & Butter in Barcelona and Berlin. These shows are mainly for retail buyers so they can view collections prior to placing orders. As well as ready-to-wear fashion shows, haute couture shows also take place separately in Paris.

Retailers might choose to put on a fashion show as part of their PR campaign or press day, or they might choose to hold an in-store event and fashion show for customers as part of their marketing and promotion strategy. Fashion shows are often the favoured choice of those organizing charity fundraiser events, especially if high-profile retailers, designers and models lend their support, which helps publicity and potential ticket sales.

Window displays

Windows provide a fantastic canvas and major marketing opportunity for retailers. Inspirational and eye-catching windows act as a powerful magnet, drawing customers in and enticing them to visit the store. Displays can be used to reinforce brand identity, attract press attention or to provide information on products, prices and promotions. Zara, for example, does not advertise, preferring to use their expansive windows and stylish displays to promote the brand. Windows can be used to promote special seasonal events, the holiday season and Christmas usually being the most important.

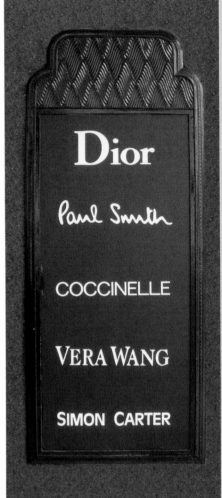

Or they can be used to tell a fashion story showcasing a hot new seasonal trend or designer collection. More pragmatic is a 'selling window', used mainly by lower-end value retailers to showcase and push specific merchandise.

Visual merchandising and signage

Once a customer is inside, then it is **visual merchandising** and signage that become important for communication, promotion and visual drama. Visual merchandising (VM) is used to create internal displays, put key looks together and outfit-build. It should be used to highlight specific looks and products that store owners or buyers wish to promote, and it is important that visual merchandisers are aware of products scheduled to be promoted in the press so that these items are given prominence. Signage can be used within the store to guide customers and indentify departments, zones or specific collections. Externally, signage can be used to indicate which brands and labels are carried. Some retailers use windows or an internal wall near the front of the store to promote what is inside.

Above left
Marking a significant milestone in a brand's history can provide an excellent opportunity to do something special. In 2009 Selfridges, the globally renowned London department store, celebrated its centenary. Stunning, yellow-themed windows paid homage to the past. Each window took a Selfridges display concept from the last 100 years and updated it, making it relevant for the modern day.

Above
Signage on the outside of a department store is used to indicate noteworthy brands carried inside on the fashion floors.

Fashion advertising

Advertising is a significant global business. Information supplied by ZenithOptimedia shows that consumer magazine advertising expenditure for 2008 in the United States was US$18.5 billion and in the UK £636 million, with US$4,511 million and £257 million being spent on promoting 'cosmetics and toiletries' and 'clothing and accessories' categories in the US and UK respectively. Generally, advertising is an expensive mode of promotion, but for big global brands with sizeable budgets, it is a highly visible facet of promotion and one of the primary methods used to transmit brand identity and communicate brand message.

Advertising is considered a non-personal form of promotion; in other words it communicates ideas using image, film or written information conveyed to an audience via mass media or the Internet. The principal objectives of advertising are to raise awareness, inform and persuade. The ultimate aim is of course to generate sales, but under the surface advertising endeavours to:

- Reinforce a brand's image
- Communicate a brand's position in the market
- Embed specific meanings into the consumer psyche
- Tap into consumer aspirations
- Create desire for the brand and its products

Most adverts developed to promote fashion work to generate desire and tap into consumer aspirations. In general, they do this by reinforcing the idea that you will be desirable, sexy, beautiful and alluring or young, cool, hip or cutting edge if you buy into a brand and purchase its clothing, accessory, fragrance, jewellery or make-up products. For men the most common messages relate to being successful, attractive, powerful, sexy, rugged, cool and so on. The dominant media for fashion advertising is the press, particularly within magazines, so the key to communicating these attributes lies in developing powerful and impactful visual imagery which can be decoded by consumers. One technique used by an increasing number of the world's most prestigious fashion brands is to employ a celebrity to become the 'face' of the brand.

Celebrity endorsement

Over the years a vast array of famous personalities from the worlds of film and music has signed deals to promote branded fashion, accessories, cosmetics and perfume. Julia Roberts signed with Italian fashion house Gianfranco Ferré for their Spring/Summer 2006 campaign; Nicole Kidman and Keira Knightley starred in mini films and print campaigns for perfumes Channel No 5 and Coco Mademoiselle respectively; actor Jude Law became the global face of the Dunhill brand and Dior Homme in 2008. Louis Vuitton pulled off a dramatic coup in signing Madonna for its Spring/Summer 2009 advertising. Emma Watson, star of the Harry Potter films, became the face of Burberry in the same year. The aim of **celebrity endorsement** is that the cachet and sparkle of the celebrity personality will become directly

"I got my MBA from Marcy Projects." -Jay-Z

i am what i am

RbK⚡

associated with the brand and that this will reinforce the brand's image and position in the marketplace. The right choice of celebrity is crucial. The Davie-Brown Index (DBI) developed by the talent division of Davie Brown Entertainment (DBE) helps advertising agencies and brands assess the suitability of a celebrity. The index has eight criteria for which the celebrity is scored and the final result is analysed using a sophisticated database. Access to this system of evaluation costs a considerable sum but if viewed as a percentage of the payment the celebrity receives, the actual cost could be considered relatively small. The eight criteria are: appeal, notice, influence, trust, endorsement, trendsetting, aspiration, awareness. They are worth considering even without the addition of complicated number crunching or analysis, as they help illuminate the essential factors that establish a celebrity's suitability to become a brand ambassador.

Appeal and notice relate to the celebrity's popularity, appeal and ubiquity within their specialist field and the media. Influence, trust and endorsement act as a measure of how strong the celebrity might be as a spokesperson or icon of the brand. Trendsetting and aspiration are concerned with how consumers might aspire to have the trendsetting lifestyle of the celebrity in question. Consumer awareness of the celebrity is, of course, essential for the endorsement to be effective.

So far we have looked at the more traditional approaches by which fashion advertising and celebrity endorsement aim to raise awareness of a brand and capture consumer imagination. In general, campaigns using celebrities are not designed to shock or be controversial as it is important for both parties to keep their reputations intact. There are instances, however, of fashion advertising that pushes boundaries or subverts normal messages. Kate Moss caused a sensation when she starred in a series of risqué and erotic promotional films, *The Four Dreams of Miss X,* for lingerie brand Agent

Provocateur, and Italian fashion house Dolce & Gabbana came under fire in 2007 for its use of controversial and sexually explicit imagery in a print campaign published in the Spanish press. The advert, showing a man pinning a woman to the ground by her wrist, was withdrawn after complaints that it was sexist and promoted gender-related violence. However as you will see in the following example, it is possible to build a strong brand image through the use of provocative and unconventional advertising.

A unique approach to fashion advertising
The United Colors of Benetton

Since its inception the United Colors of Benetton advertising initiative has used the Benetton brand name as a platform for comment on many significant global issues such as racism, war or world hunger. During its early years Benetton stocked an extensive range of sweaters in a dizzying array of colours – the original advertising slogan was 'All the colors of the world'. This was later altered to become the now legendary 'United Colors of Benetton'. The company believed the united colors concept to be so strong and its metaphor for diversity to have such potential that the slogan became an official trademark.

Top

The Africa Works global communication campaign run by the United Colors of Benetton was launched in February 2008. The adverts were designed to promote the Birima microcredit programme in Senegal. The photograph by James Mollison features Senegalese workers who have used micro loans to start small businesses. Additional graphics include the United Colors of Benetton and Birima logos and the Africa Works campaign slogan developed by Fabrica, the Benetton Group's communication research centre.

Above

The Victims advert from August 2008 shows a Tibetan monk and Chinese soldier bowing in peace.

Benetton advertising campaigns capitalize on the power of the photographic image to convey strong emotional messages and raise awareness of important universal issues.

Components of an advertising campaign

Advertising is comprised of several components. There is the message being communicated, the medium or channel used to display the advert and the timing and exposure of the advert or campaign. The following section explains each of these elements with particular focus on the message and the medium, which are of key importance to any campaign.

The message

It should already be apparent that the message is a crucial element of any advertising campaign. It is therefore vital that the purpose of the advert and its overt and subliminal messages are considered carefully. Who is the advert aiming to attract and what is it trying to communicate? What type of message will be relevant to the audience but also be coherent with the purpose of the campaign and the values of the brand? Will the message be direct and to the point – 20 per cent off all products in a coming sale, for example – or will it be more subtle, provocative and challenging? Another issue to consider is how the message will be conveyed visually – will it be via a photographic image, fashion illustration, product illustration or other graphic image? Will the advert need additional written information in order to get the message across? Should there be a slogan or strapline to accompany the image? Could the message be communicated without any image at all, or perhaps all that is needed is some written text?

When deciding upon the message the following points should be considered:

- What is the purpose of the advert? Is it to raise awareness, inform, reinforce brand values or provoke action?
- What it the most important message it needs to convey?
- Will the message be communicated directly or indirectly?
- How will the message be communicated – via image, written text or both?

Left
Milla Jovovich presents the Tommy Hilfiger limited-edition bag in a window advertisement at the Coin store in Milan, Italy. The advert combines both image and text to deliver its message.

When designing an advert or campaign, determine what will make it distinctive and how it will attract consumer attention. The message must be decided upon and an understanding of how it will be relevant and meaningful to consumers will be needed. Will the advert provide a talking point, have a story to tell, communicate ideas directly or work more obliquely through a visual subtext? Should a celebrity be linked with the campaign and will budgets allow for this? Also consider the skills that might be required and personnel needed; will there be a need for a stylist, photographer, art director or film director, or will a fashion illustrator have to be commissioned?

Advertising features and benefits
Blackspot shoes

Based in Vancouver, Canada, *Adbusters* is a not-for-profit magazine with a circulation of around 120,000. The activist magazine offers its readers philosophical articles and commentary that address social, cultural and economic global issues. The aim is to promote change in the way business is conducted and create a stronger balance between economy and ecology. To that end *Adbusters* decided to do something concrete that could challenge the status quo – so they became the first magazine to manufacture and sell a shoe.

Adbusters launched the Blackspot Shoe Campaign with the classic V1 Blackspot sneaker. They later introduced their second style, the V2 Unswoosher boot, marketed as 'The most earth-friendly shoe in the world', with a rubber sole made from recycled car tyres and organic hemp upper. The shoes are ethical, anti-sweatshop, anti-logo and pro-environmental as well as what Adbusters call 'pro-grass roots capitalism'. Every pair of Blackspots comes with a Blackspot Shareholder Document. The certificate, included in the box with the shoes, has a unique log-in number that allows the purchaser to log into the members' zone on the Adbusters/ Blackspot website and participate in shareholder online forums. Anyone buying a pair of the shoes automatically becomes a member of the Blackspot 'Anti-corporation' and receives the right to vote on a selection of company issues.

The Blackspot sneaker is a deliberate subversion of the Converse Chuck Taylor All-Star. The advertisement points out and draws attention to the specific features and benefits of this ethical, anti-logo sneaker.

The advertising medium or channel

Once the message and purpose of the advert is established, the next issue to consider is the medium. The medium, or channel, is the vehicle by which an advert is presented and reaches the public. Traditional mass media advertising channels are:

- Print media
- Cinema
- Television
- Outdoor advertising
- Radio

One of the most prevalent channels for fashion, accessory, perfume and cosmetic advertising is the printed adverts featured in the vast array of international and nationally published monthly fashion magazines. The December 2008 issue of American *Vogue* for example carried 221 pages of advertising. Although this figure represents a 22 per cent drop from the 284 pages of the previous year, it is still a substantial proportion of the magazine. Another traditional mass media print channel is the national press. Here adverts are more likely to be printed in black and white; however weekend colour supplement magazines published by most national newspapers generally carry full-page and double-page adverts for many of the luxury

fashion brands. Cinema and television advertising allows brands to tell a story in the form of a short film. Chanel, as already mentioned, uses this technique for its Chanel No 5 perfume, with both Nicole Kidman and Audrey Tautou starring. Global sports brands such as Nike and adidas also produce adverts for film and television. The adidas Originals 2008 campaign utilized print, TV, cinema and web channels. Television advertising is effective for building brand consciousness but also in reaching national and local audiences to inform them of special events and sales. Outside media or ambient advertising such as billboards, posters and adverts on the sides of buses or taxis are all typically used by fashion companies. Armani is famous for its 310-sq-m (3,337-sq-ft) billboard located at the junction of Via Cusani and Via Broletto in Milan. The final traditional medium to discuss is radio. This is a less favoured choice for fashion, mainly because fashion advertising is more suited to the visual media. However, adverts on local radio stations provide a cost-effective way to advertise sales or promotions, store openings, local fashion events or celebrity appearances.

New advertising channels

Traditional channels are highly important for fashion advertising, but the situation is changing rapidly. Promotion via the Internet, either direct from a brand website, via corporate or consumer blogs or through the spread of online viral videos, must now be considered as a supplementary or alternative platform for advertising, promotion and brand building. The European Interactive Advertising Association publishes the EIAA Online Shoppers Report, giving data on European consumers' use of the Internet for content, communication and commerce. The 2008 report shows that 59 per cent of European online shoppers cite websites of well-known brands as an important

Above left
David and Victoria Beckham advertise Emporio Armani underwear. The traffic-stopping advert displayed on a massive billboard in the centre of Milan caused a sensation.

Above
Orla Kiely advertises on buses in London and in Hong Kong. Here a London bus is decorated with the distinctive trademark Orla Kiely 'Stem' pattern.

source of information. The 2009 Nielsen Media Research Global Online Consumer Survey gauged opinions from 25,000 Internet consumers from 50 countries; 70 per cent of respondents trusted information from brand websites. Nielsen Media Research also found that 90 per cent of respondents trust recommendations from people they know and 70 per cent trusted consumer opinions posted online. The work by Nielsen also highlights regional differences. Consumer opinions posted online were trusted most by Vietnamese and Italian Internet consumers and least by consumers in Argentina. Brand websites were most trusted in China, Pakistan and Vietnam, whereas Swedish or Israeli respondents were considerably less trusting of information from this source.

Viral promotions

Seth Godin, author of *Purple Cow*, mentioned in Chapter 2, believes that marketing ideas must be 'remarkable' in order to stand out and get a foothold in consumer consciousness. Malcolm Gladwell in his book *The Tipping Point* takes this further stating that the message itself or the product it is promoting must be 'memorable'. Gladwell introduces what he calls the 'stickiness factor'; for an idea or marketing message to spread it must 'stick'. Something about the message, its content or how it is delivered must remain active in the recipient's mind – it must be remarkable, memorable and worth talking about. The new mantra being, 'ideas that spread win'.

Viral videos are becoming an important element of promotional campaigns as they have potential to reach millions of viewers; apparently, 20 hours of new videos are uploaded on to YouTube every minute of every day. Insights into how and why viral promotions work are discussed in an online interview conducted by Abbey Klassan of *Advertising Age* with Matt Cutler, Vice President of Visible Measures. Visible Measures have developed a system for monitoring and measuring online video audiences. Cutler believes that viral videos are no longer a niche marketing tool; data shows the actual size of online audiences can in certain circumstances be comparable to that of TV audiences. The first week's exposure is crucial to the success and spread of a viral video. Cutler explains

Left
This billboard, shot by Annie Leibovitz, shows Keith Richards with his Louis Vuitton guitar case. This advertising campaign was designed to link the brand with several influential figures from sport, music, film and politics. A viral video was also posted on YouTube showing Leibovitz while she photographed the legendary rock star for the campaign. An article for the Business of Fashion website stated that the viral created reverberations amongst press and consumers alike. More than 8,000 press articles were written about the campaign and numerous blogger discussions buzzed on the Internet.
(Amed. www.businessoffashion.com 2008)

that during this initial launch period it is important to have a high concentration of publicity and paid-for media exposure about the viral. Once it takes hold, however, the viral spread should accelerate mainly by peer communication via email, social networking sites and word of mouth. Videos that do not get embraced by consumers will fail to get to the first significant milestone of 1 million viewers. The next hurdle is to pass the 4 million mark. A superstar campaign is one that gets to 10 million viewers or more.

Blogs and social networking

Blogs are one of the fastest-growing areas of what has become known as **consumer-generated media (CGM)**. Bloggers are out there sharing opinions and brand experiences and as David Meerman Scott says in his book, *The New Rules of Marketing and PR*,

"There's never been an easier way to find out what the marketplace is thinking about you, your company, and your products!" Meerman Scott (2007).

The blogosphere is expanding fast; in the nine months it took authors Scoble and Israel to write their book *Naked Conversations: how blogs are changing the way businesses talk with customers,* the number of bloggers tripled from under 7.5 million to almost 20 million. Scoble and Israel envision a day when "Companies that don't blog will be held suspect…with people wondering whether those companies have something to hide." Brands are catching on to the importance of this medium, pioneers being sports brands like Nike with nikeblog.com or casual brands like Fat Face with its online community, outthere.fatface.com. Apparelsearch.com has a directory of useful fashion industry blogs. Social networking sites are also becoming vital avenues for promotion. Burberry launched its own social networking site in the autumn of 2009. The site, called Art Of The Trench, will feature user-submitted pictures of people sporting the brand's famous trenchcoat. Burberrys believes that this medium will help them attract new younger customers and strengthen ties with their existing customer base.

Timing and exposure

The next issue to consider is the timing of an advert – how long it will be published, placed on television or viewable online. A company needs to balance the spread of media used with the time-frames and costs of exposure. A fashion brand might chose to advertise twice a year with campaigns timed to coincide with the launch of the Spring and Autumn seasons. A concentrated campaign using an intense burst of advertising might be suitable to announce the launch of a new brand or product. Adverts can also be used at strategic times to promote mid-season or end-of-season sales. A permanent advertising presence is expensive, so continuous campaigns are most likely to be used by the large global brands with sizeable advertising budgets. Each advert can be considered in terms of its reach or

"I have found that after Google, Facebook actually ranks second as being the avenue that brings the most traffic to my website. It is a powerful tool. Also it allows me to communicate on a personal level with my customers and keep them updated for free with what's been happening in the shop."
Hannah Jennings

OPENED DURING RENOVATIONS

BCBGMAXAZRIA

FOR CAREER OPPORTUNITIES, PLEASE CONTACT HR.CANADA@BCBG.COM

Left
A hoarding outside the BCBGMaxazria store in Vancouver, Canada, is used to advertise the fashion brand during store renovations.

coverage – the number of people within the target market exposed to the advert over a specific length of time – and frequency, or the number of times someone is likely to view the advert during the time-frame. For television advertising it is believed that a viewer needs to see an advert between five and seven times for its message to take hold. Another issue to consider is which media will have the most impact on the target audience. The key factors to consider when deciding upon the most suitable media are:

- **The target audience:** which media are most suitable to attract desired consumers?
- **The reach:** how many people are likely to be exposed to the advert?
- **The frequency:** how often or how many times is the target consumer likely to be exposed to the advert?
- **The impact:** which media or combination of media will provide most impact?
- **The cost:** what are the cost implications of each medium, how will the advertising budget be best employed?

Planning advertising campaigns

As with all aspects of marketing, thorough research, planning and clarity of purpose are essential when developing an advert or larger campaign. The first step in the planning process is to set objectives for the advertising campaign. Is the purpose to inform about something specific such as a sale, special promotion or product launch? Or is it to maintain brand awareness and keep the brand in consumer's consciousness? Or perhaps it is to persuade a new target audience to adopt the brand. When the objective is clear it should then be possible to take the next steps and determine suitable media, consider the exact message of the advert and decide upon its style and content. It will also be necessary to calculate a budget and decide if the campaign can be

Revitalizing classic jeans
Levi's 501® Live Unbuttoned integrated advertising campaign

Left
A window display in a London department store featuring Levi's 501® jeans and promoting the Live Unbuttoned campaign.

In the spring and summer of 2008, Levi's launched 'Live Unbuttoned', a global advertising campaign designed to celebrate the classic 501® jeans. The campaign made use of a variety of traditional advertising media such as print and TV ads as well as newer advertising media, most notably viral and digital. It was the biggest integrated marketing programme the brand had undertaken, going live in 110 countries worldwide. The viral campaign generated a great deal of consumer and media interest. This signposts potential marketing directions for the future; the indication being that viral and commercial approaches do not appear to be mutually exclusive and that a number of strands of creative content can be used simultaneously to appeal to different consumer types. Robert Cameron, Vice President of Marketing at Levi Strauss & Co, San Francisco, stated in an interview with Stuart Elliott of *The New York Times* that, "Advertising and marketing are changing really radically, it's all about engagement." He added, "We try to imagine what the world will be like five, ten years from now and market that way today."

The use of new media offered the company a unique opportunity to promote the timeless straight-leg button-fly jean as a quintessential contemporary garment relevant to the lifestyle of a new generation. In order to understand why this new young consumer was so important to the future of the company it is necessary to go back in time and review certain trends that had occurred in the jeans market.

The background story

At their peak in 1996 Levi Strauss & Co had revenues of US$7.1 billion. However by 2003 the global denim brand would see this figure fall dramatically to only US$4.1 billion and between 2003 and 2007 the company's net sales remained flat. Levi's has faced intense competition and the jeans market has changed significantly over the years, most noticeably in the coveted 13–24 age group. Unfortunately Levi's was slow to catch on to demographic shifts, cultural changes and market developments affecting their business. A problem for Levi's was that young consumers were rejecting the functional classic 501® jeans – they were not cool anymore. The younger generation had no desire to wear brands or styles that their parents or grandparents favoured and were shifting their allegiance to newer, sexier, more fashionable brands. Designer denim took off during the 1980s, spearheaded by a famous Calvin Klein advert featuring a fifteen-year-old Brooke Shields, turning to camera and asking provocatively, "You want to know what comes between me and my Calvins – nothing." Although Levi's sales did not appear to be affected immediately, this seminal advert heralded the changes to come. Companies such as Gap, Old Navy and Tommy Hilfiger entered the denim market along with an increasing number of mainstream high-street fashion retailers offering own-brand jeans at affordable prices. As the new millennium took hold the market shifted once again with the rise of premium jeans and niche designer brands such as Seven for all Mankind, True Religion, Rock & Republic and Citizens of Humanity. True Religion, launched in 2003, generated sales of US$2 million

in its first year; three years later net sales had risen to over US$100 million. Individually these companies were considerably smaller than Levi Strauss & Co but their rapid growth and encroachment into the market presented further challenges to Levi's business. Clearly Levi's needed to formulate a strategy that would raise their profile and enable them to regain a credible share of the youth market.

The spirit of the brand

Levis Strauss & Co realized that the key to the future lay in repositioning the famous original button-fly 501® jeans and communicating the core values and underlying essence of the brand in a new way. Rooted in the rugged American West, Levi's 501® jeans were a classic symbol of frontier independence, democratic idealism and rebel spirit. The company recognized that they had to find a way to translate these ideals and make them relevant and accessible to a younger, free-spirited consumer. They needed a modern take that was in tune with the unrestrained and self-expressive attitude of the desired target audience. The solution, in essence, was simple and built upon one of the most symbolic aspects of the jeans – the buttons.

A modern approach to marketing

The Live Unbuttoned campaign was shrewd in linking the signature button-fly feature of the jeans with the concept of 'unbuttoning', breaking free from inhibitions and convention – an idea that resonates strongly with the youth market.

"The objective was really quite simple – to target a younger demographic of guys (young men in the 18–24-year-old range), get them to engage with our brand in a fun and meaningful way, and encourage them to check out and wear Levi's."
Erica Archambault
Levi's PR & Brand Marketing (2009)

If Levi's wished to communicate on the same wave length as the target audience it desired, it too would have to break free from traditional

The Levi's 501® Live Unbuttoned campaign made use of newer advertising media such as viral videos and free downloadable music but it also utilized more traditional advertising and marketing approaches, such as outside advertising on giant hoardings and focused window displays.

Above
A building in London's trendy Brick Lane is wrapped in a massive canvas poster advertising Levi's 501s® to the young and artistic habitués of London's East End area.

approaches to advertising and integrate viral and digital marketing media into the campaign. The first of several viral videos was seeded on YouTube prior to the main launch. Aimed at a young male demographic, Jeans Jump showed a group of guys jumping, somersaulting and back flipping from ever increasing heights into a pair of 501® jeans. The short film became a viral hit, receiving 3.5 million hits in the first ten days. The video was a seeding project or teaser but it quickly became a phenomenon reaching a further 75 million people through traditional press and media coverage. The campaign was bolstered by further viral videos and new strands of user-generated content designed to support the initial approach and offer a platform to entertain and get people talking virally. A digital program came on stream providing free downloadable music and videos of emerging new artists from music, sport, art and entertainment. Erica Archambault believes the use of viral media within the campaign worked well because "it spoke to young guys in a relevant way...guys could relate." However more traditional marketing tactics were also utilized to increase the range of the campaign at retail level – focused window displays and in-store point-of-sale materials.

carried out in-house or if an agency will need to be appointed. A simple advert might be handled in-house on a limited budget. A more complicated advert or global campaign will usually require the expertise of an advertising or communications agency. In summary the steps of the planning process are:

- Set advertising objectives
- Determine suitable media platforms
- Decide who will devise the campaign
- Set budget and time-frame
- Confirm content, style and advertising message

Measuring advertising effectiveness

Measuring advertising effectiveness is important for determining the extent to which a campaign has met its strategic objectives, which could be any of the following:

- To stimulate an increase in sales
- To build brand awareness
- To introduce a new product or collection
- To change consumer image and perception of a brand or product
- To increase customer loyalty

It is not easy to gauge results accurately. Sales increases may result from a combination of factors such as pricing compared to competitors, or whether the product is also available online. A celebrity wearing the brand might boost sales, or **product placement** in a popular TV show or film could create demand. Determining if an advertising campaign has increased consumer awareness requires research to test consumer awareness before and after a campaign; similarly, detailed consumer analysis will be required to determine if an ad campaign was effective in changing consumer image of the brand.

One aspect of advertising that can be measured is what is known as **opportunity to see** (**OTS**). This represents a frequency of exposure to an advertisement. Average OTS gives a figure to indicate how many people from a target audience have had an opportunity to see, hear or read an advertisement. Gross OTS is a cumulative figure for a campaign, derived from adding results from different adverts within a campaign and from the various media such as TV, cinema, magazines, Internet and outdoor channels. OTS figures are created using surveys, face-to-face interviews and through self-reporting, usually using diaries kept by members of the target audience.

A similar idea is that of **advertising impacts**, which refers to the total number of separate occasions when a TV or radio commercial is viewed or heard by a target audience. If an advertising campaign aired 100 times over four months and each time the advert was on air it achieved an average of 1 million viewers then the campaign would have received 100 million impacts with a monthly impact of 25 million.

"Half the money I spend on advertising is wasted; the trouble is I don't know which half."
John Wanamaker

Advertising costs can be evaluated using a **cost per thousand (CPT)** calculation. This is the average cost of reaching one thousand of the target audience. The cost of a full-page colour advert in American *Vogue* varies depending on its position within the magazine but it will be upwards of US$100,000. The CPT for the advert would be calculated by dividing this cost by the circulation number and multiplying by 1,000. So if the circulation was 1.2 million, the CPT would be just over US$83 per thousand.

Sales promotion

Sales promotion, also known as below the line marketing, works to increase demand and boost sales of specific products or services. The aim of a sales promotion is to make a brand and its merchandise or services more attractive to customers by offering additional inducements to purchase, such as a price reduction, giving a product away for free, offering an extra benefit or service with a purchase, or offering a prize. Promotions usually run for a limited and very specific time-frame and there may be certain conditions attached, such as a minimum spend. Sales promotions directed at the end-consumer are termed consumer sales promotions; those aimed at retailers, wholesalers or manufacturers are known as trade sales promotions. Trade sales promotions are offered by apparel and textile wholesalers or suppliers and manufacturers to encourage their business customers to purchase or place forward orders.

Promotions directed towards the ultimate consumer employ what can be termed as **pull strategies**, the idea being that the offer creates demand and entices or pulls the customer in, encouraging them to visit the store or website and ultimately make a purchase. **Push strategies** are geared towards trade distributers and retailers and are designed to encourage them to promote or push a brand or particular product and sell it on to the end-consumer.

The key types of consumer sales promotions are discussed below with indications as to how each might be used. The advantages of each technique and its benefit to consumers are given, as well as points to consider when planning sales promotion campaigns. Information outlining the essentials of trade sales promotions is given at the end.

Left
A Levi's store in Bangalore, India. The US jeans brand is offering Indian shoppers the opportunity to purchase a $30 pair of jeans by paying in three instalments. This age-old sales promotion technique is more commonly used to sell white goods like washing machines, but Levi's has embraced the concept to tempt Indian customers with limited budgets.

Consumer sales promotions

The purpose of sales promotions directed at the end-consumer is to generate an increase in the volume of sales in the short term, with a positive effect on overall business in the long term. Promotions generally appeal to several basic consumer instincts – to save money, get something for free, buy something unique hopefully for a reduced price, or win a prize. For retailers, the motivation for sales promotions is to increase the number of consumers visiting the store or website and increase the conversion rate; that is, the number of visitors converted into purchasers. The advantage of sales promotion campaigns is that they achieve results quickly and usually cost less than high-profile advertising.

A variety of promotional activities can be used by fashion brands and retailers, the most common being:

Above
Store windows are used to promote seasonal sales or special consumer sales promotions.

- Price reductions
- Special offers
- Gifts with purchase
- Coupons or vouchers
- Competitions

Price reductions

Price reductions are most commonly used to shift slow-selling stock. The aim is to boost sales volumes as quickly as possible by reducing the price of selected merchandise. This helps to sell stock through, brings cash into the business and helps to free up retail space for new product. A price reduction should help to increase volume sales but it will also reduce the margin and affect profit. Price reductions employed during seasonal sales will normally be planned as part of the buying and merchandising strategy. Reductions will usually be in the region of 10–30 per cent, however in a harsh trading climate retailers may be forced to offer reductions of 50–70 per cent.

Special offers

The main objective of special offers is to increase sales but they can also be employed as a technique to create desire for a brand or product or as a way to develop or reward customer loyalty. Special offers can be designed in a variety of formats; the exact nature will be dependent on the situation that needs to be addressed and the market level of the retailer. Offers such as 'two for the price of one' (known as a 2-4) or 'buy one get one free' (BOGOF) are typically used by high-street or volume retailers as a way to move old-season stock or lower-priced merchandise that is underperforming. An example would be, 'Buy a camisole and get one free'. This type of promotion could be used to shift camisoles in old season's colours so that fresh stock can be brought into the store. Another option is for retailers to offer customers a discount on a specific item when they make a purchase. A men's retailer might, for example, offer certain slow-selling tie designs at half price when a customer purchases a shirt. The advantage of a promotion such as this is twofold; it should help to improve sales of both the ties and the full-price shirts. Sales can be maximized if the offer is accompanied by clear signage and an eye-catching display. This will alert customers, inform which items are being promoted and detail prices and time-frames. Promoted merchandise can be featured on mannequins, presented on a selling table or highlighted through use of in-store posters, banners, display boards or marketing materials. **Point-of-sale** displays placed by till points can be used to encourage customers to purchase a special offer before they leave the store.

Special offers can also be used to promote a specific brand. A department store or boutique might run a campaign to introduce a new brand or create an offer to push a brand that is not performing as well as expected. An option in this instance would be to run a co-operative promotion where the retailer and the fashion brand develop a campaign together and share the costs. Special offers may be used to encourage customers to sign up to loyalty schemes or store cards or to reward loyal customers who spend over a specified amount on a card.

Limited editions

One way that a designer, brand or retailer can increase their kudos and create desire for their merchandise is to offer customers the opportunity to purchase limited-edition product. For many consumers it can be an attractive proposition to know that only a restricted number of people will have the same item. There are several ways to approach the concept of limited editions. One way is to develop a special one-off item available in limited quantity for a limited time-frame. Another option is to create a limited-edition collection rather than just one item. For Winter 2008/9 Billabong, the Australian surf and casual wear brand, introduced Designer's Closet, a limited-edition collection for the Billabong girls' European market. The British boutique retail brand, Whistles, also launched a special limited-edition collection for Autumn 2008/9. Consisting of 20 styles available in two of their stand-alone boutiques in London and their concession in Selfridges, the luxury collection was hand-made in London and comprised classic investment pieces such as cocktail dresses and timeless tailoring. Only 100 of each style was produced, making availability extremely exclusive. Yet another approach is to produce a special edition as a series that comes onto the market at regular intervals. This tactic is employed by Radley, a British handbag and accessory brand. Each season they design and produce a unique bag featuring an illustrated scene incorporating the signature Radley little black dog. These bags have become collectors' items; many customers return season after season to purchase the latest version of the series.

Above

The accessory designer Anya Hindmarch offered customers a special one-off, limited-edition 'I am not a plastic bag' reusable cotton shopper. The canvas tote was developed in partnership with the not-for-profit organization We Are What We Do. They had published a book entitled *Change the World for a Fiver*, so priced at £5 the bag represented a step people could take to stop the use of plastic bags. Launched in March 2007, the bag was originally sold exclusively in Anya Hindmarch UK stores, Dover Street Market in London, Colette in Paris and Villa Moda in Kuwait. The limited availability of the prized eco-statement bag caused a sensation; shoppers queued for hours to get their hands on one.

Later in the year the bag sold in a major UK supermarket. Again, stock was limited and customers were only allowed to buy one each; within an hour the bag was sold out.

A celebratory special offer
Diesel Dirty Thirty

Fashion companies develop limited editions as a way to differentiate themselves and offer exclusive product to customers. In 2008, the Italian jeans company Diesel developed an exclusive special offer to celebrate their thirtieth birthday and thank fans for their loyalty to the brand. The Diesel Dirty Thirty campaign offered customers the chance to purchase a unique pair of limited-edition jeans in either the Heeven style for men or Matic for women. Only 30,000 pairs were made available in 160 stores worldwide; priced at £30 (€30 or $50) the premium jeans were affordable and highly desirable. Designed with several distinctive features, each pair came with a commemorative xXx back patch (the Xs representing 30 in Roman numerals), a hand-made repair patch and an embroidered 'Dirty Thirty 1978–2008' stitched on the side seam. They were also finished with a special 'dirty' wash treatment. The Diesel promotion also had a limited and very specific time-frame – one day only from 10 a.m. on 10 October 2008. As an added incentive, the first ten customers purchasing the jeans at each store were invited to attend one of the Diesel xXx global parties which took place simultaneously in 17 locations around the world on 11 October. The Dirty Thirty promotion illustrates several important elements that go towards creating a successful special offer:

• A desirable product with unique features
• Limited availability
• A limited and specified time-frame
• A promotional price reduction

When developing a special offer, it is important to ensure that the offer is in keeping with the ethos and market level of a brand or retailer. Great special offers such as the Diesel Dirty Thirty promotion should raise the profile of the brand and achieve a sales boost in the short term but must not undermine or cheapen the image of a brand and drive customers away in the long term.

Above left
Daisy Lowe models the women's Matic style Dirty Thirty jeans.

Above
The limited-edition jeans included unique design features such as a leather back patch with the distinctive Diesel xXx sign, a hand-made repair patch and embroidery celebrating Diesel's thirtieth anniversary, 1978–2008.

High-profile designer and high-street retail collaborations

Collaborations between high-profile designers and high-street retailers is
a promotional trend that has grown rapidly in recent years, although it is
not a completely new phenomenon; the UK department store Debenhams
pioneered the idea in the 1990s with its Designers at Debenhams collections.
The collaboration concept really took off in November 2004 when the Swedish
fast-fashion giant H&M teamed up with Karl Lagerfeld to produce the
Lagerfeld for H&M collection, consisting of womenswear, menswear, a
fragrance and accessories. The collection was limited to 20 out of the 32
global markets in which H&M operated. Since then H&M has worked with
several different designers: Stella McCartney created a collection that sold in
400 stores in November 2005; in autumn 2006, the Viktor & Rolf collection
sold in 250 stores across 24 global markets; Roberto Cavalli collaborated in
2007; in April 2008 a collection by the Finnish brand Marimekko went on sale
in 28 stores; and in November 2008 the Japanese designer Rei Kawakubo
brought her Comme des Garçons label into the fold. Spring 2009 saw a
continuation of this strategy at H&M with a women's collection by British
designer Matthew Williamson and a new departure for the designer, a
menswear collection. Collaborations of this nature have become quite
a phenomenon in fashion retail. Massive crowds gather prior to a launch,
storming the store when the doors open and stock sells out in hours or days.
Another retailer that collaborates with designers is the US discount store
Target. The brand promise is, 'Expect More, Pay Less'®. One way Target
delivers on this promise is with its 'Design for All'® offering. Alliances with
fashion designer Isaac Mizrahi, accessory designer Anya Hindmarch and
the shoe brand Siegerson Morrison have allowed Target to offer customers
designer product at affordable price points. For Spring 2009 they added to
their list of luminary guest designers by inviting Alexander McQueen to

Above left
Madonna advertises and models her 2007 M
by Madonna collection, created in collaboration
with Swedish high-street retailer H&M.

Above
Film star Penelope Cruz and her sister Monica,
a dancer and television actress, collaborated with
the Spanish fashion chain Mango to produce
a limited-edition collection inspired by vintage
pieces in the Cruz sisters' own wardrobes.

collaborate with them to produce a collection aimed at the younger McQ customer. Target also do limited-edition designer promotions for one season but their main approach is to work with a designer over the long term, selling the designer's collection each season with stock levels planned to ensure that sales can be maintained during the season. H&M, on the other hand, partner with a different designer each year, the plan being to offer a short, sharp retail experience.

A variation on the collaborative theme is for a retailer to team up with a celebrity; H&M did this with Madonna, launching the M by Madonna fashion line in March 2007, and UK high-street retailer Topshop has developed an ongoing relationship with the globally famous model Kate Moss. H&M head designer Margareta van den Bosch worked with Madonna to create a collection that reflected the pop superstar's distinctive fashion style. In a similar vein, Moss works closely with the Topshop in-house design team so that they can interpret her individual and eclectic fashion sensibility, translating it into the desirable and commercially successful Kate Moss, Topshop collection. Although not explicit, it is understood that the celebrity does not design the garments themselves, they merely provide the inspirational style and lend their name to the enterprise. There is a risk to this kind of arrangement as celebrity status can be fickle – a chosen personality can go out of fashion or lose favour with the public. The key issue with celebrity collaborations is to ensure that the face fits, that the chosen celebrity enhances the profile of the brand and that target consumers connect with that person's style.

Other collaborations

The potential of collaborative initiatives continues to be harnessed by a diversity of clothing companies. Design collaborations and strategic alliances have flourished, particularly between designers or celebrities and sports brands. Each one manages to take an individual and innovative approach to the collaborative concept, utilizing its possibilities to generate new ideas and develop products designed to appeal to the targeted consumer. Puma was a pioneer of the sport-fashion collaboration, joining with model Christy Turlington as early as 2000 to produce her Nuala yoga and lifestyle collection. Puma and Turlington extended their association developing Mahanuala, a technically focused yoga apparel, footwear and accessories collection. Introduced in 2004, the collection sells online via a dedicated boutique within the Amazon Apparel & Accessories site. adidas launched its Y-3 collection in 2003, created as a strategic alliance between the German sports brand and the Japanese fashion designer Yohji Yamamoto. A key purpose of this partnership was to establish a strong fashion element within the adidas brand, giving it a distinctive platform for differentiation. Adidas developed a further partnership with Stella McCartney launching the fashion directional sports collection, adidas by Stella McCartney in 2005. Collaborative cross

The O'Neill brand was born on the beaches of California and is a recognized international label selling youthful surf and sport lifestyle clothing. The company's mission is to inject a new sense of creativity into the youth lifestyle market; to that end O'Neill have set up a collaborative initiative known as The Collective. O'Neill understand the significance of graphic art within the sports apparel and youth market, so they teamed up with Dutch artist Boxie (real name Marco van Boxtel) to create an exciting limited-edition range specifically designed for the brand. They have also collaborated with British fashion designer, Luella Bartley, who has produced surf wear and winter sportswear for the brand.

Below
Boxie designs for O'Neill

fertilizations are becoming ever more creative. Lacoste, for example, teamed up with the multi-format fashion and art magazine *Visionaire* and 12 artistic influencers from design, music, photography and art. The project utilized cutting-edge printing technology to create a wearable publication with 12 unique photographically printed Lacoste polo shirts embedded within the pages of *Visionaire No 54*, a four-volume edition of the magazine/book hybrid.

As can be seen from the variety of collaborations featured, it certainly appears that there is mileage in creative associations and opportunity for other fruitful alliances to blossom. The recent growth of the phenomenon indicates that it has been a beneficial strategy for many brands.

The benefits of collaborations

The general format for collaborations is for a large, well-known brand or retailer to join forces with a more exclusive design-led company or individual designer. For the venture to work and be profitable, each partner must gain something from the relationship. It is also important to ensure that the association does not alienate existing customers. Collaborations between high-profile designers and high-street retailers provide considerable benefits to all parties concerned. The designer gets wider exposure and should be able to attract a new audience that previously might have been excluded, usually because of the high price or exclusivity of the designer label. For the retailer, the arrangement allows them to offer increased choice, keep relevant and up to date and attract new fashion-conscious customers. In short, the high-street retailer gains prestige, the designer company is exposed to a new market, and consumers are able to buy designer fashion at an affordable price in a store that they are familiar with or in which they feel comfortable. Successful collaborative partnerships manage to build upon the power and recognition associated with each contributor, merging their strengths to accomplish something unique that could not have been achieved by each partner on their own. Collaborations allow a brand or designer to:

- Attract new customers
- Gain credibility in a new market
- Enhance kudos and prestige
- Innovate and develop alternative creative approaches
- Generate new business opportunity
- Share resources
- Reduce the risk of going it alone
- Create a buzz and attract press coverage

Limited editions and collaborative associations have become one of the foremost sales promotional tools utilized within the fashion industry. Other options that can be contemplated are to offer a gift with purchase, set up a competition of some sort or organize a coupon or voucher promotion.

Below
Luella Bartley designs for O'Neill.

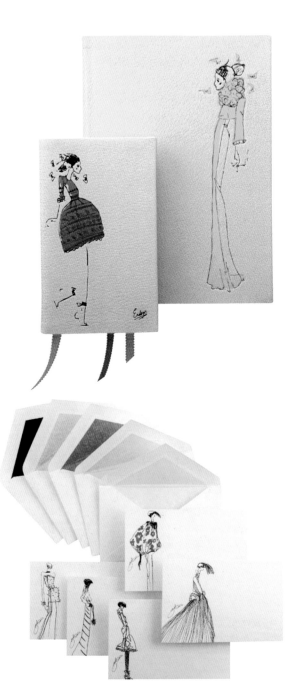

British luxury leather goods and stationery brand, Smythson, worked with Giles Deacon to produce 300 boxes of couture correspondence cards (above), each embellished with exquisite, hand-engraved pen and ink sketches. For their next collaboration, Smythson teamed with Erdem to create limited-edition, hand-made leather diaries (top) decorated with engraved, colour-blocked illustrations, and notebooks (left) lined with printed silk from Erdem's Resort 2010 collection (above left).

Gift with purchase

A gift with purchase promotion is widely used by the cosmetics and perfume industry, where trial size make-up or skincare items are given away when a customer purchases a specified number of products. Women's fashion magazines also give away free gifts with an issue. Gift with purchase promotions can be a useful tool for fashion retailers but its vital to factor in the cost of the gift item relative to how much a consumer must spend before they are entitled to receive it. Referring back to the example of the slow selling men's ties on page 175; a retailer might consider a gift promotion of a free tie when a customer buys a high-priced item such as a suit or spends over a certain amount. Giving a gift with a purchase could also be an effective promotion to use if launching a new brand such as a new perfume. In this instance a small sample of the fragrance could be given away. Overall a gift must be desirable, in keeping with the brand or retailer's image, and the scheme must have potential to increase sales.

Coupons and vouchers

Promotions using coupons or vouchers offering a discount to customers are another option that can be used. Traditionally, schemes such as this have been operated between a magazine or newspaper and a fashion retailer. Customers usually receive a discount in the region of 10 or 20 per cent when they redeem their coupon in a participating store. This type of promotion benefits the retailer and the magazine with the potential of boosting circulation for the magazine and increasing sales for the retailer.

Nowadays coupons or vouchers do not have to be printed and the rise of **e-commerce** (Internet) and the growing influence of m-commerce (mobile phone) provide increasing opportunity and potential for the development of promotional discount schemes. Consumers can pick up **voucher codes** from a website or register to have **text codes** or mobile barcodes sent to their phone. The latest innovations in mobile phone technology allow consumers to make online purchases directly from their mobiles. Camera phones with preinstalled software can be used to photograph barcodes placed in store windows or incorporated into print ads. Barcodes can also be sent straight to a consumer's mobile phone to be scanned by a retailer when the consumer wants to make a purchase or claim a promotional discount. Ralph Lauren was one of the first luxury fashion brands to integrate mobile purchasing into its retailing, launching an m-commerce site in 2008. Nike introduced an innovative mobile marketing campaign in 2008 that enabled fans to create their own colour combinations for trainers based on photos they had taken on their camera phones. Barcode and text code promotions are effective in targeting a younger audience for whom the mobile phone is one of the main modes of communication. They also offer a retailer or brand the possibility of direct communication and interaction with consumers and the opportunity to gather useful data.

Competitions and prize draws

Another promotional device that retailers or fashion brands can consider is to run a competition or prize draw. Prize draws can be operated via the Internet, mobile phone or a printed entry form available in store, in a magazine or newspaper or by direct mail. Basic competitions usually ask entrants to answer a simple question about the brand or company but competitions can be developed that are much more interesting and engaging – inviting consumers to customize or redesign garments, for example. In 2009, as part of their launch campaign for a new flagship store in London's Camden area, the charity Oxfam ran a competition, inviting entrants to customize a garment or outfit they already own and submit a photograph of their results via a link to the flickr website. The prize for the winner was a custom-made garment by celebrity stylist Mrs Jones and pictures of their winning customized outfit posted on the Oxfam website. The key point about a competition is to ensure that the prize is enticing enough; consumers must feel that it is worthwhile entering. Also for consideration is the number of prizes on offer, in other words will customers believe they have a reasonable chance to win?

Planning consumer sales promotions

One of the main advantages of sales promotional offers is that they have the potential to achieve results quickly. They can increase consumer traffic and boost sales and generally cost less than high-profile advertising. Campaigns can also be used to enhance consumer loyalty, often with the side benefit of collecting valuable data on consumers. Consumer sales promotions offer a company considerable scope but they will need to be planned with care; disadvantages can occur if a company over relies on discounts or offers that could cheapen its image. Another problem, particularly in a tough trading climate, is that consumers cut back on normal spending and purchase only during a promotion. While this can be advantageous in keeping cash flowing through the business, it can devalue the overall financial position of the company. When planning a promotion, it is important to consider the following:

- Purpose of the promotion
- Target audience
- Type of scheme most appropriate
- How it will operate
- Time-frame
- Range or reach of the offer
- How to inform customers about the promotion
- Costs
- Potential tie-ins, additional events and co-operative partners

Above
Winning shoes – DIY Oxfam competition. Patricia Stepanovic won with customized shoes inspired by a Christian Louboutin design for Rodarte.

The first consideration should always be its purpose – what it should achieve for the company and what it should offer customers. Tied to this is the next key issue, what is the target audience for the campaign? With these two points in mind it should be possible to determine the most appropriate type of sales promotion and how it will operate. The time-frame of an offer needs to be thought through with care. It is important to fix a viable time limit, long enough to allow the promotion to have an effect but not so long that consumers delay purchasing. The cut-off date must be communicated clearly so that customers appreciate the offer is limited. Hopefully this will create desire and a sense of urgency. For a price reduction on slow-selling stock, the issue will be to calculate how much the selling price needs to be reduced in order to encourage customers to purchase while also ensuring the least damage to the overall margin and profit. For a special offer promotion on product designed or ordered in specifically for a promotion, the important issue will be judging the correct quantity, particularly if it is a limited edition like the Diesel's Dirty Thirty jeans. A fine balance must be achieved between limiting availability so that customers crave the product and ensuring that there is enough stock; running out too soon could disappoint loyal customers. Equally, over-ordering and having a large amount of unsold stock would be counterproductive. The range or reach of the offer should also be determined: will it be available in every store or retail channel or in selected channels or locations only?

Consumers will need to be alerted and informed about a promotion, so an advertising campaign of some sort may be required, or some form of public relations activity. But not always. Information on a sales promotional campaign can also be disseminated using information incorporated within window displays or by using in-store and point-of-sale materials.

Finally there is the ever important issue of cost and available budget. Price reduction promotions used to shift stock will be best handled with minimum extra costs, so promotional information is likely to be simple and informative point-of-sale or window signage. Planned special offers or limited editions that require a sizeable awareness campaign with possible advertising or PR support will have significant costs that will need to be budgeted. There may, however, be potential co-operative partners or tie-ins that could extend the scope of the promotion and present possibilities to share the costs.

There is one last point to mention in conclusion. There are legal regulations governing advertising and promotions. Prize draws and competitions in particular are subject to specific restrictions. Sales promotional schemes should therefore be created with care to ensure that all aspects comply with relevant law. Professional bodies such as the Institute of Sales Promotion, the Chartered Institute of Marketing (CIM) or the American Marketing Association (AMA) can assist with information on legal matters.

Advantages and disadvantages of sales promotions

ADVANTAGES
- Creates desire and provides incentive to purchase
- Short-term increase in sales
- Brings customers in
- Supports consumer loyalty
- Improves conversion rate
- Can be used to target specific customer groups
- Lower cost compared to advertising campaigns

DISADVANTAGES
- Only provides short-term results
- Could negatively affect brand image
- Could negatively affect full-price sales
- Might run out of promotional stock early and disappoint customers
- Must comply with government regulations

Trade sales promotions

So much of the focus within fashion is on retail and the end-consumer but business to business (B2B) trade and promotions are a highly important aspect of the industry. It is common practice for companies to offer promotions, such as discounts or extended payment terms to business consumers as an incentive to purchase or place forward orders. Many companies offer special promotions at trade exhibitions, fairs or conferences to encourage customers onto a stand and place orders at the show. It is also usual to provide incremental price reductions for purchasing higher volumes. Free point-of-sale materials in the form of literature, display visuals or swing tickets with product information may also be offered by manufacturers as part of the deal. Negotiations might also take place to discuss the possibility of co-operative advertising between the supplier and a retailer, perhaps as a special campaign to promote a new product, fabric or garment technology. Promotional schemes can be used to develop an ongoing relationship with a customer or be tailored to match specific customer requirements. A promotional offer might help to finally close a sale with a customer who is wavering. Once again, it is important to consider the overall objectives of the company and its reasons for being at a fair or trade event and to ensure that promotions are fair and ethical.

Direct marketing

The aim of **direct marketing** is to establish a direct link between the business and the end-consumer. It might not be considered as high-profile as advertising but it can be cost effective and more easily controlled from within the company. Direct marketing is also effective in B2B situations; companies can send out new season catalogues to existing trade customers or send email information and updates. Direct marketing covers promotional activities such as:

- Direct mail via post or email
- Mail order catalogues
- Text message alerts
- Magazine inserts

In order to carry out direct marketing, a company will need to have a customer database (although this is not necessary for magazine inserts). This is why store cards and loyalty cards are so important to a retailer. Also of importance is the Internet, as customers ordering online will automatically be added to the database. Brochures or catalogues can be enclosed with monthly store card statements or sent out to customers who have ordered online. Email messages and text alerts can also be considered for direct marketing.

Magazine inserts are beneficial in communicating with potential customers not yet on the database; although not targeted at a specific person they can be directed at the readership of particular magazines or newspapers. Uniqlo, for example, had a ten-page insert placed within a major UK newspaper's weekend colour supplement magazine at the beginning of 2009. The insert was used primarily to promote the Spring menswear collection but it also informed readers that Uniqlo was due to open in Selfridges, gave a useful list of all other stores within the UK and promoted exclusive offers and 'first chance to buy' opportunities online. Direct marketing is a strategy also used in B2B situations. A business could pay to have an insert placed within an industry paper or magazine or carry out direct mailing. The London Edge trade fair, for example, sends out mailings to 30,000 international buyers.

Left
The Super Dry trade stand at the Bread & Butter trade fair. Fashion brands that sell wholesale will need to market and promote their merchandise to the many fashion buyers who visit the fair. It is standard practice to offer discounts on larger orders if placed during the fair. This acts as an incentive to the buyer to place an order there and then, rather than leave the stand and perhaps purchase from a competitor brand. Trade discounts are usually incremental, in other words the amount of discount offered increases in line with the size of order placed.

Fashion PR and publicity

PR and publicity are another vital component of the fashion promotional mix. The overall aim of PR is to get media coverage and establish and generate a favourable image of an organization, brand or fashion label. Positive publicity and well-handled PR has a great advantage for fashion companies – not only does it have potential to enrich the image, kudos or reputation of the company or brand but it can be lower in cost compared to advertising. Advertising and PR do often achieve similar end results; however, companies have to pay substantial sums to place an advert in a major magazine or in the cinema or on TV. The costs incurred with PR on the other hand are generally much lower and relate either to the operational costs of running an internal PR department or paying a PR agency – they normally charge a monthly retainer and/or a fee for their work. PR ensures that newsworthy stories attributed to a brand, fashion shows, product launches and information about seasonal collections are covered by the international, national and local press and that garments and accessories are featured in magazine editorial fashion pages.

Dependent on the requirement and the size of a company, it can be possible to handle publicity and PR in-house. Smaller companies with lower budgets may find they can manage most of the day-to-day aspects of publicity themselves, appointing an agency if necessary to handle special projects or events. Larger companies may employ a specialist PR agency or they may be able to afford to run their own dedicated PR or press department. Other companies may generally use outside PR agencies and employ a communications manager to oversee projects and liaise with the agency.

Measuring PR effectiveness

Although PR may be more cost effective relative to advertising, it is still important to be able to determine and measure its effectiveness. There are several ways this can be achieved:

- Clip reports
- Column inches
- Advertising value equivalent (AVE)
- Public opinion or audience sentiment
- Share of voice

The most traditional method is to monitor the number of press articles that are published, known as press clippings. **Clip reports** will give details on which publications the coverage appeared, the topic of the article published and the circulation of the publication. This information can be further refined by measuring the amount of **column inches** printed. **Advertising value equivalent (AVE)** measures the benefit to a client of a PR campaign. AVE compares the cost of the column inches achieved with how much the equivalent space would have cost as advertising. Another option is to gauge public opinion or

audience sentiment relating to a particular brand or PR campaign. This is time consuming and requires complex data collection and analysis using focus groups or surveys. Another technique that requires data analysis is **share of voice**. This compares a company's press results with those of its main competitors and determines who got the most coverage.

Basic PR techniques

The following section looks at a selection of basic techniques employed by fashion PR, namely product placement, **celebrity seeding**, events and product launches, fashion shows and press days.

Product placement

A company can raise awareness of its brand and products by having them feature in a film, television show, music video or digital game. Known as product placement, this form of promotion can generate considerable desire for a particular product. One of the most notable examples of fashion product

Left
This set of Louis Vuitton luggage featured in the Wes Anderson movie *The Darjeeling Limited*. The luggage was designed by Marc Jacobs with the help of Anderson's brother, Eric, who created the distinctive jungle pattern that decorated the surface of the cases. Not only did the luggage feature in the film, but it became the centrepiece of a window display at the Louis Vuitton store in New York.

placement was in the *Sex and the City* television show and films. The first movie, which came out in May 2008, featured clothing by Vivienne Westwood, Prada, Jimmy Choo, Louis Vuitton, Christian Lacroix and Chanel to name but a few. Shoe designers Manolo Blahnik and Jimmy Choo became household names after their product first featured in the show. The association between the Blahnik and *SATC* brands became so integral to the concept that a link to the Blahnik website was included on the *SATC* movie website.

Product placement can have a dramatic effect on sales, as was evidenced when the movie *The Queen* was released in the United States in 2006. Immediately after the film opened in New York, visitor numbers at the Barbour by Peter Elliot store on Madison Avenue increased dramatically, as did demand for two classic Barbour jackets, the 'Beaufort' and 'Lisdale' worn by the actress Helen Mirren when she portrayed the Queen in the film.

Product placement provides an important revenue stream for film financing. According to Reuters, in 2006 companies worldwide spent nearly US$3.4 billion to have their products appear in films and TV shows. Companies do not always have to pay to have their products showcased; some manage to achieve this privilege for free. In 2007, for example, a set of Louis Vuitton luggage became the surprise star of *The Darjeeling Limited* after it was commissioned by director Wes Anderson for his movie.

Celebrity seeding or celebrity product placement

The cult of celebrity and its relationship to the world of fashion is becoming an increasingly important factor within the fashion PR remit. Many agencies have had to add a dedicated celebrity division to handle 'buzz press', which refers to the new speed at which agencies have to pump out stories concerning a brand's links with celebrities or what clothing or accessory brands famous personalities are wearing. This fascination with celebrity and fashion has occurred partly as a result of the proliferation and high circulation of weekly celebrity gossip magazines such as *Hello*, *OK!* and *Heat*. One consequence of all this interest in celebrities is the PR activity known as **celebrity seeding** or celebrity product placement. As discussed earlier, celebrity product placement occurs when a celebrity signs a contract to become the face of a brand. Seeding, on the other hand, is when a designer or brand loans or donates product to a celebrity so that they will be seen wearing the brand's products. This is usually handled via a PR agency. The aim of celebrity endorsement is of course to choose a suitable celeb with a personality and reputation that enhances the brand's status, and who is regularly in the public eye and constantly snapped by the paparazzi; the result should be massive media coverage and a high volume of column inches.

Press days

PR agencies and in-house press offices organize press days to showcase next season's collections to the fashion press. Magazines work on long lead-times so press days are held well in advance of the season so that editors can

Above
Elizabeth Hurley at a dinner and fashion show held in honour of Salvatore Ferragamo.

request samples from designers and start developing ideas for fashion shoots and editorial. Press days can be held to promote trade fairs or a group of designers; the British Fashion Council, for example, held a press event to promote estethica, their trade initiative for sustainable fashion, showcasing 23 ethical labels.

Above
Grazia fashion magazine holding a week-long event in Westfield shopping centre. *Grazia* set up a temporary office inside the London shopping mall, where shoppers could view production staff produce and edit the magazine. The event also offered shoppers free makeovers, fashion advice and style seminars.

Special events

Special events are designed to suit a variety of situations which might include:

- Product launches
- Charity events
- Sponsorship events
- Fashion seminars and style clinics
- Fashion shows
- Private shopping evenings
- Designer guest appearances

Special events can be aimed either at the press, industry professionals and business customers or at the end-consumer. They will either be organized by a PR agency or an in-house events office or press office. With product launches, the product need not necessarily be apparel or accessories but could be a trade initiative. For example, an evening drinks event was held in a prestigious hotel in the centre of Colombo in Sri Lanka to promote the first ever Apparel South Asia Conference and two forthcoming trade exhibitions, the Apparel Industry Suppliers Exhibition (AISEX) and Fabric and Accessory Suppliers Exhibition (FASE) in 2008. Special events aimed at end-consumers have two main purposes; one is to offer something extra to reward loyal customers or store card holders and the other is to promote sales or specific designers and brands. Organizing a special event will require that a press release and invitations are sent out.

Personal selling

Personal selling refers to promotional or sales activities that take place face to face with personal contact. There are two key interfaces for personal selling within the fashion industry. The first, most obviously, is in-store, where sales personnel interact directly with customers. The customer experience in-store can be a make-or-break factor in terms of whether customers purchase or not, so this element of personal selling is vital for the industry. This topic was discussed in Chapter 2 in terms of 'process' within the marketing mix (*see* page 47). This concept views the entire process of purchasing from the consumer's point of view, of which personal selling will be a part. Many boutique owners know their customers intimately; they often purchase items directly from design houses and fashion retailers with a specific customer in mind and will call their most loyal customers to inform them that they have an item especially for them. There is report of a personal stylist ordering three Balenciaga cocktail dresses priced around £3,000 each for her various clients at a Harrods pre-season trunk show.

The other important area for personal selling is in business to business (B2B) situations. Much of the global fashion and textile industry operates at manufacturing and wholesale level, requiring sales representatives and agents to foster and develop profitable business relationships with appropriate buyers. Personal selling occurs at a variety of industry trade fairs for fabric, trimmings, apparel and accessories and other industry resources. Fibre manufacturers must sell their products to textile manufacturers, who in turn need to capture the imagination of, and sell fabrics to, fashion designers and retailers. Each of these businesses will utilize personal selling as a key promotional tool.

The advantage of personal selling is that it affords customers a high level of personal attention. Sales representatives can tailor their message and information to suit the needs of specific customers. Personal selling presents the opportunity to build a long-term business relationship, offer good technical advice and background information on products and services, and solve the numerous problems that occur within fashion design, manufacturing, supply and retail.

7.

Fashion is an international industry with potential for employment across a wide range of disciplines. This final chapter outlines the key skills required to work as a professional within fashion design, fashion retail management and fashion marketing and promotion. It provides information on some of the day-to-day tasks and responsibilities involved to help you determine which options to explore further so you can decide upon a potential career direction.

Marketing is an essential function of the industry, and affects the entire supply chain, from production and wholesale of raw materials to the design, development, manufacture and promotion of fabrics, garments and accessories, right through to fashion retail and the sale of products to the end-consumer. Marketing is the common denominator linking all the processes together, so whatever role you intend to pursue within the industry, an understanding and appreciation of marketing is becoming an ever more essential skill.

Fashion and textile supply chain

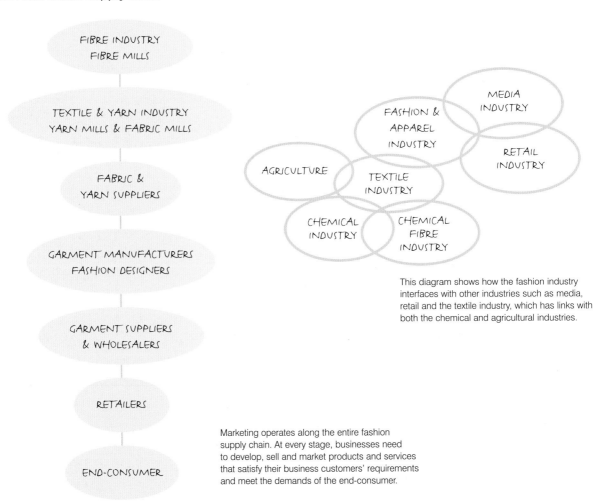

FIBRE INDUSTRY
FIBRE MILLS

TEXTILE & YARN INDUSTRY
YARN MILLS & FABRIC MILLS

FABRIC &
YARN SUPPLIERS

GARMENT MANUFACTURERS
FASHION DESIGNERS

GARMENT SUPPLIERS
& WHOLESALERS

RETAILERS

END-CONSUMER

MEDIA INDUSTRY

FASHION & APPAREL INDUSTRY

RETAIL INDUSTRY

AGRICULTURE

TEXTILE INDUSTRY

CHEMICAL INDUSTRY

CHEMICAL FIBRE INDUSTRY

This diagram shows how the fashion industry interfaces with other industries such as media, retail and the textile industry, which has links with both the chemical and agricultural industries.

Marketing operates along the entire fashion supply chain. At every stage, businesses need to develop, sell and market products and services that satisfy their business customers' requirements and meet the demands of the end-consumer.

Professional skills

Fashion can be glamorous and exciting, but it is important to remember that fundamentally it is a commercial business producing and selling fashion and textile products. These must satisfy customer demand and produce profit for the business concerned. To work in the industry you need to be ambitious, self-motivated, creative, energetic and passionate about fashion and have a working knowledge of marketing and business. Employment within fashion is very competitive and you will find that you are required to work at a much faster pace than you did as a student. If you are lucky enough to land a job you should be prepared to put in long hours and be willing to deal with the constant barrage of tight deadlines that most fashion professionals accept as the norm. It is also likely that you will work on more than one project or fashion season at a time, so it is vital that you are organized, accurate and pay attention to detail. Employers will expect you to understand the market, be aware of customer requirements and work within set financial parameters.

An understanding of the target market No matter what role you take on within the industry, you will be expected to understand and grasp the particulars of the specific market targeted by the company for which you are working. Although you might not be required to carry out detailed consumer research yourself, you must make sure that you are informed and aware of relevant consumer and market trends and appreciate the way in which the identity and values of the brand are reflected in the product and services offered to customers.

Commercial awareness If you remember back to the marketing definitions in Chapter 2, you will recall that "marketing is the management process responsible for identifying, anticipating and satisfying customer requirements profitably". The bottom line is that individual products, collections, marketing schemes and promotional strategies must all be commercially viable and contribute to the profitability of the company. It is important therefore that you grasp the bigger picture and ensure that your creative ideas are also commercial and profitable.

Awareness of corporate business objectives Whether you work for yourself or for a company, you will always have a desired outcome or specific objectives to achieve and there may be key performance indicators set by the company by which you will be judged. It is vital that you always have the business objectives and company strategy in mind when you develop designs or propose schemes for marketing and promotion.

Communication and presentation skills Presentations and meetings are an essential part of professional life so it is important to develop competent skills in this area. The fashion industry operates on long lead-times – product can take anywhere from 1–18 months to be developed. This means that the textiles, garments or accessories under discussion might not actually exist yet, so excellent communication skills, both visual and verbal, will be required in order to explain ideas, discuss concepts and describe products

accurately during meetings. Designers, product development teams and buyers developing own-label collections for high-street retailers or purchasing for department stores will be expected to present their product ranges, explain the rationale behind their designs and communicate how the collection and pricing strategy will achieve the company's overall strategic and financial objectives. It may also be necessary to present to key suppliers and manufacturers so they are aware of the types of styles, detailing and fabrications that they will be required to source, produce or supply.

Team-work Getting on with and working alongside others is a key professional skill and whatever role you are employed in within the industry, team-work and good communication will be required. Even the most talented designer will not be able to make it totally alone, they are only one facet of the overall picture. Even if it is their name on the label or they are the figurehead behind the brand, they still rely on a team of professionals across a wide selection of disciplines, from pattern cutting, sewing, managing production, sales, promotion, business and marketing.

Above
Confidence with communicating ideas and presenting collections is essential for fashion. Jason Wu presents his collection to Anna Wintour, Editor-in-chief of American *Vogue*.

Skills required to progress within the fashion industry

- Creative flair and commercial awareness
- Evaluating market and business trends
- Strategic thinking and awareness of corporate business objectives
- Ability to research trends and intuit future fashion and market direction
- Team-working skills and ability to work with others
- Ability to negotiate and network
- Strong organizational skills and ability to work to tight deadlines
- Presentation skills and ability to communicate information clearly
- A proactive and flexible approach
- Ability to multitask and work on more than one project or fashion season at a time
- Problem-solving, creative process management and project planning

Career choices

This section shows how an understanding of marketing principles is integral to many key job roles within the fashion industry.

Fashion design

Jobs exist within fashion design at every level of the industry from haute couture, designer ready-to-wear through to high-street fashion or designing for a garment manufacturer. Designers will usually specialize in womenswear, menswear, accessories or childrenswear, although it is possible to work in more than one area. They also tend to stick to a particular market level such as couture, luxury or streetwear. Designers working for a large organization may work for a specific department, such as casual wear, knitwear, outerwear, formal wear or separates. Depending on the type of market and the direction you wish to take you can be employed as a designer or as a fashion and trend forecaster.

Fashion designer

The fashion designer's role is to design and develop individual fashion products or product ranges appropriate for a specified target market. It is important for designers to have a clear understanding of trends in the overall fashion market as well as solid background knowledge of their particular market and target consumer. This knowledge should assist the designer in determining the correct design concept, product details, fabrications and pricing for their proposed collection or product range.

Typical work activities:

- Reviewing sales results from current and previous season
- Researching trends and undertaking inspirational shopping trips
- Developing and presenting concepts for the new season

Above
The ability to work as a team is another vital skill. Designers rely on a team of skilled technicians to help them realize their creative ideas.

- Sourcing fabrics, materials, components, trims and embellishments
- Designing and developing product ranges
- Overseeing creation of prototypes, producing accurate product specifications for samples and production
- Managing sampling process and fittings
- Liaising with manufacturers and suppliers for sampling and production
- Confirming range selection with management, buyers and other relevant personnel. Presenting final range to internal staff or external buyers.
- Approving final colours, bulk fabric and trimmings
- Presenting ranges to management, sales staff and buyers

Fashion designer: key skills
- Professional knowledge of fabrics and materials
- Ability to illustrate and draw technical details accurately
- Creative flair and commercial awareness
- Good eye for proportion and colour
- Self-motivated
- Ability to research and monitor trends

Roles and departments that interface with design

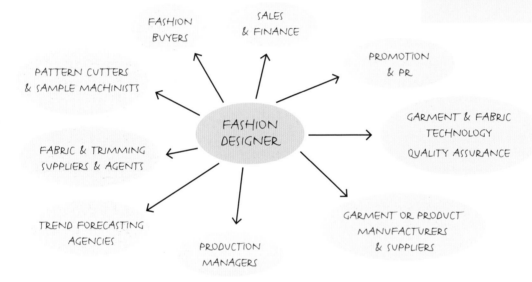

Left
The team behind the streetwear label Durkl Clothing working in their studio in Washington, DC.

Fashion and trend forecaster

Fashion and trend forecasters work approximately 18 months to two years ahead of the season in order to develop and compile trend and market reports purchased by the industry. Fashion forecasting and prediction agencies provide information on current and developing consumer trends and emerging fashion and textile trends in womenswear, menswear and childrenswear. They produce presentations and printed and/or online reports that include colour palettes, design illustrations, print and fabric designs and technical flat drawings of product so that companies who purchase their services can see how the predicted trends will translate into product designs.

Typical work activities:

- Visiting trade fairs or working on an agency stand to sell prediction packages at fairs like Première Vision
- Travelling to research trends
- Compiling visuals and colour palettes for key trends and fashion themes
- Researching technical developments in fabrics, materials, components, trims and embellishments

Trend forecaster: key skills

- Self-motivated and ability to research
- Awareness of what is going on culturally in music, art, street fashion and film
- Creative flair and commercial awareness
- Good eye for colour
- Ability to produce fashion illustration and technical flat drawings to a high standard
- Good networking skills
- Ability to analyse trend data

Roles and departments that interface with forecasting

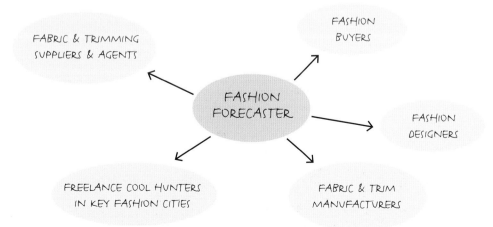

FABRIC & TRIMMING SUPPLIERS & AGENTS

FASHION BUYERS

FASHION FORECASTER

FASHION DESIGNERS

FREELANCE COOL HUNTERS IN KEY FASHION CITIES

FABRIC & TRIM MANUFACTURERS

Fashion retail management

Retail culture is high pressure and demanding. Stores are open six or seven days a week, virtually 365 days a year. If you want to work in this sector you will need to be committed and proactive – retailing is never fully predictable and the situation changes daily so you will need to be able to respond to each challenge that arises. The head-office or behind-the-scenes jobs outlined in this section are retail buyer, merchandiser and visual merchandiser.

Retail buyer

Buyers source, develop and select product ranges. They must understand customer needs and predict consumer demand in order to select commercially viable ranges of merchandise that appeal to the target market. Career opportunities for fashion buyers exist in two main areas, either working for retailers selling their own label ranges or for an individual boutique, small boutique chain or department store selling wholesale and designer fashion labels and brands. Retail buyers have considerable responsibility to achieve a company's financial targets and create profit, so they must have a good head for business, be aware of current trends and shifts in consumer demand, keep up to date with what competitors are up to and respond effectively to change.

Typical work activities:

- Researching fashion trends and analysing consumer buying patterns
- Attending fabric and trade fairs
- Sourcing, developing and selecting product ranges
- Working with a merchandiser to create range plan
- Negotiating with suppliers and manufacturers
- Reviewing and analysing sales performance
- Managing supplier relationships and sourcing new suppliers
- Travelling to manufacturers both in home market and overseas
- Visiting stores to review performance and meet with store managers
- Writing reports and presenting ranges to management

Retail buyer: key skills:

- Keen eye for fashion
- Excellent commercial awareness
- Strong communication and negotiation skills
- Numerate
- Accurate
- Ability to work to tight deadlines
- Ability to monitor fashion trends
- Awareness of competitors within the market

Left
Buyers placing orders with Danish label nümph on their stand at the Bread & Butter trade fair in Berlin.

Roles and departments that interface with fashion buying

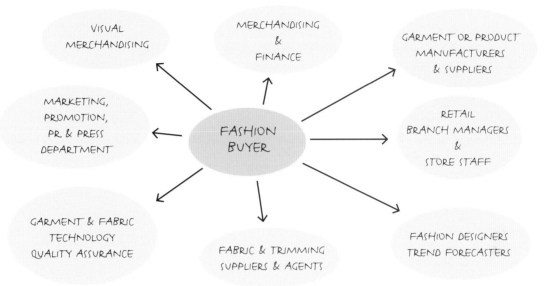

VISUAL MERCHANDISING

MERCHANDISING & FINANCE

GARMENT OR PRODUCT MANUFACTURERS & SUPPLIERS

MARKETING, PROMOTION, PR & PRESS DEPARTMENT

FASHION BUYER

RETAIL BRANCH MANAGERS & STORE STAFF

GARMENT & FABRIC TECHNOLOGY QUALITY ASSURANCE

FABRIC & TRIMMING SUPPLIERS & AGENTS

FASHION DESIGNERS TREND FORECASTERS

Garment fitting and approval

Designers, buyers and product technicians usually work as a team to fit garments and approve product specifications.

At American outdoor brand, Nau, the team pay meticulous attention to key details as well as to the look, fit and feel of a garment. Every aspect of the jacket being fitted, right down to buttons, closures, pockets, zips and stitching, has to be approved and specified accurately. At Nau garments are specifically cut to increase ease of movement. Sleeves are cut longer than average, to ensure wrist coverage when reaching for a hold while climbing or holding bicycle handlebars, and tops are cut lower in the rear to keep wearers warm when bending. The designers also work closely with fabric suppliers to create new, more sustainably produced technical fabrics that deliver on performance, hand-feel and drape.

Merchandiser

Merchandisers are responsible for the budget and work to maximize a retailer's profitability by ensuring that products appear in the right store at the appropriate time and in the correct quantities. Merchandisers work very closely with buyers to plan ranges and determine what quantity of each style should be bought. They must make sure the buyer stays within budget and that the range will achieve margin and profit targets. Merchandisers must also co-ordinate and liaise with suppliers to monitor deliveries and work with the distribution and warehouse departments to ensure the right amount of stock is sent to the correct stores. Merchandisers monitor the daily and weekly sales figures and must be proactive in devising markdown or promotion strategies. In a small company, the same person may have to do the buying and handle the merchandising.

Merchandiser: key skills
- Numerate with excellent analytical skills
- Accurate
- Strong computer skills and ability to use IT packages
- Understanding of product manufacture
- Strong negotiation skills

Typical work activities:
- Budget planning
- Working with buyer to plan product ranges
- Liaising with buyers, suppliers, distribution, stores and management
- Analysing financial data
- Forecasting potential sales, profits and stock figures
- Devising markdown and promotional strategies to mitigate losses and maximize sales and profit
- Presenting financial data, sales forecasts and stock information to management
- Negotiating delivery dates and stock quantities with suppliers
- Travelling with buyers to visit manufacturers

Roles and departments that interface with fashion merchandiser

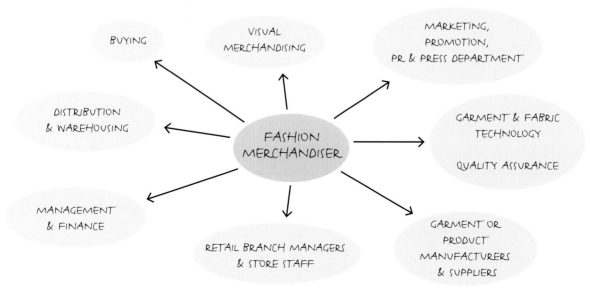

Visual merchandiser

A visual merchandiser is responsible for creating and installing schemes for windows and in-store displays with the aim of drawing customers into the store, promoting merchandise and maximizing potential sales. Displays and promotions will be designed to fit in with important annual events such as the launch of the Spring and Autumn seasons and Christmas, Valentine's Day or Easter. Large and medium-sized companies may employ their own visual merchandising (VM) team, but they could also use the services of a specialist retail or VM consultancy. Owners of smaller businesses may 'do it themselves' or use the skills of a freelancer. If you are interested in working in VM, then be prepared to lift and carry props and mannequins, climb ladders, adjust lighting and paint backdrops. You may also be required to travel, usually from store to store, and work unsociable hours – changes in displays and installations usually take place at night when the store is closed to avoid disruption or loss of sales.

Above
SAKS Christmas windows 2008.

Roles and departments that interface with visual merchandiser

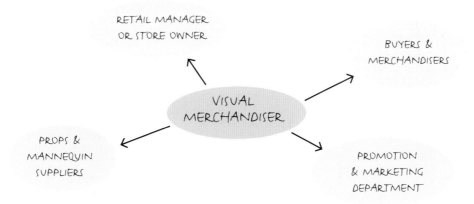

RETAIL MANAGER
OR STORE OWNER

BUYERS &
MERCHANDISERS

VISUAL
MERCHANDISER

PROPS &
MANNEQUIN
SUPPLIERS

PROMOTION
& MARKETING
DEPARTMENT

Typical work activities:

- Researching and devising display concepts and schemes
- Creating concept boards and presenting schemes to colleagues
- Technical drawing by hand or CAD of windows and floor plans
- Sourcing materials and display elements, such as lighting, props and accessories
- Installing and dismantling displays
- Dressing mannequins
- Creating VM informational packs sent out to stores
- Visiting stores and training sales staff

Visual merchandiser: key skills

- Creative flair and good eye for composition, proportion and colour
- Understanding of how to communicate brand identity within visual displays
- Good knowledge of fashion trends
- Strong display techniques
- Ability to work to tight deadlines

Fashion marketing and promotion

Describing the career options within fashion marketing is somewhat complicated by the fact that interpretations of exactly what comes under the banner of marketing vary considerably depending on the requirements and structural set-up of a particular company. This makes it much harder to define individual job roles, as some view marketing as a sales-related role, others regard it as a management function, and there are those that consider it to mean promotion and PR, so job options could be in any of the following:

- Sales and marketing
- Brand management/product management
- Promotion and PR

To work in sales, marketing or promotion you will need to be a people person and a good communicator with strong verbal and written communication skills. You should enjoy networking and be willing to socialize as part of your work. You should also be proactive, organized and flexible.

Brand management/product management

Brand management focuses on the strategic management of a brand and the development and maintenance of the brand identity. Marketing management encompasses a variety of roles and again these will be dependent on each company's requirements. If you check recruitment agency websites for fashion marketing jobs you will notice adverts for product management. Product managers are responsible for overseeing the overall process of developing product and bringing it to market. They usually handle a specific product or product category, overseeing the entire process of conceptualization, design, production, selling and distribution of a manufacturer or designer's products. With so much responsibility it is no surprise that a product manager is a senior level job; you will probably need to start in an assistant position and work up. You will also need a degree in business administration, marketing, or apparel production. As product managers gain extensive experience and knowledge of the manufacturer's operations, they can be promoted into an executive leadership position.

Typical work activities:

- Working with a technical team on product design, construction and manufacture
- Sourcing manufacturers and negotiating production contracts
- Planning production and delivery schedules
- Negotiating distribution rights
- Writing detailed marketing and business reports
- Reviewing sales results and analysing data
- Monitoring fashion and market trends
- Forecasting and preparing monthly and annual sales targets for specific regions
- Researching and developing new product lines
- Travelling to visit overseas manufacturers and distributers

Brand management: key skills

- Highly analytical
- Numerate with strong skills in maths
- Knowledge of apparel manufacture
- Ability to analyse and utilize data from sales, production and fashion forecasts
- Well-organized
- Attention to detail
- Ability to deal with pressure and tight deadlines
- Ability to present and communicate detailed information to others
- Good negotiation skills

Promotion and PR

Fashion PR is about promotion and image. The aim of PR is to gain media coverage to promote and generate a favourable image of an organization, brand or fashion label. To work in PR you will need to get on well with a broad spectrum of people, be sociable and a good networker. PR people need to build strong working relationships with their clients and with members of the fashion press.

Typical work activities:

- Writing press releases and handling press enquiries
- Creating press packs and goodie bags for fashion shows and events
- Sending garments out to magazines to be featured in fashion shoots and editorial
- Creating look books and style books to give to press and buyers
- Running press days to view collections
- Developing and managing product launches, special events or parties
- Managing the guest lists for fashion shows, events, store openings, shopping evenings, retail events or product launches
- Managing business communication or news stories concerning announcements on trading figures
- Informing press of newsworthy stories, sponsorship deals, celebrity endorsements or designer collaborations
- Handling negative news stories and limiting any damage that might be caused

Above
PR personnel are responsible for sending sample garments out to the fashion and national press so they can be featured in editorial fashion spreads or in articles on key trends or what's hot in the shops.

Promotion and PR: key skills
- Strong verbal and written communication skills
- Good networker and confident in social situations
- Proactive, organized and flexible

Roles and departments that interface with fashion PR

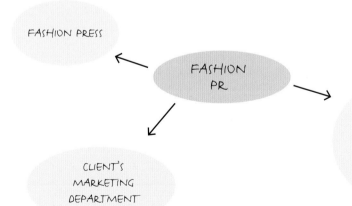

FASHION PRESS

FASHION PR

CLIENT'S MARKETING DEPARTMENT

CLIENTS:
FASHION DESIGNERS
BRAND MANAGERS
MARKETING MANAGERS
FASHION BUYERS
RETAILERS

Applying for a job

When applying for a position, you need to consider the type of organization you wish to work for, which level of the market your skills are best suited to, and whether you wish to work in womenswear, menswear, childrenswear, accessories or specific sectors such as sportswear or knitwear. Research the market to determine which companies are doing well; you are most likely to be employed by a company experiencing growth. Read the business sections of newspapers and check out industry websites for information. You can find out about appointments and employment opportunities from:

- Recruitment agencies
- Trade fairs, exhibitions and graduate employment expos
- College and university careers departments
- Appointment sections in industry publications such as *Drapers* or *Retail Week*
- Networking and word of mouth
- Contacting companies directly by calling their HR department and sending out your CV and a covering letter

Research into companies you might be interested to work for. Most company websites have a section where you should be able to find annual reports and financial results. Check out the size of an organization, number of employees, sales turnover and profits. Take a look at the company mission statement, brand values and objectives and consider if you might fit in to the organization. Go to the press section of the website and look at the most recent press releases.

If you are happy to work in a corporate environment and want a job in mass market fashion, you could consider retail organizations like Gap, Marks & Spencer, H&M, Zara, Topshop, Mango or Banana Republic. If you are more independently minded then you might prefer to work for a smaller organization. Salaries tend to be lower and there are fewer benefit packages but with fewer employees, you are likely to get exposure to more aspects of the business and gain excellent first-hand knowledge. Another option is to work for a supplier or manufacturer. Designers employed by this sector may meet with buyers from high-street retailers to discuss trends and decide what type of styles they wish you to develop. You might present ideas you have researched on their behalf, show them designs or development samples and hopefully take orders if samples are approved. Working for a supplier can be very hands-on and exciting but it is also pressurized. Clothing and footwear prices fell by 8 per cent in the 12 months to May 2009 in the UK; suppliers are challenged to keep cost prices low and they may be dropped by a retailer if they do not perform, so jobs in this sector are not always secure.

Work experience and internships

Work placements and internships are a good first step for your career. Although you might not be paid, you will benefit from gaining first-hand industry knowledge. If work placements are not offered as part of your course curriculum, then it is advisable for you to seek an internship or paid work during your holidays so that you can practise skills, gain professional knowledge and increase your confidence. The reality of working life can be very different from your college studies. An investigation into Employer Engagement, Work-Related Learning and the Student Experience by Catherine McConnell (Skillfast-UK, 2008) described student experiences of the workplace. One student found it hard to think about structure and design first and not about theme and colour as they had at college. The experience helped them realize how quickly you have to work in the industry and why there isn't time to get arty and spend weeks on sketchbooks. Some students find the work they undertake as an intern boring or repetitive, but it is worth persevering, as one student discovered when they had to mount a large volume of fabric swatches onto card; the experience helped improve their attention to detail and presentation. Industry experience is extremely valuable and will help you learn how to conduct yourself and carry out work in a professional manner.

Writing a CV and covering letter

A CV (curriculum vitae) or résumé is an important professional tool used to advertise your experience and skills. A CV should summarize your work experience to date, outline your skills and detail your education and academic accomplishments. There are two types of CV you can consider. A chronological CV gives details of your employment history in chronological order; this format should be used if you have industry experience. A functional CV is more suitable for graduates and college leavers; this format focuses on skills and qualifications.

A CV should begin with your name, address, contact details and date of birth. The next section should be the professional profile, a concise statement describing your experience, skills, abilities and personal qualities. On a chronological CV the profile will be followed by your work experience and educational details in reverse chronological order. On a functional CV the profile will be followed by a section listing your skills. Additional information can then be listed, making sure it is relevant to the job. Interests come last. For references, it is best to state, 'references available on request'. It is courteous to ask someone if they are willing to be your referee and if they agree for you to give out their details.

The CV should be sent out with a covering letter outlining why you want to work for the organization in question. The letter should be brief, no more than one side of A4. It should state which post you are applying for, why you want the job and indicate the experience, skills and personal qualities that you believe meet the requirements of the company and the role they are advertising. Make sure the letter is typed (unless a handwritten letter is specified by the company). Use top-quality white or cream A4 paper, ideally the same as you have used for your CV. If you are writing to a specific person, then the letter should start 'Dear (insert correct name)' and end 'Yours sincerely'. If you do not have a specific name, then begin, 'Dear Sir/Madam' and finish 'Yours faithfully'.

It is possible that a company you wish to work for is not currently advertising for a position. In this instance you can send out a speculative CV and covering letter explaining what type of job you are interested in. Many companies keep CVs on file, and they may contact you if they are interested in you and a suitable position should arise. It is important to address a speculative CV to a specific person, so contact the company by phone and find out who you should send the letter to, making sure you spell their name correctly.

CV tips:

- CV's should be typed

- First impressions count so print your CV on best quality white or cream paper

- The CV should be on one (maximum two) A4 pages

- Do not print double sided; make sure each page is printed separately

- Do not use coloured paper or coloured ink as CVs are likely to be faxed, scanned or photocopied by potential employers

- The layout should be simple and look professional. Make sure the CV is easy to read; use white space to separate sections and keep to one font throughout. Headings can be in bold or a bigger font size to make them stand out.

- Send your CV out unfolded in an A4 envelope

- Use a spell check and double check your CV for mistakes. A good idea is to ask someone else to proofread it – they will usually spot spelling mistakes and typos that you might have let slip through.

- Avoid using jargon and acronyms

Interviews

Interviews vary enormously depending on the job role, the level of the job and the type of company involved. The interview may be an informal chat or could involve a panel of interviewers, you might be expected to make a presentation, or the recruitment process might be conducted in a group with other candidates.

Informal interview These may be carried out by telephone or in a public place like a hotel lounge or café. They are often used by a company when they wish to meet or talk to someone informally to learn more about them and see if they might fit into their organization.

Pre-screening Companies use a recruitment agency or someone within their own Human Resources department to conduct an interview to pre-screen candidates. This may take place face to face or on the telephone; the purpose is to verify details of your CV and check you have the minimum qualifications required.

Selection interview This is the next step in the process. Interviewers already know that pre-screened candidates have the right skills, so are looking to see who has the right attitude and personality and could fit in with other employees within the organization. Interviews may be carried out by one person, a series of different people who each interview the candidate one by one, or by an interview panel. If successful, you may be offered the job or invited back for a second interview.

Panel interview Panel interviews are conducted by several people at once. The panel is usually made of managers from departments you will work with if you get the job. Members of the interview panel will take it in turn to ask you questions. Keep calm and make eye contact with each panel member when you respond to them.

Group interviews and assessment centres Candidates may be interviewed as a group; this allows an organization to see how candidates interact with each other and assess if they are team players or have leadership potential. Assessment centres are special recruitment days where candidates perform a series of tasks and exercises such as group discussions, presentations and leadership exercises.

You should get an opportunity to ask questions at the end of the interview. Start with questions about training and appraisals. You can ask about career

Interview tips:

- Prepare thoroughly, research the company and gather background information on the skills required for the job.

- Research latest industry developments and trends so that you are knowledgeable and informed if asked during your interview.

- Confirm beforehand if you are expected to take anything with you such as examples of previous work or a portfolio.

- Make sure you know exactly where to go, how to get there and allow enough time for transport problems or hold-ups. It is better to be early than late. Try to arrive about ten minutes ahead of your interview time so that you can take time to breathe and unwind from the journey.

- Think about a suitable outfit to wear and make sure it is clean, presentable and still fits! It's a good idea to try your outfit on well before the day of the interview, check for missing buttons, holes or dropped hems.

- Take a copy of the job application and your CV with you. You can read these in preparation while travelling or waiting.

prospects and opportunities for growth and clarify any queries about job specification and responsibilities. Save questions about pay and holidays until last or, even better, double check details with Human Resources before or after the interview. Find out when you can expect to hear if you have been successful, and don't forget to thank the interviewer for their time before you leave.

It is worth considering the type of language you use within a professional situation. Below is a list of positive words and action words you might find useful when compiling your CV or attending an interview. Make sure you choose ones that are suitable, relevant and true to you.

POSITIVE WORDS

Accurate	Co-operative	Experienced	Knowledgeable	Precise	Self-motivated
Adaptable	Creative	Expert	Literate	Productive	Self-reliant
Ambitious	Decisive	Fast	Mature	Professional	Serious
Analytical	Dedicated	Flexible	Motivated	Proficient	Skilled
Articulate	Dependable	Friendly	Objective	Punctual	Smart
Assertive	Diligent	Hardworking	Open-minded	Qualified	Talented
Astute	Diplomatic	Honest	Organized	Quick-thinking	Tenacious
Bright	Dynamic	Imaginative	Outgoing	Rational	Thorough
Calm	Educated	Independent	Patient	Realistic	Trustworthy
Capable	Effective	Informed	Perceptive	Resourceful	Versatile
Competent	Efficient	Innovative	Persistent	Responsible	Willing
Confident	Energetic	Intelligent	Personable	Self-assured	
Consistent	Enthusiastic	Inventive	Practical	Self-confident	

ACTION WORDS

Achieved	Co-ordinated	Facilitated	Invented	Oversaw	Reorganized
Administered	Created	Formulated	Investigated	Participated	Researched
Advised	Delegated	Founded	Launched	Performed	Resolved
Analysed	Demonstrated	Generated	Led	Pioneered	Restructured
Arranged	Designed	Guided	Liaised	Planned	Reviewed
Assisted	Developed	Handled	Maintained	Presented	Revised
Attended	Devised	Headed	Managed	Prepared	Scheduled
Broadened	Directed	Identified	Marketed	Processed	Secured
Collaborated	Edited	Implemented	Monitored	Produced	Set up
Completed	Effected	Improved	Motivated	Programmed	Solved
Communicated	Established	Increased	Negotiated	Promoted	Structured
Conceived	Evaluated	Initiated	Opened	Proposed	
Conducted	Expanded	Installed	Operated	Recommended	
Controlled	Explored	Instructed	Organized	Recruited	

Source: The Careers Department, Plymouth College of Art

Portfolios

A portfolio of work that shows off your abilities and skills is an important marketing tool for those seeking employment as a fashion designer. Make sure your portfolio is organized, neat and professional and that the work displayed plays to your strengths. Select work that showcases your skills in fashion drawing and illustration, technical drawing, fabric selection, range building, print design, use of colour, creating colour palettes, computer-aided design (CAD), Photoshop, photography or fashion styling.

Consider the content and layout; it is advisable to put your best quality work at the front, making sure it is targeted at the company and the job for which you are applying. Each project or section within the portfolio should start with an inspiration or concept page followed by 4–6 pages of design work. These should include illustrations of your proposed collections as well as professional flat technical drawings and fabric swatches. Flat working drawings should be precise and neat so viewers can easily see design details, stitching and closures. Update your portfolio with new work on a regular basis; remove older material – anything over two years old should be taken out or kept to a minimum.

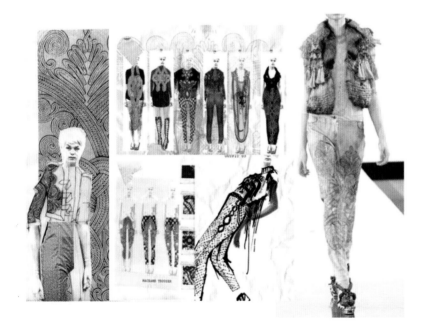

Above
Portfolio design work by fashion graduate Beatrice Newman featured online on the recruitment website, www.artsthread.com. Newman's collection, entitled 'Opulence of Empires', is inspired by the sumptuousness of Russian Tsars and *The Arabian Nights*. The collection incorporates rich colours such as gold and coppers and uses embellishment, pattern and prints from palace interiors and Russian carpets.

Portfolio tips:

- Choose the best size portfolio to showcase your A3 and A4 work well. You can use A2 but don't go too big as you will have to carry the portfolio around and potential employers can find it frustrating to handle overly large or unwieldy folios.

- Each project in the portfolio should be presented in a style that is both professional and reflective of the market and consumer for which it is intended. Give each project a title, include a limited amount of explanatory text and annotate designs. A viewer should be able to understand your work without you having to give lengthy verbal explanations.

- Take the time to double check all written content, especially titles, technical terms and designer or brand names to make sure they are spelt correctly.

- Present work either in landscape or portrait format; try not to mix the two as it can be annoying for a viewer to have to keep turning the portfolio to view the work.

Further reading

D. Adcock, A. Halborg, C. Ross. *Marketing Principles and Practice*, Financial Times/Prentice Hall, 2001

Teri Agins, *The End of Fashion*, HarperCollins, 2000

Michael J. Baker, *The Marketing Book*, Financial Times/Prentice Hall, 2001

J.A. Bell, *Silent Selling: Best Practices and Effective Strategies in Visual Merchandising*, Fairchild, 2006

Sandy Black, *Eco-chic: The Fashion Paradox*, Black Dog Publishing, 2008

Sandy Black, *Knitwear in Fashion*, Thames & Hudson, 2002

Sarah E. Braddock Clarke and Marie O'Mahony, *Techno Textiles 2: Revolutionary Textiles for Fashion and Design: Bk 2*, Thames & Hudson 2007

Evelyn L. Brannon, *Fashion Forecasting: Research, Analysis, and Presentation*, Fairchild Books; 2nd revised edition, 2005

Michael Braungart, William McDonough. *Cradle to Cradle: Remaking the Way We Make Things*, Vintage, 2009

Martin Butler. *People don't buy what you sell: They buy what you stand for*, Management Books 2000 Ltd, 2005

Leslie de Chernatony & Malcolm McDonald, *Creating Powerful Brands*, Butterworth-Heinemann, 3rd edition 2003

Michel Chevalier & Gerald Mazzalovo. *Luxury Brand Management*, John Wiley & Sons 2008

Pamela N. Danziger. *Let Them Eat Cake: Marketing Luxury to the Masses – as Well as the Classes*, Dearborn Trade Publishing, 2005

Scott M. Davis & Michael Dunn. *Building the Brand-driven Business*. Jossey-Bass. 2002

Kate Fletcher. *Sustainable Fashion and Textiles: Design Journeys*, Earthscan Publications Ltd, 2008

Mary Gehlhar, *The Fashion Designer Survival Guide: An Insider's Look at Starting and Running Your Own Fashion Business*, Kaplan Publishing, 2005

Malcolm Gladwell, *The Tipping Point*, Abacus, 2000

Seth Godin. *Purple Cow*, Penguin Books, 2005

Helen Goworek. *Fashion Buying*, Blackwell Science, 2001

Helen Goworek. *Careers in Fashion & Textiles*, Blackwell Publishing, 2006

Eric von Hippel. *Democratising Innovation*, MIT Press, 2005.

Jeff Howe. *Crowdsourcing: Why the Power of the Crowd is Driving the Future of Business*, Crown Business, 2008

Neil Howe and William Strauss. *Millennials Rising*, Vintage Books, 2000

Mark Hughes, *Buzzmarketing: Get People to Talk About Your Stuff*, Portfolio, 2005

Tim Jackson and David Shaw. *Mastering Fashion Buying and Merchandising Management*, Macmillan, 2001

Tim Jackson and David Shaw, *The Fashion Handbook*, Abingdon, Routledge, 2006

Sue Jenkyn Jones. *Fashion Design*, Laurence King, 2nd edition, 2005

Richard M. Jones, *The Apparel Industry*, Blackwell Publishing Ltd, 2nd edition, 2006

Jean-Noël Kapferer. *Strategic Brand Management*, The Free Press, 1992

J.N Kapferer & V. Bastien, *The Luxury Strategy: Break the Rules of Marketing to Build Luxury Brands*, Kogan Page, 2009

Philip Kotler. *Marketing Management: Analysis Planning, Implementation and Control*, Prentice Hall, 1994

Philip Kotler, *FAQs on Marketing*, Marshall Cavendish Business, 2008

P. Kotler, G. Armstrong, V. Wong, J. Saunders. *The Principles of Marketing*, Financial Times/Prentice Hall, 2008

Suzanne Lee, Warren de Preez, *Fashioning the Future: Tomorrow's Wardrobe*, Thames & Hudson, 2007

Martin Lindstrom, *Buyology: How Everything We Believe About Why We Buy Is Wrong*, Random House Business, 2008

Margaret McAlpine, *So You Want to Work in Fashion?*, Hodder Wayland, 2005

Malcolm McDonald, *On Marketing Planning: Understanding Marketing Plans and Strategy*, Kogan Page. 2007

Geoffrey Miller *Spent: Sex, Evolution and the Secrets of Consumerism*, William Heinemann Ltd, 2009

David Meerman Scott. *The New Rules of Marketing & PR*, John Wiley & Sons, 2007

Tony Morgan. *Visual Merchandising*, Laurence King, 2008

Bethan Morris, *Fashion Illustrator*, Laurence King, 2nd edition, 2010

Don Tapscott. *Grown up digital*, McGraw Hill, 2009

Wally Olins, *Wally Olins: The Brand Handbook*, Thames & Hudson, 2008

Faith Popcorn, *EVEolution: The Eight Truths of Marketing to Women*, HarperCollins Business, 2001

A. Ries, J. Trout. *Positioning: The Battle for Your Mind*, McGraw-Hill Professional, 2001

Lon Safko, David K Brake. *The Social Media Bible: Tactics, Tools and Strategies for Business Success*. John Wiley & Sons, 2009

Marian Salzman & Ira Matathia, *Next Now: Trends for the Future*, Palgrave Macmillan, 2008

Bernd H. Schmitt. *Experiential Marketing*, The Free Press, 1999

Robert Scoble & Shel Israel. *Naked Conversations: How Blogs Are Changing the Way Businesses Talk with Customers*, John Wiley & Sons, 2006

Simon Seivewright, *Basics Fashion Design: Research and Design*, AVA Publishing, 2007

Michael R. Solomon and Nancy J. Rabolt. *Consumer Behaviour in Fashion*, Prentice Hall, 2008

Mark Tungate. *Fashion Brands*, Kogan Page, 2004.

Sophie Sheikh. *The Pocket Guide to Fashion PR*, Preo Publishing, 2009

Rosemary Varley. *Retail Product Management*, Routledge, 2002

R Varley and M Rafiq. *Principles of Retail Management*, Palgrave Macmillan, 2004

Peter Vogt, *Career Opportunities in the Fashion Industry*, Checkmark Books, 2nd revised edition, 2007

Nicola White and Ian Griffiths. *The Fashion Business. Theory, Practice, Image*. Berg, 2000

Judy Zaccagnini & Irene M. Foster, *Research Methods for the Fashion Industry*, Fairchild, 2009

Reference notes

1 Structure of the Fashion Market

p12   LVMH First half results for 2009.

p14   Christian Dior 2008 Annual Report.

p15   *Value Clothing Retailers Shine Amid Recession*. Just-style.com (22.09.09).

p17   www.theuniformproject.com

p18   Mintel report on ethical clothing 2009.

p23   American Apparel and Footwear Association, *Trends: An Annual Statistical Analysis of the U.S. Apparel and Footwear Industries*, 2007 Edition.

2 The Marketing Toolkit

p26   Philip Kotler quote: *FAQs on Marketing*, Marshall Cavendish Business, 2008.

p27   Martin Butler quote: *People don't buy what you sell: They buy what you stand for*, Management Books 2000 Ltd, 2005.

p29   Seth Godin quote: *Purple Cow*, Penguin Books, 2005.

p30   Mark Hughes quote: *Buzzmarketing: Get People to Talk About Your Stuff*, Portfolio 2005.

p34   Neil H. Borden quote: The Concept of the Marketing Mix, Journal of Advertising Research, Cambridge University Press 1964.

p53   Ries & Trout quote: *Positioning: The Battle for Your Mind*, McGraw-Hill Professional 2001.

The concept of Positioning was developed by Ries & Trout and first took hold in 1972 with a series of articles entitled The Positioning Era, published in *Advertising Age*.

p57   Lisa Armstrong quote: *Asos.com: As Seen on the Screens of the Fashion Savvy*, www.timesonline.com (21.01.09).

3 Research and Planning

p62   Philip Kotler quote cited by G. Lancaster & P. Reynolds. *Management of Marketing* (2005).

p71   The North Face – Sustainable Store, JGA Press release 2009. www.jga.com

p87   Uniqlo Reigning Supreme. W. David Marx, www.thebusinessoffashion.net (25.01.09).

p88   Retail insight on Uniqlo and Japanese consumer market. www.japanconsuming.com (06.01.09).

p96   Stuart Rose quoted in *The Financial Times*, 'M&S admits Shanghai errors. Patti Waldmeir' (10.02.09).

4 Understanding the Customer

p105   John Rocha quote: *The Times Magazine* (22.09.07).

p109   Erdem Moralioglu quoted in *Elle Magazine* 2007.

p109   Quote by Douglas posted on www.jonathanpontell.com. Jonathan Pontell is a cultural historian and writer whose website has a section devoted to information on Generation Jones.

p110   The Bosanquet & Gibbs report, *Class of 2005: The IPOD generation* was published by the influential think-tank, Reform in 2005. www.reform.co.uk

p113   It is estimated that every year in the UK consumers purchase two million tonnes of clothes of which 1.2 million tonnes end up in landfill.

p113   The term 'conspicuous consumption' was coined by Thorstein Veblen in *The Theory of the Leisure Class* (1899).

p115   Jennings sourced information from *Drapers* article: 'Portas Says Future is Bright for UK's Indies'. Khabi Mirza. (24.11.07).

p121   Information on Generation G can be found on www.trendwatching.com

5 Introduction to Branding

p128   Chartered Institute of Marketing online pamphlet, *How Brands Work*. www.cim.co.uk

p134   Quotation: *The Economic Importance of Brands – Seven Reasons Why Brands Really Matter*, Clamor Gieske of FutureBrand, The British Brands Group 2004.

p146   Harmonizing Your Touchpoints, Scott Davis & Tina Longoria. Brand Packaging 2003 www.prophet.com

p150   *Strategic Brand Management*, Kapferer 1992. Kapferer attributes this new view of USP to Ted Bates.

p151   Danziger quote: *Let Them Eat Cake: Marketing Luxury to the Masses – as Well as the Classes*, Dearborn Trade Publishing, 2005.

p152   Quotation by Sean Chiles of IPincubator, specializing in brand development and licensing.

p155   Luxury Retailers Left High and Dry During Slowdown, Ann Hynek. www.foxbusiness.com (05.03.09).

6 Fashion Promotion

p 161   ZenithOptimedia sourced US advertising information from Magazine Publishers of America 2009 and UK data from Nielsen Media Research 2009.

p165   For Luxury Brands, Less Money to Spend on Ads, Stephanie Clifford, www.nytimes.com (23.11.08). Clifford cites information from the Media Industry Newsletter.

p.167   Tracking the Giants of Viral Video: New Data Insights, Abbey Klassen, *Advertising Age*. http://adage.com (07.06.09) Abbey Klassen interviews Matt Cutler VP of Visible Measures.

p170   Levi's Unbuttoned and Out of the Closet, Stuart Elliott, www.nytimes.com. (14.09.08).

p170   Financial data; Levi Strauss & Co Annual Financial Report 2007.

p170   According to research carried out by the Zandl Group, Levi's lost 30 per cent market share for males aged 13–24 and 38 per cent for girls in the same age group in the year 1997–98.

Denim Turned Every Which Way But Loose, Anne-Marie Schiro, www.nytimes.com (02.02.99).

p171   CNBC American Originals: Levi's, Sewing A Legend (2007).

p172   This famous quote is most usually attributed to John Wanamaker who opened Philadelphia's first department store, Wanamaker's, in the second half of the 19th century. Wanamaker developed the first ever copyrighted store advertisements in 1874.

Trade publications and magazines

Adbusters

Advertising Age

Adweek

Amelia's Magazine

Arena

Bloom

Brand Republic

Daily News Record (DNR)

Dansk

Dazed and Confused

Drapers: The fashion business

The Economist

Elle

Encens

Fantastic Man

GQ

Harpers Bazaar

i-D

In Style

International Textiles

L'Officiel

Marketing Week

Nylon

Plastic Rhino

Pop

Purple

Retail Week

Selvedge

Sneaker Freaker

Tank

Textile View

V

View on Colour

Viewpoint

Visionaire

Vogue

Women's Wear Daily (WWD)

Zoom on Fashion Trends

Useful addresses

UK

The British Fashion Council (BFC)
Somerset House, South Wing
Strand
London WC2R 1LA
tel +44 (0)20 7759 1999
www.britishfashioncouncil.com

The British Fashion Council provides support to emerging British fashion designers with schemes ranging from business mentoring and seminars to competitions and sponsorship.

Organizes the annual fashion awards and supports initiatives such as: estethica, Fashion Forward and NEWGEN.

Fashion Awareness Direct (FAD)
10a Wellesley Terrace
London N1 7NA
tel/fax: +44 (0)20 7490 3946

A charitable organization committed to helping young designers succeed in their careers by bringing students and professionals together at introductory events.

UKFT – Centre of the UK Fashion and Textile Industry
5 Portland Place
London W1B 1PW
tel +44 (0)20 7636 7788
fax +44 (0)20 7636 7515
www.5portlandplace.org.uk

UKFT advises members on running a business and supplying clothing and knitwear to the global marketplace. Its export division, UK Fashion Exports, gives advice on how to achieve sales in overseas markets.

US

Council of Fashion Designers of America (CFDA)
1412 Broadway, Suite 2006
New York NY 10018
+1 212 302 1821
www.cfda.com

A not-for-profit trade association that leads industry-wide initiatives and hosts the annual CFDA Fashion Awards, which recognize the top creative talent in the industry. Offers programmes to support professional development and offers scholarships, including the CFDA/Vogue Fashion Fund, the Geoffrey Beene Design Scholar Award, the Liz Claiborne Scholarship Award, and the CFDA/Teen Vogue Scholarship.

The American Apparel and Footwear Association (AAFA)
1601 No. Kent Street
12th floor
Arlington VA 22209
tel + 1 703 524 1864

The AAFA is a national trade association representing apparel and footwear companies and their suppliers.

United States Small Business Administration
26 Federal Plaza, Suite. 3100
New York, NY 10278
tel +1 212- 264-4354
fax +1 212- 264-4963

The SBA assists with small business start-up and development.

Additional resources

International fashion and textile trade fairs

The Accessories Show
New York & Las Vegas.
www.accessoriestheshow.com

Atelier
Accessories and apparel trade show.
New York
www.atelierdesigners.com

Bread & Butter
Street and urban wear.
Berlin, Germany
www.breadandbutter.com

CPD - Düsseldorf
International trade fair for
womenswear and accessories.
Düsseldorf, Germany
www.igedo.com

CPH Vision
Exhibits established and up-and-coming
contemporary fashion brands.
Copenhagen, Denmark.
www.cphvision.dk

CURVExpo
Designer lingerie and swimwear.
New York & Las Vegas
www.curvexpo.com

GlobalTex
LA International Textile and Sourcing Fair.
Los Angeles
www.globaltex.com

Expofil
Yarn, fibre and knitwear show.
Paris
www.expofil.com

Futurmoda
Leather and footwear trade show.
Alicante, Spain.
www.futurmoda.es

HMD – Herrenmode Düsseldorf
International trade show for menswear
and accessories.
Düsseldorf, Germany
www.igedo.com

Lineapelle
Trade fair for leather, accessories and
components for footwear, leather goods,
garments and furniture.
Bologna, Italy
www.lineapelle-fair.it

London Edge
Street and clubwear trade show.
London
www.londonedge.com

**The Los Angeles International Textile Show
(L.A. Textile)**
Cutting-edge fashion direction,
textiles and creative design resources

from around the globe.
Los Angeles
www.californiamarketcenter.com

Modacalzado + Iberpiel
Footwear and leather goods.
Madrid, Spain
www.ifema.es

Modafabriek
Womenswear, menswear and children's fashion.
Amsterdam
www.modefabriek.nl

Pitti Immagine
Organize a wide range of fashion and textile
fairs including:
Pitti Bimbo – Childrenswear
Pitti Filati – yarn show
Pitti Uomo – menswear
Pitti W – women's pre-collection
All the above in Florence, Italy.
Modaprima – Apparel and accessories Milan
www.pittimmagine.com

Première Vision
International fabric trade fair.
Paris
www.premierevision.fr

Pulse
Gifts, interior and fashion accessories.
London
www.pulse-london.com

Pure Womenswear
Womenswear, accessories and footwear.
London
www.purewomenswear.co.uk

Terminal 2
Denim and urban fashion brands.
Copenhagen, Denmark
www.terminal-2.dk

Top Drawer
Gifts, interior and fashion accessories.
London
www.topdrawer.co.uk

International fashion weeks

Amsterdam International Fashion Week
www.amsterdamfashionweek.com

Audi Joburg Fashion Week, South Africa
www.africanfashioninternational.com

Bangalore Fashion Week, India
www.bangalorefashionweek.in

Cape Town Fashion Week, South Africa
www.africanfashioninternational.com

Colombo Fashion Week, Sri Lanka
www.colombofashionweek.com

Durban Fashion Week, South Africa
www.africanfashioninternational.com

Hong Kong Fashion Week
www.hktdc.com/fair/hkfashionweekfw-en/

Japan Fashion Week in Tokyo
www.jfw.jp

Lakmé Fashion Week, Mumbai, India
www.lakmefashionweek.co.in

London Fashion Week
www.londonfashionweek.co.uk

Los Angeles Fashion Week
www.fashionweek.la.com

Mercedes-Benz Berlin Fashion Week
www.mercedes-benzfashionweek.com

Mercedes-Benz New York Fashion Week
www.mbfashionweek.com

Milan Fashion Week
www.milanomoda.it

Paris Fashion Week
www.modeaparis.com

Paris Haute Couture Fashion Week
www.modeaparis.com

Rome Haute Couture
www.altaroma.it

Rosemount Australian Fashion Week
www.afw.com.au

Stockholm Fashion Week
www.stockholmfashionweek.com

**Wills Lifestyle India Fashion Week,
New Delhi**
www.fdci.org

Marketing, advertising and promotion associations

Advertising Research Foundation (ARF)
www.thearf.org

The American Marketing Association
www.marketingpower.com

Chartered Institute of Marketing
www.cim.co.uk

**European Association of Communications
Agencies (EACA)**
www.eaca.be

**European Interactive Advertising
Association (EIAA)**
www.eiaa.net

Institute of Direct Marketing (IDM)
www.theidm.com

Institute of Practitioners in Advertising
www.ipa.co.uk

Institute for Public Relations (IPR)
www.instituteforpr.org

Institute of Sales Promotion (ISP)
www.isp.co.uk

International Licensing Industry
Merchandisers' Association (LIMA)
www.licensing.org

The Internet Advertising Bureau
www.iabuk.net

Marketing Agencies Association
Worldwide MAAW
www.maaw.org

PMA – The Association for
Integrated Marketing
www.pmalink.org

World Advertising Research Centre
(WARC)
www.warc.com

Trend forecasting and fashion intelligence

The Carlin Group
www.carlin-groupe.com

Colour & Trends
www.colour-trends.com

BrainReserve (Faith Popcorn)
www.faithpopcorn.com

The Future Laboratory
www.thefuturelaboratory.com

Li Edelkoort
www.trendunion.com

Marian Salzman
www.mariansalzman.wordpress.com

Mudpie
www.mpdclick.com

Nelly Rodi
www.nellyrodi.com

Pantone Inc
www.patone.com

Peclers Paris
www.peclersparis.com

Promostyl
www.promostylamericas.com

Style.com
www.style.com

Stylesight
www.stylesight.com

Trendstop
www.trendstop.com

Trendzine
www.fashioninformation.com

Trendwatching
www.trendwatching.com

WGSN
www.wgsn.com

Fashion and textile market information

American Apparel and Footwear
Association
www.apparelandfootwear.org

Clothesource
www.clothesource.com

Cotton Incorporated
www.cottoninc.com

The Doneger Group
www.doneger.com

Drapers
www.drapersonline.com

Euromonitor International
www.euromonitor.com

Fashion Incubator: industry information
www.fashion-incubator.com

Fashion Infomat
www.infomat.com

Fashion Reporter
www.thefashionreporter.com

Fibre2fashion
www.fibre2fashion.com

First Research
www.firstresearch.com

Just-style
www.just-style.com

Mintel Reports
www.mintel.com

My Fashion Life: industry analysis
and news
www.myfashionlife.com

NPD Group
www.npd.com

TNS Worldpanel Fashion
www.tnsglobal.com

The Tobé Report
www.tobereport.com

Verdict Research
www.verdict.co.uk

Women's Wear Daily
www.wwd.com

Marketing, branding, advertising and retail information

Advertising Age
http://adage.com

Adweek
www.adweek.com

The American Marketing Association
www.marketingpower.com

Brand Republic
www.brandrepublic.com

Fashion Windows: Visual Merchandising
www.fashionwindows.com

The Gallup Organization
www.gallup.com

Interbrand Brandchannel
www.brandchannel.com

Landor & Associates
www.landor.com

The Market Research Society
www.mrs.org.uk

The Retail Bulletin: Fashion Merchandising
www.theretailbulletin.com

Retail Week
www.retail-week.com

Visual Store: Visual Merchandising
www.visualstore.com

Unity Marketing
www.unitymarketingonline.com

Wally Olins
www.wallyolins.com

World Luxury Association
www.worldluxuryassociation.org

Blogs, social networking and street fashion

Fashionising.com
Fashion social network.
www.fashionising.com

HypeBeast
http://hypebeast.com

Japanese Streets
www.japanesestreets.com

Lookbook
www.lookbook.nu

Mashable
Social media news and web tips.
www.mashable.com

The Sartorialist
www.thesartorialsit.blogspot.com

Sustainability and eco-fashion

Better Cotton Institute
www.bettercotton.org

British Association for Fair Trade Shops
www.bafts.org.uk

Department for Environment,
Food and Rural Affairs
www.defra.gov.uk

Eco Fashion World
www.ecofashionworld.com

Environmental Justice Foundation
www.ejfoundation.org

Ethical Fashion Forum
www.ethicalfashionforum.com

Ethical Trading Initiative (ETI)
www.ethicaltrade.org

Fair Wear Foundation
www.fairwear.nl

Fashioning an Ethical Industry
www.fashioninganethicalindustry.org

Futerra Sustainability Communications
www.futerra.co.uk

Global Organic Textile Standard (GOTS)
www.global-standard.org

International Labour Organization
www.ilo.org

Material Connexion
Sustainable fabric library.
www.materialconnexion.com

New Economics Foundation
www.neweconomcis.org

Oeko-tex
Sets standards for manufacture.
www.oeko-tex.com

Pesticide Action Network
www.pan-uk.org

Soil Association
www.soilassociation.org

Sustainable Cotton
www.sustainablecotton.org

United Nations – Global Compact
www.unglobalcompact.org

World Fair Trade Organization (WFTO)
www.wfto.com

Company profiles & data

Dun and Bradstreet
www.dnb.co.uk

First Research
www.firstresearch.com

Hoover's
www.hoovers.com

LexisNexis
www.lexisnexis.co.uk

Zandl Group
www.zandlgroup.com

Government census and trade data

US Census Data
www.census.gov

UK National Statistics
www.statsbase.gov.uk

Information on starting a fashion business

Designer Forum
www.emtex.org.uk/df/designerforum

Design Trust
www.thedesigntrust.co.uk

Fashion Capital
www.fashioncapital.co.uk

Skillfast
www.skillfast-uk.org

The UK Department for Business,
Innovation & Skills
www.bis.gov.uk

Fashion recruitment agencies

Arts Thread:
Student and industry website.
www.artsthread.com

Fashion Personnel
www.fashionpersonnel.co.uk

FJobs
www.fashionjob.com

Fusion Consulting
www.fusion-consulting.com

Indesign Recruitment
www.indesignrecruitment.co.uk

Jobs in Fashion
www.jobsinfashion.com

People Marketing
www.peoplemarketing.co.uk

Retail Choice
www.retailchoice.com

Smith and Pye
www.smithandpye.com

Vanessa Denza
www.denza.co.uk

Glossary

Advertising channel The medium by which an advert reaches the public; for example, cinema, magazine, internet or newspaper.

Advertising exposure The length of time an audience is exposed to an advert.

Advertising impacts The total number of separate occasions that a TV or radio commercial is viewed or heard by a target audience.

Advertising message The message conveyed by an advert.

Advertising reach The number of people within a target market exposed to an advert over a specific length of time.

Advertising Value Equivalent (AVE) Measurement to compare the cost effectiveness of PR against advertising.

Audience sentiment Audience opinion relating to a particular brand, advertising or PR campaign.

Brand A trademark name that distinguishes a product or brand company from others in the market.

Brand architecture The way a company structures and names its brands.

Brand awareness The number of customers or potential customers with awareness of a particular brand.

Brand equity A brand is a valuable asset to a company. The power of the brand name and the accumulated goodwill that exists towards a brand gives it an extra value known as brand equity.

Brand essence The essential nature of a brand. The core or heart of the brand expressed in clear and simple terms.

Brand extension Expansion of a brand by developing and selling new products in a broadly similar market. The term 'brand stretching' is used if a brand takes its name into a very different and unrelated market.

Brand identity The elements of a brand that define its identity, for example, identifying colours, logo, product, window displays and advertising. The brand's identity is its fundamental means of consumer recognition and symbolizes the brand's differentiation from competitors.

Brand image The consumer's view and perception of a brand and its identity. For users of a brand this will be based on practical experience. For non-users it will be based on impressions gathered from media sources or the opinion of others.

Brand licensing A brand owner can lease the use of the brand name and logo to another company. A licensing fee or royalty rate will be agreed for the use of the brand name.

Brand loyalty Refers to how loyal consumers are to a brand. In the fashion market it is possible for consumers to be loyal to several brands simultaneously.

Brand management Strategic management of a brand. Brand managers ensure the identity and values of the brand are maintained.

Brand message This is the message that a brand organization wishes to communicate about the qualities and ideas behind the brand and its product. The message can be communicated via the logo, strapline, slogan and advertising as well as via the press.

Brand personality Brand personality works on the idea that a brand has a distinct personality and that it is possible to attribute human personality traits to a brand.

Brand positioning This is both the strategic management of a brand's position relative to competitors in the market as well as the perception of the brand's position in the mind of consumers. Positioning strategy is a key component of marketing and branding strategy.

Brand proposition Statement encapsulating what the brand offers its customers. It defines the brand benefits and what makes the brand unique.

Brand repositioning The process of redefining a brand's identity and position in the market.

Brand strategy Refers to the strategic plan used to enable the development of a brand so that it meets its business objectives. The brand strategy should influence the total operation of a business and be rooted in the brand's vision and values.

Brand touchpoints A brand touchpoint is a point of interaction between a brand and consumers, employees or stakeholders.

Brand values These form the code by which a brand operates. Internally, the brand values act as a benchmark to measure behaviours and performance. They should be connecting and engaging and can also be used to market and promote a brand to consumers.

Bricks and mortar retail Retail that takes place in-store as opposed to online.

Bridge line American term for diffusion line or a collection placed between designer and high-street fashion.

B2B (Business-to-business) Trading that takes place between one business and another.

B2C (Business-to-consumer) Trading that takes place between a business and the consumer.

Celebrity endorsement A celebrity signs a contract to act as a brand ambassador and to be seen wearing and advertising the brand.

Celebrity seeding A brand loans or donates product to a celebrity for free so that they are seen wearing the brand's products.

Clip report A report giving information on the effectiveness of a PR campaign. Indicates which publications covered the story and their circulation figures.

Co-brand or Partnership brand A brand created when two brand names work together. Y3 by Yohji Yamamoto and adidas is an example.

Co-creation A company designs and creates its products with co-operation and input from consumers.

Column inches Indication of effectiveness of a PR campaign. Measures amount of column inches printed in press.

Comparative shopping (comp shop) Designers and fashion buyers research the marketplace to compare products and prices from competitors.

Competitive advantage A specific advantage one company or brand may have over competitors within the market.

Concession A store or department store leases space within their store to another brand.

Consideration set The set of potential brand or product choices a customer may consider when purchasing.

Consumer-generated media (CGM) Refers to web-content generated by consumers through blogs or sharing on social media websites.

Consumer profile Description of a typical customer or targeted customer. The profile is derived from analysis of market research data.

Cost per thousand (CPT) Calculation to determine the average cost of an advert reaching one thousand people within the target audience.

Cost-plus pricing Formula used to calculate minimum price at which a product must be sold in order to recoup original costs.

Country of origin effect (COOE) The perception that products made in certain countries may be of better quality, for example French perfume or Italian leather.

Crowdsourcing A company outsources design or other functions to the public, usually via the internet.

Customer pen portrait A written portrait used to describe a typical customer or core customer.

Customer segmentation Analysis of customers, grouping them into clusters with similar characteristics.

Demi-couture Luxury-level fashion positioned between couture and ready-to-wear.

Demographics Analysis of a population by gender, age, occupation and social class.

Differentiation Strategy used to ensure a brand and its products are distinct from those of competitors.

Diffusion line Collection developed by a designer or brand to be sold at a lower price than main collection; allows a wider range of customers to buy into the brand.

Direct marketing When a company markets directly to the end-consumer via mail outs, emails, text messages or magazine inserts.

Distribution channel Route by which product is distributed and reaches the market.

E-commerce Business and retail conducted via the internet.

End-consumer The eventual user or wearer of the product. It may not always be the customer: a baby may be the end-consumer but the mother might be the customer.

Endorsed brand Parent brand endorses one of its own sub-brands: Obsession by Calvin Klein for example.

Experience marketing Focuses on experience as a way to create connection between a brand and its audience.

Fad A short-lived fashion that does not survive long enough to become a trend.

Fascia Shop front and signage displaying brand logo and name.

Fashionability A term used to describe a garment or brand in terms of how fashionable it is.

Focus group Products or collections shown to a test group of people in order to gain feedback on their opinions, perceptions and attitudes.

Franchise A type of business model where a parent company grants permission for an individual business to trade using the main company brand name. The franchisee pays a fee and percentage of profits to the parent company.

Geo-demographics A combination of geographic and demographic analysis used to classify customer types.

Haute couture French term for 'high sewing' meaning the highest quality of made-to-order clothing made in a studio known as an 'atelier'. Only design houses approved by the Chambre Syndicale de la Haute Couture in Paris may be classified as haute couture.

Lab-dips Fabric swatches sent to the dye lab to test and approve colours for a collection.

Lead-time Time between placing a fabric, component or garment order with a supplier or factory and delivery of the order.

Licensee Refers to the company purchasing the right to use the brand name.

Licensing A brand company sells the right for a company to produce and market branded product under licence. Most commonly used by fashion brands wishing to create a perfume, cosmetics or hosiery.

Licensor Refers to the company selling the right to use a brand name.

Like-for-like (LFL) product comparison Direct comparison of similar product sold by a range of competitive brands. Product can be compared in terms of price, quality, fabrication and design.

Likert scale A system used for setting questions on a questionnaire using a five-point scale so answers can be numerically analysed.

Manufacturer brand Branded manufacturer goods, usually fibres or fabrics such as Lycra® by DuPont™.

Margin The percentage of the final selling price achieved as profit. A product costing £10 and selling for £20 would have 50 per cent margin.

Market research Research into a specific market including investigation of consumers.

Market segmentation A system of dividing a market into smaller subsections; segmentation enables a company to focus their marketing more accurately.

Market share The share a particular company or country has of a specific market. Market share figures are expressed as a percentage.

Marketing environment Refers to factors that impact on an organization and its marketing.

Marketing mix Refers to key elements that must be balanced in order to develop an organization's marketing. There are two versions: the 4P (product, price, place, promotion) and 7P with additional criteria (people, physical evidence and process).

Marketing plan A formalized plan outlining an organization's marketing strategy.

Marketing research The full range of aspects that must be researched in order to determine a marketing strategy.

Mark-up The amount added to the cost price in order to achieve the selling price. Mark-up is usually expressed as a percentage, a product costing £10 and sold for £20 would have 100 per cent mark-up.

Mark-up factor A multiplication factor used to calculate a selling price. A product costing £10 and selling for £20 would have a mark-up factor of 2.

Mystery shopping The process of researchers visiting stores anonymously to assess the quality of service and product on offer.

Opportunity to see (OTS) Frequency of exposure of an advert; relates to how many people have the opportunity to see, hear or read the advertisement.

Own label, Private brand or Private label When a department store or retailer creates their own in-house brands. Marks & Spencer Autograph or Macy's I.N.C are examples.

Partnership brand See Co-brand.

Peer marketing Recommendation and promotion of products among consumers.

Perceptual map A map showing consumer perception of a brand in comparison to competitor brands.

PEST analysis Investigation and analysis of political, economic, social and technological factors affecting a business and its marketing.

Point-of-sale (POS) The actual place where product is sold to the customer; usually used in reference to the till-point or in the case of point-of-sale marketing, material used within store.

Pop-up store Refers to a temporary store set-up for a limited time frame. Pop-up stores often include some kind of special event designed to create a buzz.

Positioning The position a brand or product occupies in the market relative to competitors.

Positioning map A brand management tool used to indicate the current position or proposed future position of a brand in comparison to competitors in the market.

Prêt-à-porter French term for ready-to-wear clothing.

Price architecture The way a company structures pricing across the product range balancing the offer of low-, medium- and high- priced product.

Price point Product within a collection or product range will be priced at various price points according to type of product, quality or exclusivity.

Private label See Own label.

Product attribute Refers to the features, functions and uses of a product.

Product benefit Relates to how a product's attributes or features might benefit the consumer.

Product placement A company raises awareness of its products by ensuring they are seen in films and television shows.

Promotional mix Refers to key types of promotion (advertising, sales promotion, PR and personal selling) that must be balanced in order to develop an organization's promotional strategy.

Psychographic segmentation Analysis of consumer type based on their lifestyle, personality, motivations and behaviour.

Pull strategy Sales promotions directed towards the end-consumer. The offer creates demand and entices the customer to the store or website.

Push strategy Sales promotions geared towards trade distributers or retailers with the aim of encouraging them to promote the brand to their customers.

Ready-to-wear Fashion that is not couture or custom made. *See also* Prêt-à-porter.

Relationship marketing Focuses on the relationship between a brand or business and its customers with the aim of building long-term relationships and loyalty.

Sales channel Route by which a product reaches the market and is made available to consumers.

Sales promotion Promotional offers designed to encourage consumers to purchase. Also termed below the line marketing.

Segmentation Process of subdividing and classifying a market and consumers.

Segmentation variable Criteria used to analyse and classify markets or consumers.

Share of voice Comparison of a company's press results with its main competitors to determine which achieved most coverage.

Signature style A unique and identifiable style attributable to a particular designer, brand or fashion label.

Situation analysis An audit of the internal situation within a company and analysis of the external market situation.

Sourcing The search for, and procurement of, fabrics, materials, trims and manufacturing at required prices and delivery time-frames.

Specification sheet or Spec sheet A technical design drawing with measurements used to communicate precise details of a product's design and manufacture.

STP marketing strategy A strategy that makes use of segmentation, targeting and positioning.

Style tribe A group of individuals who dress in a common distinctive style.

Supply chain The network of suppliers, manufacturers, agents and distributers involved in the process of producing a garment.

SWOT analysis Analysis of the strengths and weaknesses of an organization and investigation of opportunities and threats in the marketplace. SWOT analysis is carried out as part of the development of a marketing plan.

Targeting The strategy of developing products or services specifically aimed to appeal to a particular group of consumers.

Text code A code sent by text to a consumer's mobile allowing them access to a promotional offer.

Tipping point The moment when a trend or idea crosses a significant threshold; it then spreads exponentially through a population.

Total product concept A model created by Theodore Levitt to explain the tangible and intangible elements of a product.

Trademark A logo, symbol, brand name, slogan or design detail protected by law as a registered trademark.

Trend scout Also known as a Cool hunter. A person who seeks out and reports on emerging trends in fashion, street fashion, music, design and culture.

Triple bottom line An ethical accounting system that measures a company's success in economic, social and environmental terms.

Trunk show Designers or sales representatives go on tour to show or preview collections to buyers, invited guests and customers. Trunk shows are usually held in boutiques or hotels.

Unique Selling Proposition (USP) Also known as Unique Selling Point. The distinguishing factors that differentiate one brand from another.

Value fashion or value sector Fashion produced in large volume at cheap prices by retailers such as Primark, H&M, New Look, Takko and Kiabi.

Vertical supply chain When one company or conglomerate owns all the manufacturing resources within the supply-chain.

Viral marketing Marketing campaigns where the message is spread by consumers on the internet.

Visual merchandising Promotion of fashion through window display, store layout and in-store product displays.

Voucher code A code available on the internet allowing customers to take advantage of a promotional offer.

Index

Page numbers in *italic* refer to captions/illustrations

Picture credits

p6 Karl Prouse/Catwalking/ Getty Images.
p7 Mel Risebrow. p8 Getty Images. p11 bl: Julien
Hekimian/Getty Images; br: Mel Risebrow. p12 t:
Apic/Getty Images ; m: Advertising Archive; b:
Harriet Posner. p14 FRANCOIS GUILLOT/AFP/
Getty Images. p15 t: Biasion Studio/Getty Images;
m: Gabriela Maj/Getty Images. p16 l–r: Karl
Prouse/Catwalking; Karl Prouse/Catwalking;Karl
Prouse/Catwalking; Kristian Dowling/Getty Images.
p17 www.theuniformproject.com. p18 Marc Hom.
p19 PIERRE VERDY/Getty Images. p20 Courtesy
Old Town. p21 Courtesy Erdem. p22 Londonedge
Ltd. p23 DON EMMERT/Getty Images. p24 t: Anna
KO, http://www.myspace.com/annako ©
breadandbutter.com; b: Jonatan Fernström DR
DENIM JEANSMAKERS. p28 Richard Valencia.
p29 Courtesy LittleMissMatched. p31 Ari Versluis
and Ellie Uyttenbroek. p33 Allan Faustino for
Threadless.com©2007. p35 Courtesy Regatta.
p36 t: Theo Wargo/Wire Image/Getty Images;
b: © Frederique Veysset/Sygma/Corbis. p38
Angela Weiss/Getty Images. p42 Barry
Brecheisen/Getty Images. p43 Mark A. Steele
Photography Columbus, OH. p44 Courtesy
Massey & Rogers ph. Rick Tailby. p45 Courtesy
Prey. p46 Courtesy Camper ph. Nienke Klunder.
p48 Courtesy Earnest Sewn. p51 Stuart Wilson/
Getty Images. p52 Mel Risebrow. p57 Frazer
Harrison/Getty Images. p58 t: Lipnitzki/Roger
Viollet/Getty Images; m: © WWD/Condé Nast/
Corbis; b: FRANCOIS GUILLOT/AFP/Getty
Images. p59 Courtesy Orla Kiely. p62 NOAH
SEELAM/AFP/Getty Images. p65 Scott Olson/
Getty Images. p67 Nicolai. p68 Courtesy
Bodymetrics. p69 Bill Ray/Time & Life Pictures/
Getty Images. p70 China Photos/Getty Images.
p71 Haszlo Regos, Berkley, Michigan. p75 Dave
M. Benett/Getty Images. p77 l: TORU YAMANAKA/
AFP/Getty Images; r: Andreas Wijk. p78 l:
Courtesy LuisaViaRoma; r: Courtesy Colette. p79
Rob Loud/Getty Images. p80 John Shearer/Getty
Images. 81 b: Courtesy of Rita Nazareno, ph.
S.S.de Guzman; r: © ZACARIAS by S.C.Vizcarra.
p85 l: Lesley Taylor; r: Draught Associates. p87
Jeremy Sutton-Hibbert/Getty Images. p88
Courtesy of Mudpie. p89 © Premiere Vision. p90
© Stephane Cardinale/People Avenue/Corbis. p91
STAN HONDA/AFP/Getty Images. p95 © David
Gray/Reuters/Corbis. p100 Andrew H. Walker/
Getty Images. p101 Chris Moore/Catwalking. p105
Hannah Markham. p107 l: Bloomberg via Getty
Images; r: Courtesy Gooey Wooey. p108
Keystone/Getty Images. p109 David Newby/
Guardian News & Media Ltd 2009. p110 Courtesy

Celeste Cerro. p113 Laura-Michelle Moore.
p114-115 Ian Rummey. p118 t: Joy Prater; b:
Thomas Concordia/Getty Images. p120
Courtesy Fitflop. p122 l: Lisa Marie Thompson;
r: Dan Duchars. p124 t: Harriet Posner; b:
James Hayes. p125 James Hayes. p129 l: Mel
Risebrow; r: Noel Vasquez/Getty Images. p130
Courtesy adidas. p131 Karl Prouse/Catwalking/
Getty Images; Karl Prouse/Catwalking/Getty
Images; Alberto Tamargo/Getty Images. p132
adidas. p133 Courtesy Australian Wool
Innovation Limited. p134 Harriet Posner. p135
Mel Risebrow. p136 t: Gareth Andrew Gatrell; b:
Harriet Posner. p138 Courtesy David Delfin, ph.
Gorka Postigo. p142 Courtesy Nau; t: Eugénie
Frerichs; b: Shawn Linehan. p143 Advertising
Archive. p144 © Oliver Knight / Alamy. p145 t:
Oliver Knight / Alamy; b: Harriet Posner.p148
Hannah Markham. p153 l: Jeff J Mitchell/Getty
Images; r: AFP/Getty Images. p155 Courtesy
MCM. p156 Nick Turner; Sam Robinson; fascia
and interiors by Pope Wainwright www.
popewainwright.co.uk. p158 Andrew H. Walker/
Getty Images. p159 t: Eric Ryan/Getty Images;
b: Mel Risebrow. p160 l: Andrew Meredith; r:
Harriet Posner. p162 Advertising Archive. p163
Benetton Group Photographer James Mollison;
Benetton Group Photographer: Erik Ravelo/
Fabrica, Piero Martinello/Fabrica. p164 Vittorio
Zunino Celotto/Getty Images. p165 Courtesy
Adbuster/Blackspot. p166 Raffaela Lepanto
www.nomads.com. p167 Bloomberg via Getty
Images.
p169 Mel Risebrow. p170 Mel Risebrow. p171
Mel Risebrow. p173 DIBYANGSHU SARKAR/
AFP/Getty Images. p174 t: James Doiron www.
mannequindisplay.com; b: Harriet Posner.
p175 Courtesy Anya Hindmarch. p176 Courtesy
Diesel. p177 l: Chris Jackson/Getty Images; r:
Courtesy Mango. p178-179 Courtesy O'Neill.
p180 Courtesy Erdem. p182 Courtesy Oxfam.
p185 © Bread and Butter. p187 Mark Von
Holden/WireImage. p188 J.Tregidgo/WireImage.
p189 Oli Scarff/Getty Images. p190 ©Premiere
Vision. p194 Jason Kempin/WireImage. p195 t:
JEAN-PIERRE MULLER/AFP/Getty Images; b:
Francois Durand/Getty Images. p196 David S.
Holloway/Getty Images. p197 Courtesy Premiere
Vision. p198 Anna KO, http://www.myspace.
com/annako © breadandbutter.com. p199
Shawn Linehan. p201 James Doiron www.
mannequindisplay.com. p202 Mel Risebrow.
p203 Dan Kitwood/Getty Images. p204
Brendon Thorne/Getty Images. p210
Beatrice K. Newman.

Acknowledgements

Special thanks and gratitude go to all those who
have contributed in so many different ways to the
creation of this book. To Ursula Hudson for her
years of friendship and for putting me forward
for this project. To the team at Laurence King for
their guidance and constant encouragement –
Helen Evans for commissioning the book,
Anne Townley for steering me through the writing
process with such grace and clarity, Peter Jones
and Helen Turner for transforming the manuscript
into a fully-fledged book and Annalaura Palma for
the picture research.

I wish to acknowledge, Peter Lewis-Crown,
Jane Barran, Vanessa Denza, Karin Koeppel and
Caroline Morgan for the pivotal role each played in
shaping my career in fashion. Special thanks go to
Shirley Messam for her patience and flexibility in
helping me juggle commitments to both teaching
and writing and to Claire Swift, Carmel Kelly,
Heather Pickard, Wendy Malem and Kirsten Scott
for continuing to invite me to teach.

Thank you to all students past and present who
have shared a passion for fashion; you have
helped me learn and grow as a teacher and it
has been a joy to see your careers take root
and blossom. In particular; Erdem Moralioglu,
Hannah Jennings, Hannah Markham, James
Hayes, Joy Prater, Laura Moore, Jazmin Buxton,
Maria Castro, Geetika Kumar, Linn Westedt,
Jessica Wu, Julia Crew, Nimish Shah and
Rita Nazareno – thank you for your support and
contribution to this book.

To all the companies and individuals who
generously agreed to be interviewed, contribute
material or put me in touch with someone
who could help. With special mention to;
Erica Archambault, Helga Ying, Lynn Downey,
Orla Kiely, Basia Szkutnicka, Mey Ali, Eugenie
Frerichs, Shawn Linehan, Jerry Small, Jan Chul
Hansen, Rina Hansen, Marcy Goldstein,
Charlie Bolton, Geraldine & John Sanglier,
Rachel Saunders, Emma Woolley, Liz Leffman,
Sally Bain, Jackie Naghten, Sean Chiles,
K.M. Wong and Chris Thierry.

To all my friends and family who have cared
enough to listen, been tough enough to push and
kind enough to give me a hug when needed –
thank you Emma Ganderton, Gail Rundle, Belinda
Hill, Sophie & Nick Lerner, Janey Hunt, Minni Jain,
Anne-lise & Brian Miller, Sally Wilson, Lesley &
Tony Taylor, Cathy Rowlandson, Pauline Boorman,
Letitia Blake, Pete Crone, Fliss Jay, Jerry & Toby
Levine, Jonathan & Helena Posner, Gillian Duncan
and my dad Geoffrey Posner. With special
thanks to Anna Lodge for taking the time to
read the manuscript and offering valuable
feedback and comments.

And last, but in no way least, a very special
mention and heartfelt gratitude to Mel for his
patience, guidance and love. Thank you for
being by my side day in and day out through
all the ups and downs of this project.